Lethal Injection

Lethal Injection

Capital Punishment in Texas during the Modern Era

JON SORENSEN AND ROCKY LEANN PILGRIM

Foreword by Evan J. Mandery

University of Texas Press ◥◤ *Austin*

Copyright © 2006 by the University of Texas Press
All rights reserved
Printed in the United States of America

First edition, 2006

Requests for permission to reproduce material from this work should be sent to:
    Permissions
    University of Texas Press
    P.O. Box 7819
    Austin, TX 78713-7819
    www.utexas.edu/utpress/about/bpermission.html

♾ The paper used in this book meets the minimum requirements of ANSI/NISO Z39.48-1992 (R1997) (Permanence of Paper).

Library of Congress Cataloging-in-Publication Data
Sorensen, Jonathan R. (Jonathan Roger), 1965–
    Lethal injection : capital punishment in Texas during the modern era / Jon Sorensen and Rocky LeAnn Pilgrim. — 1st ed.
       p.   cm.
    Includes bibliographical references and index.
    ISBN 0-292-71264-2 (cloth : alk. paper) — ISBN 0-292-71301-0 (pbk. : alk. paper)
    1. Capital punishment — Texas. 2. Lethal injection (Execution) — Texas.
  3. Punishment — Texas . I. Pilgrim, Rocky LeAnn, 1978– II. Title.
    HV8699.U6S67   2006
    364.66'09764—dc22
                                        2005022215

For
Jerry and Hyon Suk Pilgrim
and
Amy and April Sorensen

Contents

Foreword

It is meaningless, really, to speak about the death penalty in America without being geographically specific. Each death penalty state, as well as the federal government, has its own system for determining who shall be subject to capital punishment. These systems share some basic features, but they are each unique, and some are more problematic than others. It is eminently reasonable to be against the death penalty as practiced in one state but to support it as practiced in another.

Massachusetts, for example, is currently considering a proposal to reinstitute the death penalty with significant procedural protections to ensure against the execution of an innocent person and against discrimination in charging and sentencing. The Massachusetts proposal provides, among other things, that guilt be proved beyond any doubt, that separate juries be charged for the guilt and sentencing phases of the trial (many argue that death-qualified juries are conviction prone), that DNA testing be made available to the defendant, that an independent commission review claims of innocence, and that death sentences be imposed only if physical evidence incriminates the defendant. The Massachusetts proposal addresses the exhaustive list of faults (other than the immorality of execution) that abolitionists have found with the death penalty as applied by the various states and the federal government. All but the most moralistic objectors to capital punishment would have to take a hard look at the Massachusetts plan, which provides, insomuch as it is humanly possible to assure this, that only the guilty and only the most culpable will be executed.

Texas is at the other end of the spectrum. The Texas sentencing statute is arguably the most troubling in the nation. At its inception, the statute was structured to narrowly restrict the lens through which the capital jury could consider mitigating evidence submitted by a defendant. Some observers have legitimately criticized the Supreme Court for allowing irrelevant mitigating evidence to infect capital trials. The Court's rule—established in *Woodson v. North Carolina*—is that mandatory death-penalty statutes are unconstitutional and that a defendant in arguing for his life must be allowed to present any and all mitigating evidence he deems relevant. In Texas, defendants could offer any mitigating evidence they deemed relevant, but the evidence could be considered by the jury only in connection with three special issues to be addressed during its deliberations. A defendant named Jerry Jurek argued to the Supreme Court that this scheme effectively amounted to a mandatory death penalty—it did not allow for meaningful consideration of mitigating evidence. The Court rejected Jurek's claim in 1976, and the Texas scheme has been churning out executions since. Although Texas modified its statute to require separate consideration of mitigating evidence in 1991, the Texas statute still controversially focuses jury deliberations on the question of the "future dangerousness" of the defendant, and its motor continues to purr.

Texas's death output is prodigious. In 2002, a total of seventy-one executions were carried out in the United States. Texas accounted for thirty-three of these. Oklahoma had the next highest number with seven. Four hundred fifty prisoners were under sentence of death in Texas at the end of 2002, almost 15 percent of the national total. Only California, with 614, had more. But while Texas executed thirty-three persons in comparison to 450 prisoners under sentence, California executed one. Texas, Virginia, Missouri, Oklahoma, and Florida are collectively responsible for more than two-thirds of the executions that have been carried out in the United States since 1977. In 2002, 159 prisoners were sentenced to die in the United States. Texas was again the leader with thirty-seven admissions to death row. California followed with fourteen.

A host of questions come to mind. Why has Texas been so fervent in pursuing capital punishment? Why has it succeeded (if the number of sentences and executions is a measure of success)? Has an aggressive death penalty produced any benefits? Have rights been trampled in the process—has racism resulted, have innocents been executed? Have the dangerous criminals been incapacitated? The death penalty in Texas is clearly a phenomenon worth studying, and there are few people better equipped to study it than Jon Sorensen and Rocky Pilgrim.

Jon Sorensen is one of the three or four most important researchers who regularly devote their attention to the subject of capital punishment in America. In 1972, in *Furman v. Georgia,* the Supreme Court commuted the sentences of more than 600 death-sentenced defendants when it ruled the death penalty as then applied unconstitutional. Professor Sorensen, together with James Marquart, studied the *Furman* commutees to see whether it was in fact true, as proponents of the death penalty argued, that capital murderers posed a risk to commit future violent crime above and beyond the risk posed by noncapital murderers. The Sorensen-Marquart study remains to this day the most significant study of the question whether the death penalty is justified from the standpoint of incapacitation. Professor Sorensen has since produced a host of enormously significant empirical studies on, among other topics, deterrence, racial disparity, and the likelihood of incarcerated capital murderers to violate prison rules. He is notably one of the few honest brokers in the field. Most scholars consistently find evidence that supports one side or the other (usually their own). Jon Sorensen has published some studies that support the abolitionist side and has offered other data that support the death penalty. His work is thorough and unbiased. This book is no exception.

Death by Lethal Injection is conspicuously balanced. The authors ask all the right questions. Does the death penalty deter? Is it administered fairly? Their answers are nuanced, as any honest answers to the key questions in this area must be, and bear directly on the debate of the morality of the death penalty. Their discussion of incapacitation includes the relevant fact that capital murderers are not substantially more likely to recidivate or commit prison crime than other inmates, and the details of some of the crimes that released inmates have committed. The authors have complete command of the literature in this field. They present all of the relevant data, and do so even-handedly.

This is the kind of book that is needed in this field. It is not a polemic. It raises the level of the debate by educating readers about both sides of the issue. There is no agenda or bias here. *Death by Lethal Injection* is an important book that deserves to be read and discussed.

Evan J. Mandery
John Jay College of Criminal Justice
New York, New York
November 2004

Acknowledgments

We would like to extend our sincerest gratitude to all of the people and organizations that have assisted in the preparation of this manuscript.

We would first like to thank Allison Faust, associate editor at UT Press, and Lynne Chapman, manuscript editor, for their encouragement, patience, and sound advice from the very beginning of this project. Kip Keller deserves credit for a superb job of copyediting. Our appreciation is also due Philip Wischkaemper and Evan Mandery for their careful reviews of and thoughtful comments on previous drafts of the manuscript.

We would also like to thank the Texas Department of Criminal Justice and its staff. We could not have gathered the necessary data for this text without the patient assistance of Frank Aubuchon, Sammy Buentello, Judy Mancil, Marty Martin, Thomas Warren, Paul Williams, Margie Wilkins, and the wonderful staff in the classification and records department.

Our thanks also go out to former state senator Bill Meier, Midland County Judge Robin Sams, McLennan County District Attorney Mike Freeman, defense attorney John Niland, and Dallas County District Attorneys Patricia Hogue, Rick Jackson, and Patrick Kirlin for their insights and assistance.

Finally, we would like to express our gratitude to the University of Texas–Pan American, Prairie View A&M University, and Boston College Law School for their financial and academic support.

Lethal Injection

CHAPTER 1

The Modern Era

Being a horse farmer and horse raiser, I know what it's like to try to eliminate an injured horse by shooting him. Now you call the veterinarian and the vet gives it a shot [injection] and the horse goes to sleep—that's it. I myself have wondered if maybe this isn't part of our problem [with capital punishment], and maybe we should review and see if there aren't even more humane methods now—the simple shot or tranquilizer.

RONALD REAGAN, GOVERNOR OF CALIFORNIA, QUOTED IN "THEY SHOOT HORSES, DON'T THEY," *TIME*, OCTOBER 8, 1973

On July 30, 1964, Joseph Johnson, a black man convicted of murdering a Chinese grocer during a robbery in Houston while on parole, walked the infamous "last mile" at the Walls Unit of the Texas State Penitentiary at Huntsville, from death row to the death chamber. An eyewitness to the execution reported his final minutes:

> He entered the Death House at 12:02 a.m. He was carrying a white bible. He asked for and was granted permission to kneel and pray. "Oh God, have mercy on these people," he intoned. "Have mercy on me, and bless these people." He died with the bible in his lap. When the electricity shocked him, the bible spun from his lap with such speed that it landed in the witness area. The doctor pronounced him dead at 12:08 a.m., July 30, 1964.[1]

Unbeknown to those present, Joseph Johnson's death signaled the close of an era: he was the last inmate to be electrocuted in Texas's electric chair. Johnson was the 361st Texas inmate to take part in a macabre tradition: the ritualized walking of the last mile to the execution chamber for an appointment with "Old Sparky." With the passage of Senate Bill 63 in 1923, executions had been removed from local authorities and centralized in Huntsville, the site of the new electric chair. This technological innovation was heralded as a major advance over its predecessor, the hangman's noose, and ushered in a new era of capital punishment in Texas. The ritual that had begun with the electrocution of five black murderers from East Texas counties on February 8, 1924, had effectively come to a close with the electrocution of Joseph Johnson in 1964.

Overcrowding caused by increased delays in federal courts prompted officials to move death row inmates from the Walls Unit in Huntsville to the rural Ellis Unit shortly after the last electrocution. These court delays were the result of a concerted strategy by the NAACP Legal Defense Fund to halt executions by raising every possible constitutional claim in every death row inmate's case in an effort to clog up the court system.[2] The strategy resulted in a de facto moratorium on executions from the late 1960s (the last U.S. execution of this era taking place in June 1967) until the late 1970s (the first execution of the modern era taking place in January 1977). This de facto moratorium resulted in a pile-up on death rows across the United States as civil-rights attorneys battled the death penalty in federal courts.

This movement culminated in *Furman v. Georgia* (1972), in which the U.S. Supreme Court announced, in its lengthiest decision, that the death penalty, as imposed, constituted cruel and unusual punishment.[3] In this *per curiam* decision (one written as if by the entire court rather than a particular justice), each justice offered a separate opinion. One issue on which the five majority justices did agree was that a lack of juror guidance in sentencing deliberations had resulted in the arbitrary, and sometimes discriminatory, imposition of the death penalty.

The Texas case of Elmer Branch, joined with two Georgia cases in *Furman*, illuminated the worst aspects of the death penalty.[4] All three death-sentenced inmates were black, and each had had a white victim. Worse still, two of the appellants, Branch and Jackson, had raped but not killed their victims. It was fairly clear that the historical practice of lynching black offenders for raping white victims in the South had been merely transformed and legitimized by subsequent "legal" executions by the state. This evidence provided the strongest argument against the death penalty, on the grounds that it was an antiquated, racist vestige of slavery.

Across the United States, more than six hundred inmates were released from death row as a result of the *Furman* decision. In Texas, forty-seven death-sentenced inmates had their sentences commuted to life imprisonment. The moratorium imposed by court delays and the subsequent decision in *Furman* effectively brought to a close the second major era of capital punishment in Texas.

At the dawning of the modern era, a great deal of uncertainty existed surrounding the future of capital punishment. Public-opinion polls showed that support for the death penalty, although rising, had been at its lowest recorded level just a few years earlier. The ambivalence of the public was reflected in the nine opinions by the justices in *Furman*. Many observers believed that *Furman* signaled the end of the death penalty in the United States. Indeed, from the timing of the decision it appeared that the United States was simply following an international trend in abolishing the death penalty. However, by declaring the death penalty unconstitutional *as then imposed,* but not cruel and unusual punishment per se, the Supreme Court left the door open for states hoping to devise constitutional death-penalty statutes.

The separate opinions in *Furman* were subjected to intense scrutiny by state legislatures in an effort to determine exactly where a majority of the Court stood on the issue of capital punishment. Careful reading of the opinions revealed that only two justices opposed the death penalty as cruel and unusual in all situations. Capital punishment, at least in theory, was acceptable to the majority of the justices as long as it advanced a "legitimate penological purpose." The more pragmatic concern then became one of properly constructing a death-penalty statute that would pass constitutional muster when reviewed by the Court. It is within this ambiguous context that state lawmakers in Texas and elsewhere debated the future of capital punishment during their 1973 legislative sessions.

Reinstatement of the Death Penalty

One certainty derived from *Furman* was that any death-penalty legislation would have to include safeguards against the arbitrary or discriminatory imposition of death sentences. The discretion of juries would have to be either severely curtailed or completely eliminated to ensure a degree of regularity in the process. States could take one of two paths to accomplish this goal. First, they could pass statutes to make capital punishment automatic upon conviction for certain narrow categories of murder, such as killing a police officer or killing during the course of a robbery. This was the tack taken by members of the House of Representatives in Texas. They proposed that death be mandatory for those convicted of murders committed within a limited range of situations.

Second, states could establish criteria to guide jurors' sentencing deliberations. States taking this approach typically borrowed from the American Law Institute's Model Penal Code to compile a list of aggravating and mitigating circumstances that would serve to guide jury deliberations. This was the approach taken by the Texas Senate, following closely in the footsteps of Florida, the first state to reenact the death penalty after *Furman*.[5]

The debates in the Texas House and Senate over the potential infirmities of each other's proposed versions of a new death-penalty bill highlighted the problems with these approaches and the uncertainty legislatures across the country faced.[6] Members of the House did not believe that the Senate's version would meet the dictates of *Furman*, because it left too much discretion to the jury in making a sentencing recommendation and because it left the judge, who was to be the final arbiter, completely unguided in that role. Representatives thus believed that the only way to make sentencing consistent was to force its imposition in every capital-murder case resulting in conviction, which would purge any potential arbitrariness or discrimination from its application.[7] Critics in the Senate noted that even under the House's version of a "mandatory death penalty," discretion still existed in prosecutors' charging decisions and in juries' ability to convict defendants of lesser degrees of murder, which would not carry the possibility of death sentences. Further, senators who had carefully analyzed the dicta of the separate justices' opinions determined that a mandatory death penalty did not enjoy support among a numerical majority of the justices.

As the sixty-third legislative session neared its end, neither side was willing to accept the core portion of the other's bill. However, members of the "Reform Legislature," so called because nearly half of the senators and a large number of representatives had been replaced because of the Sharpstown scandal, were particularly anxious to fulfill their obligations to the public and to Lieutenant Governor William Hobby, and both Hobby and the public fervently supported the reenactment of capital punishment.[8] During the final week of the legislative session, a conference committee feverishly sought a compromise between the House and Senate versions of the bill, one that would pass muster with both sides. The compromise resulted in a uniquely hybrid capital-sentencing scheme.

First, the conference committee adopted a circumscribed list of criteria for defining capital murder, as suggested by the House and expanded by the Senate.[9] The categories of capital murder passed into law in 1973, as well as those added since, include the following:

(1) the person murders a peace officer or fireman who is acting in the lawful discharge of an official duty and who the person knows is a peace officer or fireman;

(2) the person intentionally commits the murder in the course of committing or attempting to commit kidnapping, burglary, robbery, aggravated sexual assault, arson, or obstruction or retaliation;

(3) the person commits the murder for remuneration or the promise of remuneration or employs another to commit the murder for remuneration or the promise of remuneration;

(4) the person commits the murder while escaping or attempting to escape from a penal institution;

(5) the person, while incarcerated in a penal institution, murders another:
   (A) who is employed in the operation of the penal institution; or
   (B) with the intent to establish, maintain, or participate in a combination or in the profits of a combination;

(6) the person:
   (A) while incarcerated for an offense under this section or [for murder], murders another; or
   (B) while serving a sentence of life imprisonment or a term of 99 years for [aggravated kidnapping, aggravated sexual assault, or aggravated robbery], murders another;

(7) the person murders more than one person:
   (A) during the same criminal transaction; or
   (B) during different criminal transactions but the murders are committed pursuant to the same scheme or course of conduct; or

(8) the person murders an individual under six years of age.[10]

By utilizing the House's narrowed definition of capital murder as a starting point, the Texas statute resembled those of other states enacting mandatory death-penalty schemes. However, senators' demands that death not be automatic upon conviction meant that some mechanism for allowing discretion in sentencing deliberations had to be devised. Representatives were adamant that such discretion be extremely limited, which ruled out the Senate's scheme of allowing jurors to weigh a long list of aggravating and mitigating factors during their deliberations. Instead, sentencing considerations were to be structured so that jurors' discretion would be almost completely constrained. The result was a series of questions, or "special issues," to be answered by jurors during deliberations:

1. Whether the conduct of the defendant that caused the death of the deceased was committed deliberately and with the reasonable expectation that the death of the deceased or another would result;

2. Whether there is a probability that the defendant would commit criminal acts of violence that would constitute a continuing threat to society; and
3. If raised by the evidence, whether the conduct of the defendant in killing the deceased was unreasonable in response to the provocation, if any, by the deceased.[11]

Depending on the answers given by the jurors to these special issues, the defendant automatically received a sentence of either life in prison or death. The jury was not directed to vote specifically for a death sentence or a life sentence, but rather just to answer the special issues to the best of its ability. Affirmative responses by all twelve jurors to each of these three questions would result in a sentence of death. A negative response by at least ten jurors to one or more of these questions, or a failure of the jury to answer any special issue, resulted in a life sentence.[12]

Along with other states, Texas began sentencing inmates to death using its newly enacted death-penalty statute, and waited for a determination of its constitutionality by the U.S. Supreme Court. The Court's decision concerning the constitutionality of Texas's death-penalty statute, along with those of four other states, was handed down in 1976. This series of decisions confirmed the view held in the Texas Senate: guided discretion was a necessary component in building a constitutional death-penalty statute. In two of these decisions, the Supreme Court struck down mandatory death-penalty statutes, holding that capital-punishment statutes must allow for individualized consideration of the defendant's culpability and the circumstances surrounding the crime.[13] In the three other cases, the Supreme Court upheld the "guided discretion" statutes of Georgia, Florida, and Texas.[14]

The Texas statute stood apart from those of Georgia and Florida, as well as any others then in existence. Commentators noted that the Texas death-penalty scheme was the closest to a mandatory death penalty imaginable in its original incarnation, with virtually no room for individualized consideration.[15] Although the special sentencing issues appeared quite restrictive, the Court held that the second special issue, concerning the defendant's potential for future violence, was broad enough to allow jurors the discretion necessary to consider aspects of a case that might be viewed as mitigating in regard to the sentence:

[T]he constitutionality of the Texas procedures turns on whether the enumerated questions allow consideration of particularized mitigating factors. . . . In the present case, however, [the Court of Criminal Appeals] indicated that it will interpret this second question so as to allow a defendant to bring to the

jury's attention whatever mitigating circumstances he may be able to show.
. . . Texas law essentially requires that one of five aggravating circumstances
be found before a defendant can be found guilty of capital murder, and that in
considering whether to impose a death sentence the jury may be asked to consider whatever mitigating circumstances the defense can bring before it. It thus
appears that, as in Georgia and Florida, the Texas capital-sentencing procedure guides and focuses the jury's objective consideration of the particularized
circumstances of the individual offense and the individual offender before it
can impose a sentence of death.[16]

Although it initially affirmed that the Texas statute allowed jurors individualized consideration, the Supreme Court was later faced with an unforeseen
circumstance. In *Penry v. Lynaugh,* a defendant with a low IQ who had also
suffered abuse as a child charged that the second special issue actually worked
as an aggravator in his case: jurors were likely to view Penry as a greater future
threat because of his low IQ and history of abuse, and would thus fail to give
proper weight to these as mitigating factors.[17] The Supreme Court agreed, and
the Texas special sentencing issues were amended for the first and only time
since the legislative reimplementation of capital punishment.

To meet the Court's concerns in *Penry,* the Texas legislature added a sentencing issue that explicitly called for the jury to consider the defendant's mitigating
circumstances. Simultaneously, the legislature rescinded the first and third special sentencing issues, relating to deliberateness and lack of provocation.[18] In
their place, the legislature added another special issue that is asked only in cases
involving accomplices who did not actually commit the murder.[19] Under the
revised sentencing scheme, jurors are first directed to consider "whether there
is a probability that the defendant would commit criminal acts of violence that
would constitute a continuing threat to society," formerly the second special
issue and the only original sentencing inquiry remaining. In applicable cases,
jurors are then asked "whether the defendant actually caused the death of the
deceased or did not actually cause the death of the deceased but intended to kill
the deceased or another or anticipated that a human life would be taken."[20] A
negative response to either inquiry results in a life sentence. If the jury answers
these questions in the affirmative, it is then directed to consider

> [w]hether, taking into consideration all of the evidence, including the cir-
> cumstances of the offense, the defendant's character and background, and the
> personal moral culpability of the defendant, there is a sufficient mitigating
> circumstance or circumstances to warrant that a sentence of life imprisonment
> rather than the death sentence be imposed.[21]

An affirmative response to this inquiry results in a life sentence, whereas a negative response results in a death sentence.

The Development of a New Technology

A murder committed in Utah only two weeks after the Supreme Court upheld the constitutionality of death-penalty schemes in guided-discretion jurisdictions resulted in the first death sentence actually carried out during the modern era. On July 19, 1976, Gary Gilmore murdered a gas station attendant during a robbery. The following day he murdered a motel manager, the crime for which he received the death penalty. Upon conviction, Gilmore waived his appeals in what has become one of the most celebrated cases in American jurisprudence. After two reprieves granted against his wishes and two unsuccessful suicide attempts, Gilmore was executed on January 17, 1977, ending a nearly decade-long moratorium in the United States.

Gilmore's case attracted widespread media attention. In addition to being the first person set to be executed in nearly a decade, Gilmore actively sought his own execution and sold the rights of his story to a publisher for $50,000. Perhaps the most intriguing part of the story was the method of execution. Gary Gilmore was to be executed by firing squad. Since the last execution by firing squad had been seventeen years earlier, when Utah executed James Rodgers, it took some time for those charged with performing the execution to come up with a suitable protocol. Utah was not unique in this regard. Although trial procedures had been updated as a result of *Furman*, jurisdictions had simply carried over their methods of execution from the previous era of capital punishment, including hanging, the gas chamber, and, most commonly, the electric chair.

When the sixty-fifth session of the Texas Legislature convened in January 1977, the death penalty was an issue again ripe for consideration. After the U.S. Supreme Court's stamp of approval in *Jurek* (the case that legitimized Texas's revamped death-penalty law), and as several death-sentenced cases neared the end of their scheduled round of appeals, Texas's first execution of the modern era was imminent. A federal district judge in Dallas had recently ruled that the state's first execution could be televised, promising a media event comparable to Gilmore's execution. Like other states, Texas had maintained its mode of execution, electrocution, from the previous era of capital punishment. Although more common than death by firing squad, electrocution was certainly no less grisly.

Given this confluence of events, it is not surprising that the idea of using lethal injection as a method of execution resurfaced. At the close of the nineteenth century, concern over botched hangings led to the appointment of a committee in New York to recommend a new method of execution. Although finally settling on electrocution, the committee reported favorably on the "injection of a lethal dose of prussic acid [cyanide]."[22] Facing enormous publicity at the outset of the modern era, legislators sought a form of execution that would be more palatable than electrocution and more likely to withstand public scrutiny.

Legislation was introduced simultaneously in the Texas House and Senate to change the mode of execution from electrocution to lethal injection. Statements by the sponsors of the bills showed that electrocution had come to be viewed as an inhumane relic of a previous era. Of electrocution, Representative Close stated, "It's a very scary thing to see. Blood squirts out of the nose. The eyeballs pop out. The body almost virtually catches fire. I voted for a more humane treatment because death is pretty final. That's enough of a penalty."[23] Senate sponsor Bill Braecklein introduced the bill in response to the federal judge's ruling that executions could be televised, stating that he "was repulsed by the idea of an electrocution taking place in someone's living room."[24]

Advocates of lethal injection feared that the sensationalism surrounding an electrocution would send the wrong message, possibly making a hero or martyr out of the condemned, as had happened with Gilmore's death by firing squad. This would not vindicate the murdered victim, nor could an execution carried out under such circumstances be expected to prevent others from committing murder. By introducing the lethal-injection bill, Representative Ben Z. Grant hoped to avoid the negative aspects associated with Gilmore's execution. He stated that "the death penalty should be swift and sure punishment, not something that takes away from the dignity of the state. The way we do it now creates a circus atmosphere that makes heroes out of criminals."[25]

Grant credited a previous discussion in the legislature over the humane disposal of animals for the idea that lethal injection could be used for executions:

When we reinstated the death penalty a few years back, I was taking testimony before the Judiciary Committee, and we had some folks [from the Humane Society] testifying about humaneness to animals. I asked them, "If we had a dangerous animal and we decided that it had to be put to death because it was dangerous, what if we burn it to death with electricity?" And the man said, "Oh, we'd bring a lawsuit and enjoin that. That would be cruel and inhumane." And I said, "That's ironical. That's what we just voted to do to people."[26]

Those intimately involved with the task of executing condemned inmates viewed lethal injection as a more humane alternative to electrocution. W. J. (James) Estelle, Jr., director of the Texas Department of Corrections and the man charged with carrying out the task, stated, "[I]f we're going to retain the death penalty, the lethal injection method suits our state of civilization more than electrocution."[27] Reverend Clyde Johnston, a prison chaplain who had provided solace to fourteen men executed in the electric chair, presented an idyllic vision of how the alternative method could be conducted:

> I would like to see this carried out in a nice clean room, something that doesn't look like a prison. Certainly not the death cell. I can conceive of how this could be handled in such a way that it could be considered gentle, humane, if done with care. I hesitate to use the word pleasant, but it would be just like someone going in, laying down, and going to sleep.[28]

The apparent ease of performing lethal injections, which would lack the horrific trauma to the body associated with electrocution, led most to willingly accept this proposed alternative. Psychologist Verne Cox noted that it was likely that "people are responding to [death by injection] favorably because of the way we were reared. As children, we were often told that [death] was like sleep. And here we have a method of killing people that is like sleep."[29]

Most of those questioning the use of lethal injection stated their opposition to the death penalty generally, using broad moral terms. However, they also cautioned that this new method, in particular, would make it too easy for the public to accept the taking of life, opening the execution floodgate. The insidious nature of lethal injection led one opponent, John Duncan of the Texas Civil Liberties Union, to comment that "[n]eedle injections by executioners in white coats in a hospital are the Orwellian equivalent of the 19th and early 20th-century phenomenon of people gathering for miles around in a picnic atmosphere to watch a public hanging."[30] Tom Flowers, of the Texas Coalition to Abolish the Death Penalty, warned:

> I have heard it said that there is [*sic*] some people in society that we just don't know what to do with, and these people have to be eliminated. And, that's the word that has been used several times in the past few weeks. There is a certain class of people that have to be eliminated. And, it seems to me that this is a very tragic word. We can look back thirty and thirty-five years in history and see what happened when a certain class of people were considered worthy of elimination, a criminal class of people according to a certain country, whether

they were gypsies, Jews, homosexuals, communists, socialists, whatever type of undesirable.[31]

Another outspoken opponent, former representative Maury Maverick, Jr., questioned supporters' "humaneness" as a motivation for switching to lethal injection, stating that "death by painless injection is not for the benefit of the deceased, but for the benefit of the affluent white majority which kills blacks, browns and poor 'white niggers' in the name of Texas." Speaking further about the racially biased implementation of the death penalty, he posed the question, "Why don't we extend this base cruelty all the way and give blacks poisoned watermelon in the hope that they will come out of the death chamber grinning from ear to ear?"[32]

One supporter of capital punishment, Kenneth Wayne Roberts, also criticized the use of lethal injections, but for different reasons, stating:

> The testimony that's been presented thus far has said that we should treat human beings like the way, as humanely as we do animals. But, I would like to say this, that animals do not go out and slaughter innocent people like Gary Gilmore, Charles Manson, and some of the other vicious murderers. I personally feel it is an easy escape hatch for some of these murderers because many of them have been on drugs before or been alcoholics. They won't mind taking another drug injection. What I'd like to know is how this drug injection is going to deter a would-be murderer from doing it.[33]

Notwithstanding such jaundiced criticisms, the bill passed, and was signed into Texas law on May 12, 1977, only one day after Oklahoma became the first state to officially switch to lethal injection. The law provided for execution "by intravenous injection of a substance or substances in a lethal quantity sufficient to cause death and until such a convict is dead, such execution procedure to be determined and supervised by the Director of the Department of Corrections."[34] In the week before Texas's first scheduled execution, that of Howard Lincoln, Director James Estelle decided, in consultation with medical experts, that the anesthetic sodium thiopental would be the substance administered in a dosage sufficient to cause death.[35] The muscle relaxant pancuronium bromide, which collapses the diaphragm and the lungs, and potassium chloride, which stops the heartbeat, were subsequently added to the lethal potion before the first execution took place.

Lincoln's execution was not carried out as scheduled, because of a legal challenge that temporarily stayed all death sentences. Kenneth Granviel, another condemned inmate scheduled to die in September of 1977, filed a lawsuit with the Texas Court of Criminal Appeals, challenging the use of lethal injection as a cruel and unusual punishment and attacking the new law for vagueness, in that it failed to specify which substances would be used. The court held that lethal injection did not violate "evolving standards of decency that mark the progress of a maturing society" and as such did not violate the Constitution's prohibition against cruel and unusual punishments. The court further rejected Granviel's vagueness argument after reviewing state statutes authorizing hangings, firing squads, and electrocutions, none of which specified in detail the manner of execution (i.e., height of fall, type of bullets, or amperage).[36] Granviel survived another nineteen years before being executed by lethal injection; Lincoln's sentence was commuted.

Legal challenges to other general procedures in the implementation of capital punishment continued to prevent any lethal injections from taking place in the 1970s. Two procedural challenges that affected many of Texas's death row cases were finally decided by the U.S. Supreme Court in the early 1980s. In *Adams v. Texas,* the Court held that potential jurors could be removed from the jury pool during *voir dire* "for cause" only if their opposition to the death penalty would interfere with their ability to apply the law.[37] In *Estelle v. Smith,* the Court ruled that state psychiatric examinations of defendants were subject to the Fifth Amendment protection against self-incrimination and the Sixth Amendment right to counsel.[38] Not only did these and similar legal claims prevent executions from going forward in the state, but they also resulted in a number of overturned cases.

Lethal Injection Moves to the Fore

Executions got off to a slow start in the modern era while condemned prisoners pursued a variety of legal challenges. Inevitably, however, the time came when one of the condemned murderer's appeals had run their course and the state was cleared to perform its first lethal injection. This occurred on December 7, 1982, when Charlie Brooks became the first criminal ever executed by lethal injection.

Rather than walking the fabled "last mile" as so many condemned inmates had done during the electrocution era, Brooks left his fellow death-row inmates behind at the Ellis Unit on his final journey. He was housed alone on the old death row at the Walls Unit, down the hall from the death cell. While Chaplain Johnston had hoped that a more serene atmosphere would be chosen, the death cell had simply been converted to serve more practical needs. A gurney now occupied the place of the electric chair. Just before the appointed time of the execution, witnesses entered the chamber and found Brooks strapped to the gurney with the intravenous (IV) lines already inserted and the saline solution flowing. The lines ran to an IV stand and a drip bag concealed in a booth behind a one-way mirror, next to the decommissioned electric box, where Director Estelle and other unnamed participants stood ready. When asked if he had any final words, Brooks prayed to Allah in Arabic and told his girlfriend, "I love you" and "Be strong." At 12:09 a.m., Warden Pursley said, "We are ready." The executioners inserted the fatal combination of drugs into the drip line.

A journalist present at the execution noted that tiny air bubbles were clearly visible to witnesses and to the condemned as the lethal drugs snaked through the lengthy intravenous line. According to this account, Brooks's obvious "agony of anticipation" before succumbing to the effects of the drugs seemed to cause him more discomfort than the remainder of the process:

> It was perhaps a minute, perhaps two minutes, before he felt death creeping in. Then he slowly moved his head toward the left shoulder, and back toward the right, then upward, leftward again, as if silently saying no. . . . Charlie's head stopped midway on its second turn to the left. His mouth opened and a sound came from between his parted lips. . . . The groan that started out as "Ahlllll" ended up as a long, protracted "Uhmmmmm," and his eyes had closed by the time his lips went shut. . . . His head pointed up, his body lay flat and still for seconds. Then a harsh rasping began. His fingers trembled up and down, and the witnesses standing near his midsection say that his stomach heaved. Quiet returned, and his head turned to the right, toward the black dividing rail. A second spasm of wheezing began. It was brief. Charlie's body moved no more.[39]

Doctors pronounced Charlie Brooks dead at 12:16 a.m., seven minutes after the process of execution had begun. Other witnesses agreed that the process was "peaceful and humane." The tranquility of the execution was in sharp contrast to the crime that landed Brooks on the gurney. After stealing a car from a used-car lot during a test drive, Brooks murdered an accompanying mechanic with one shot to the head after binding and gagging him with duct tape and a wire clothes hanger. Witnesses to the lethal injection reported that Brooks appeared to go to sleep and that any suffering was brief. The first lethal injection of a condemned prisoner had gone off without a hitch.

Fifteen months passed before the next lethal injection was carried out in Texas, on March 14, 1984. In 1980 James Autry shot a forty-three-year-old female convenience-store clerk between the eyes with a .38 caliber pistol after arguing over the price of a six-pack of beer, and was sentenced to die for her murder. Autry also shot two witnesses in the head, including a forty-three-year-old former Roman Catholic priest, who died instantly, and a Greek seaman who survived the gunshot but was seriously injured.

The next execution, that of Ronald O'Bryan, followed closely, on March 31, 1984. On Halloween night in 1974, O'Bryan returned from a neighbor's house with some Pixy Stix candy for his son, his daughter, and some of their friends who were trick-or-treating. After ingesting the candy, which had been poisoned with cyanide, his eight-year-old son died a slow, painful death. (None of the other children ate the Pixy Stix.) The motive for the killing was money: O'Bryan had recently increased to $20,000 the amount of life insurance he carried on his son. He made the poisoned Pixy Stix and handed them out to the children after pretending to get them from a neighbor's house. This crime earned O'Bryan, who ironically was a dentist, the nickname "Candyman."

The next execution was that of Thomas Barefoot on October 30, 1984. Barefoot was convicted of capital murder for the August 7, 1978, shooting death of police officer Carl Levin, age thirty-one, of Harker Heights, Texas, outside Killeen. Barefoot, an oilfield roughneck from Louisiana, was wanted in New Mexico for the rape of a three-year-old girl, and killed Levin to avoid arrest. He had previously been arrested for molestation, aggravated assault, attempted rape, armed robbery, assault and battery, burglary, hit and run, possession of a sawed-off shotgun, possession of amphetamines, possession of marijuana, possession of an unregistered firearm, escape, theft, and driving while intoxicated.

Executions increased during the mid-1980s, with six in 1985 and ten in 1986, but then declined to six in 1987 and averaged only four a year through 1991. Compared to the rest of the country, however, Texas experienced an unparalleled wave of executions during the 1980s. Yet by the close of the decade, the total number of removals from death row by commutation or reversal outpaced executions by a ratio of 3:1 (99 versus 33). By the early 1990s, most of the roadblocks to lethal injection had been removed, and executions began in earnest. The relationship between executions and removals from death row for other reasons was reversed, as executions outpaced removals by a ratio of 3:1 (166 versus 54) in the 1990s. From 2000–2003, the difference between executions and other removals broadened to nearly 13:1 (114 versus 9). Currently, the number of executions has nearly managed to keep pace with the relatively stable influx of inmates to death row, resulting in a consistent death row population of about 450 inmates at any given time.[40]

Since 1984, the performance of lethal injections has been constantly refined.[41] For those charged with carrying out lethal injections, none of whom were licensed medical personnel, but rather a group of handpicked correctional

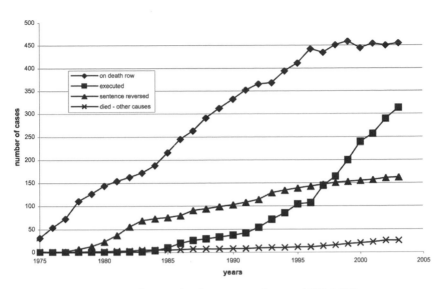

Figure 1.1. Disposition of Texas death-sentenced cases, 1975–2003

officers, a great deal of uncertainty surrounded the procedure. Although the initial execution of Charlie Brooks appeared to have gone off without a hitch according to witnesses, behind the curtain the execution team had actually run into a problem. Their first attempt at the injection was foiled when the three lethal substances, mixed together in the same syringe, coagulated to form a jelly-like substance. Introducing the drugs consecutively solved this problem. During one of the early injections, excessive pressure applied to one of the plungers caused the lethal injection line to dislodge from the condemned's arm and spray witnesses who had come to view the execution. On another occasion, when the lethal drugs had been purchased from another vendor, the execution-ers, unaware that the concentrations of the drugs were different, were surprised when the usual dosage failed to accomplish the objective. After considering whether to inject air bubbles through the line or to use the cyanide kept nearby as a fail-safe, either of which would likely have caused an unsettling response in the condemned, the executioners decided to simply inject all of the remaining drugs from the vials, which proved a timely solution. Nonetheless, the closely knit execution team, members of which typically alternated between perform-ing suicide watches, handling "tie downs," and manning the phone behind the curtain, where a detailed account of the procedure was forwarded to, and transcribed by, the governor's office, experienced little turnover. As such, they were able to refine and carry out the process of lethal injection with dignity and efficiency and without the dramatic or grisly side effects of its predecessors.

Table 1.1 Death sentences, death row populations, and executions, by jurisdiction, 1973–2003

Jurisdiction	Sentenced to death, 1973–2002	On death row, Dec. 31, 2002	Executed, 1977–2003
United States	7,254	3,557	885
Texas	925	450	313
Florida	872	366	57
California	795	614	10
North Carolina	504	206	30
Ohio	367	205	8
Pennsylvania	352	241	3
Alabama	342	191	28
Oklahoma	313	112	69
Georgia	299	112	34
Illinois	294	159	12
Arizona	239	120	22
Louisiana	214	86	27
Tennessee	204	95	1
South Carolina	179	72	28
Mississippi	173	66	6
Missouri	167	66	61
Virginia	137	23	89
Nevada	135	83	9
Arkansas	99	40	25
Indiana	97	36	11

(continues)

The new technology of lethal injection quickly spread to other jurisdictions, becoming the predominant mode of execution during the modern era. Some states initially employed methods of execution left over from the previous eras, but the older methods quickly fell out of favor. Each of the three executions carried out during the 1970s involved a different method of execution: firing squad, electrocution, and lethal gas. Of the 117 executions carried out nationwide during the 1980s, only 36 percent were performed by lethal injection, most of them in Texas; most of the others were performed by electrocution. In the 1990s, 83 percent of the nation's 478 executions were performed by lethal injection. In 2003, all 65 executions carried out across the United States were performed by lethal injection.[42]

Even so, Texas remains the most prolific user of lethal injection, as well

Table 1.1 (*continued*)

Jurisdiction	Sentenced to death, 1973–2002	On death row, Dec. 31, 2002	Executed, 1977–2003
Kentucky	75	36	2
Maryland	52	15	3
New Jersey	51	14	0
Oregon	51	26	2
Delaware	48	14	13
Idaho	40	20	1
Washington	38	10	4
Federal prisons	32	24	3
New Mexico	28	2	1
Nebraska	27	7	3
Utah	26	11	6
Colorado	19	5	1
Montana	15	6	2
Wyoming	11	2	1
New York	9	5	0
Connecticut	8	7	0
Kansas	6	5	0
South Dakota	5	5	0
Massachusetts	4	0	0
Rhode Island	2	0	0

Note: No persons were sentenced to death in the following jurisdictions during the modern era: Alaska, the District of Columbia, Hawaii, Iowa, Maine, Michigan, Minnesota, New Hampshire, North Dakota, Vermont, West Virginia, and Wisconsin.

as the most prolific executioner during the modern era. Of the 885 executions performed in the United States during 1977–2003, over one-third (313) were carried out in Texas. The jurisdiction with the next highest number of executions was Virginia, with 89. Why is it that Texas accounts for so many of the executions carried out in the United States? Although many attribute this to an almost mythical "frontier justice" mentality on the part of Texans, a number of pragmatic reasons actually account for the disproportion.

The first and most obvious reason is that Texas is one of the largest states, with many highly populated urban centers. Although by the end of 2002 Texas had sentenced more offenders to death than any other state, California and Florida, two other large states with similar demographics, had each sentenced nearly as many offenders to death. The high number of death sentences handed down in these jurisdictions is a direct result of the sheer volume of capital murders. As shown with regard to the deterrence hypothesis, tested in Chapter 2, the use of capital punishment tends to increase in direct proportion to the increased need for the sanction, which is based on the number of murders occurring in a jurisdiction.

The peculiarity of the state's capital-murder statute is often implicated in Texas's large number of executions. Some point to the near mandatory nature of the special-issues framework, which directs jurors to answer questions rather than to debate the type of sentence the defendant is to receive. The data used to test the incapacitation hypothesis in Chapter 3 partially support this contention. During the penalty phase of capital-murder trials, Texas juries sentence over 80 percent of defendants to death, whereas juries in other jurisdictions routinely sentence less than 50 percent of defendants to death. If the near mandatory nature of the special-issues framework were the entire explanation for this difference, however, the percentage of defendants sentenced to death by juries should have decreased after the framework was changed to include explicit consideration of whether the presence of mitigating evidence warrants a sentence of life imprisonment. Yet the percentage of penalty trials resulting in death sentences has remained as high since the addition of this mitigating question.

Others have suggested that the cause of these high death-sentencing rates rests with the special issue requiring juries to consider the likelihood that defendants will "commit criminal acts of violence that would constitute a continuing threat to society." This provision invites the jury to speculate about the "future dangerousness" of the defendant. The evidence presented in Chapter 3 suggests that juries are influenced by considerations of future dangerousness, but this cannot be the entire explanation. The death-sentencing rate in Oregon, the only state with a statute modeled after Texas's, is closer to that of states that ask jurors to weigh mitigating and aggravating factors than to the rate in Texas.

The data presented in the analysis of retribution in Chapter 4, however, illuminate how another aspect of the statute may lead to high death-sentencing rates among capital juries in Texas. First, the types of cases that may be considered death-eligible are somewhat restricted by the statutory definition of capital murder in Texas; most other jurisdictions include a broad array of aggravating factors that allow almost any murder to be eligible for the death penalty. A death sentence is more likely to be viewed as an appropriate sentence for murders committed in this limited range of situations. Second, prosecutors appear to utilize informal yet routine criteria that further narrow their selection of cases to those for which they are most confident the defendant will receive the sanction.

Finally, Texas has simply been more successful in executing those sentenced to death than most other states. Texas has executed more than one-third of those sentenced to death in the state during the modern era (313 of 925). Compare this to California, where only a little more than 1 percent of those sentenced to death have been executed so far (10 of 795). Some states have been even more successful than Texas in clearing obstacles to execution. Virginia, for example, has successfully executed 65 percent of its death-sentenced population (89 of 137).[43]

The data and discussion in Chapter 5 illuminate some additional reasons for Texas's level of success in administering capital punishment. First and foremost, all three branches of government in Texas have upheld the will of its citizens, who have been shown to support capital punishment; many other U.S. jurisdictions are currently battling a lack of comparable unanimity. Several other states are also faced with continued setbacks. In Illinois, Governor Ryan commuted the sentences of all death row inmates because of problems discovered in the processing of capital cases and, to a lesser extent, questions raised concerning the innocence of a few of the death-sentenced. In the day-to-day processing of appeals, Texas courts and the federal courts directly overseeing Texas capital cases have been less willing to intervene and halt executions than those in other states. Although Texas experienced some setbacks in its legal procedures early on, the attorney general's office, the governor's office, and the legislature have all worked together to address any problems discovered in the statute or its implementation.

Texas's experience with capital punishment should be instructive as other states continue to process capital cases and to push toward the final resolution of death-sentence appeals. Exactly what can the Texas experience tell us about capital punishment? In arguments over the death penalty, the perennial questions are the following: Does the death penalty prevent others from committing murder? To what extent does the death penalty prevent future murders by those who are executed? Are those sentenced to death among the murderers most deserving of the ultimate sanction? Beyond shedding light on these questions, this study addresses more pragmatic issues concerning the administration of capital punishment. Can the death penalty be imposed in a manner that is unbiased, reliable, and cost-efficient?

Many of these questions could be addressed from historical, moral, philosophical, or legal points of view, but the analysis that follows relies mainly on the social-scientific method in a search for answers. As such, it is best equipped to answer certain questions, but leaves others to the discretion of the reader.

CHAPTER 2

Deterrence: Does It Prevent Others from Committing Murder?

The death penalty is a warning, just like a lighthouse throwing its beams out to sea. We hear about shipwrecks, but we do not hear about the ships the lighthouse guides safely on their way. We do not have proof of the number of ships it saves, but we do not tear the lighthouse down.

HYMAN BARSHAY, POET, QUOTED IN *NEITHER CRUEL NOR UNUSUAL* BY FRANK CARRINGTON

When Texans entered the fray over capital punishment in 1973, events occurring throughout the nation impinged on the nature and outcome of the debate. The nation had witnessed the struggle related to the civil-rights movement, the rise of the counterculture, student protests over the Vietnam War, and the breaking Watergate scandal. The events of this period fostered a high degree of distrust of the government and an unprecedented level of concern for the rights of minorities. Social movements spilled over into the courts and legislatures, where minorities pressed for recognition of their rights. Two key examples were the passage of the historic Civil Rights Act of 1965 and the Supreme Court's decision in *Roe v. Wade*.[1] Benefits were also extended to other downtrodden groups. The mentally ill were deinstitutionalized, and a series of Supreme Court cases restricted the power of the police and offered those accused of crimes many additional legal protections, such as the right to counsel for indigents.

Although these events signaled for many the promise of a social transformation that would create a more just and inclusive society, for others these and associated occurrences signaled a deterioration of the social fabric that could lead to chaos and anarchy if not checked. Worsening disorder and crime—rates of serious crime in the United States doubled during the 1960s—were seen by many as evidence of both a dangerous trend and the failure of liberal social policies.[2] The riot at Attica State Prison in New York in September 1971 and the subsequent prison takeover by inmates exemplified the dangers that could result from this revolutionary movement. The response to Attica, a poorly planned counterattack by state police and corrections personnel that left ten hostages and twenty-nine inmates dead, along with another three hostages and eighty-five inmates wounded, typified the larger social backlash by conservatives attempting to prevent further deterioration of the social order.[3] Battle lines between the two increasingly polarized groups had been clearly drawn a year earlier when four student protesters at Kent State University were shot and killed by National Guardsmen. While the social movements begun in the 1960s continued to make headway, the country was on the verge of a law-and-order movement that gained momentum during the early 1970s and influenced crime policy for decades to come.

It was during this critical period that the U.S. Supreme Court decided the case of *Furman v. Georgia,* essentially overturning a case decided only a year earlier.[4] *Furman* was a five-four decision in which each of the nine justices penned a separated opinion. The debate over capital punishment, embodying issues of race relations and the ultimate power of the government, symbolized the larger social battle taking place between those who viewed the criminal-justice system as a tool of government oppression and those who viewed it as a vehicle for preserving social order. Perhaps no other single societal issue was more controversial than the death penalty. Within the death-penalty debate itself, deterrence surfaced as its primary justification and became a major dividing point. As Justice Marshall wrote in *Furman,* "[T]he most hotly contested issue regarding capital punishment is whether it is better than life imprisonment as a deterrent to crime."[5] At this time, few were willing to support the sanction merely for its retributive potential, a sentiment seen as akin to seeking revenge. Supporters were most likely to express support for the death penalty because of its ability to protect the public, a sort of necessary evil. Those opposed to the sanction, therefore, seldom had to argue the issue on moral grounds, but rather on its lack of effectiveness in protecting the public. Those opposed to the death penalty often conceded their willingness to impose the penalty if it could be shown to benefit society by reducing crime.

Texas legislators charged with reimplementing capital punishment were not themselves immune from controversy. In what became known as the Sharpstown scandal, many legislators, the Speaker of the House, the lieutenant governor, the attorney general, and even the governor had been implicated in a bribery-and-fraud scheme involving businessman Frank Sharp.[6] As a result of the scandal, new members constituted fully half of the House of Representatives at the beginning of the sixty-third legislative session. The legislature, stacked with neophyte representatives elected under the rubric of reform, would be forever known as the reform legislature, as much for its composition as for the series of laws it enacted to prevent future government corruption. The freshman lawmakers also overhauled the Texas criminal code, making it one of the most sophisticated in the country and a model for other states to follow.

It is within this context that the public debate over capital punishment took place on the floor of the House on February 6, 1973. Two bills were open for debate: House Bill 200, which proposed general categories of capital murder that could be subject to the death penalty, and House Bill 229, which singled out police officers for special protection. As elsewhere, much of the discourse focused specifically on the issue of deterrence. Those on both sides provided arguments, emotional appeals, anecdotal evidence, and varying levels of statistical proof.

Representative Baker, an opponent of the death penalty, asked each of those speaking either in favor of or in opposition to House Bills 200 and 229 whether they were aware of any statistics suggesting that the death penalty was a deterrent. Baker often prefaced this inquiry with a statement concerning states and countries that had abolished the death penalty, such as Minnesota and the Scandinavian countries: he claimed that they had experienced decreases in murder rates after abolition and that their rates of murder had remained lower than those in retentionist jurisdictions. This assertion was challenged by Carol Vance, the Harris County district attorney, who countered that most of those jurisdictions were experiencing decreasing murder rates before abolition and therefore had less need for the death penalty. According to Vance, the causal order posited by Baker was reversed. States that had less need for the death penalty were more likely to do away with it, whereas those with higher rates of homicide continued to utilize it.

Proponents of capital punishment were also quick to point out that major differences other than the legal status of the death penalty existed between Texas and abolitionist jurisdictions, and that it was these other differences that accounted for the abolitionist jurisdictions' lower homicide rates. In one heated exchange, attorney Fred A. Semaan argued that abolitionist states such as Minnesota differed considerably from Texas. When Representative Washington asked him if he believed Texans were more inclined to violence than residents of abolitionist states, Semaan agreed that they were: "I don't think in Maine, New Hampshire, Vermont and those states people go to a beer joint the way some people here do in Texas—sit there and drink beer, and because somebody goes up and puts a nickel in a jukebox and plays a tune that somebody else don't like, kill him for it [sic]. That's been done here."[7]

Proponents charged that a more appropriate measure of the deterrent effect of capital punishment could be found closer to home. Vance stated that he had tried armed robbers who claimed that they would have killed the witnesses had it not been for the possibility of receiving a death sentence. On the House floor, John Green, district attorney for Ector County, showed a filmed interview with a serial killer from West Texas who had killed six women. In the interview, the serial killer, Johnny Meadows, stated that he was aware that the death penalty had not been carried out, and estimated that he would serve about twelve years for this string of killings. During the questioning of a witness opposed to the House bills, Representative Sullivan stated that he knew of a murderer who had killed two women and weighted them down in a stock tank, but had left a three-year-old alive, purportedly because he did not want to be given the death penalty as had Michael Paprskar, a defendant recently sentenced to death for the murder of a child. Defense attorney Frank Maloney, the witness being questioned, mentioned a weakness in this sort of evidence supporting deterrence, namely, that the defendant's explanation could have been the result of hindsight.

Proponents of the legislation also presented some crude statistics in support of deterrence. In response to a question from Representative Baker, Vance stated that since the beginning of the de facto moratorium on capital punishment in Texas, murder rates had increased dramatically in Harris County, especially for those types of murders that were likely to be deterred by capital punishment. Although lacking exact figures, he estimated that, in his jurisdiction alone, robbery murderers, crimes that had traditionally garnered a death penalty, had increased from about three a year before the moratorium in 1964 to over twenty a year since that time. Specifically concerning HB 229, Ted Butler, district attorney for Bexar County, stated that from 1942 to 1968 no police officers had been murdered in San Antonio, but one had been killed in 1969, one in 1972, and three in the first few weeks of 1973, killings he directly attributed to the abolition of the death penalty.

The strongest statistical evidence, however, was presented by those testifying in opposition to House Bills 200 and 229. Three professors—the Reverend Daniel B. McGee, professor of religion at Baylor University; Alan M. Sager, a law professor at the University of Texas; and Dr. Harold M. Hyman, the William P. Hobby Professor of History at Rice University—presented the hard statistical facts of the day. The information they relied on came from a recently published anthology by Hugo Adam Bedau, *The Death Penalty in America,* and research published in the appendices to Justice Marshall's opinion in *Furman;* the material presented by both Bedau and Marshall relied heavily on the research of Thorsten Sellin, the famous criminologist who had pioneered the methodology used to test the deterrence hypothesis.[8]

Sellin compared homicide rates among and within jurisdictions in which the legal status of the death penalty differed. If the death penalty acted as a deterrent, Sellin assumed, then comparing the rates of homicide in neighboring abolitionist and retentionist jurisdictions should show that states with the death penalty have a lower homicide rate than states without it. Sellin asserted that states closest in physical proximity would share other factors that might also influence homicide rates, thus leaving the presence or absence of capital punishment as the primary distinguishing feature between them. Sellin also compared the rates of homicide in states before and after the abolition or reinstatement of the death penalty, assuming that if the death penalty were a deterrent, rates of homicide within a jurisdiction should be higher during periods of abolition and lower during periods of retention.

The three professors took to the House floor and gave varying renditions of the evidence related to the deterrence hypothesis, and each concluded that none of the statistical evidence supported it.

Although the statistical methodology used to study this question has become more sophisticated over time, criminologists still rely on comparative approaches similar to those expounded in the House debates. When examining the issue of deterrence and the death penalty, criminologists typically compare the rate of homicide, or of some subset of homicides, according to the legal status (or, more often, according to the actual use) of the death penalty across jurisdictions at one point in time or within particular jurisdictions over time. This chapter combines the use of various statistical designs using a comparative methodology similar to Sellin's to determine whether rates of homicide are lower in Texas relative to other jurisdictions that do not utilize capital punishment, and whether rates of homicide are lower in Texas when capital punishment is more heavily utilized.

The results from this exercise could suggest several possibilities. First, an inverse relationship between the death penalty and homicide rates, in the absence of other plausible alternatives, would suggest that the death penalty acts as a deterrent. Second, a direct relationship between the death penalty and homicide rates, again in the absence of other plausible alternatives, would suggest that the death penalty might actually increase the rate of homicide. Researchers refer to this as the "brutalization effect," and have suggested that the use of the death penalty may actually encourage citizens to follow the lead of the state in committing acts of murder against their transgressors.[9] A null finding (i.e., one that showed neither an inverse nor a direct relationship) would suggest that capital punishment neither deters nor brutalizes, or that any such effects elude current measurement capabilities.

A Comparison of Homicide Rates in Texas to Those in Other States

The first step in testing the deterrence and brutalization hypotheses involves comparing the rate of homicide in Texas to those of all other states using a simple cross-sectional design. In a cross-sectional design, the target is analyzed against the comparison group within a particular span of time. In this case, the annual homicide rate per 100,000 residents in Texas is compared to the same measure for other states during the millennial years, 1999–2001. The states are listed in descending order of homicide rates in Figure 2.1.

Immediately noticeable is that states retaining the death penalty tend to have higher homicide rates than abolitionist states. The rate of homicide ranges from 1.1 per 100,000 residents in North Dakota, an abolitionist jurisdiction, to nearly 11.5 per 100,000 residents in Louisiana, a retentionist jurisdiction. The median homicide rate, 5.03, falls between the retentionist jurisdictions of New York and Pennsylvania. Only two of the twelve abolitionist jurisdictions, Michigan and Alaska, have homicide rates above the median, while the remaining ten abolitionist jurisdictions are clustered among states with the lowest homicide rates.

This pattern is even more pronounced when looking at the actual use of capital punishment. States above the median homicide rate executed 237 convicted murderers during this period; those states below the median put only 10 to death. Texas has the eighteenth highest homicide rate among all states. Having performed 37 percent (92 of 247) of the nation's executions during this period, this ranking, on its face, appears to support the abolitionist side of the deterrence debate. If the death penalty were a deterrent, the argument goes, then Texas should be located among those states with the lowest homicide rates. These findings are consistent with those of previous studies performing similar analyses, which have failed to find evidence of a deterrent effect.[10]

Without delving further, this simple correlation might even be construed as support for the brutalization hypothesis. Supporters of deterrence, however, may counter that such a simple analysis suffers from a number of flaws. One criticism is that the comparison includes all types of homicides, many of which are not subject to the death penalty. Given that capital-murder statutes limit the circumstances under which a penalty of death can be imposed, only a

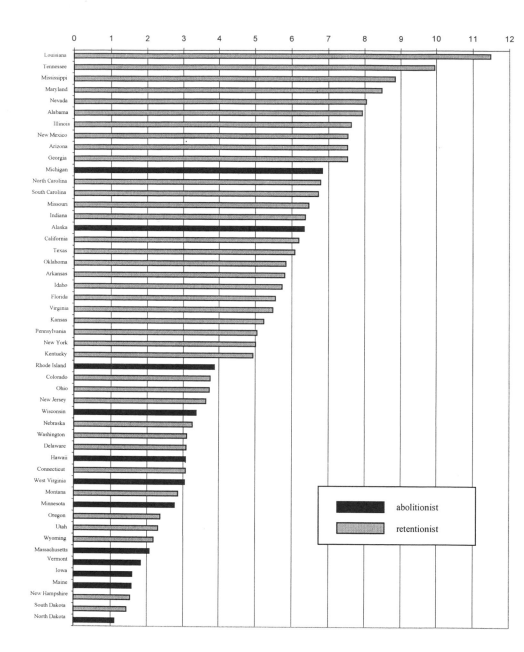

Figure 2.1. Homicide rates for abolitionist and retentionist states, 1999–2001

small subset of the total number of homicides could possibly result in a death sentence and eventual execution. It is not reasonable to suppose that homicides ineligible for the death penalty would be deterred by the threat of capital punishment, hence there is no reason to expect lower rates of these noncapital murders among retentionist states. The strength of the previous analysis rests on the assumption that general homicide rates are a reasonable proxy for death-eligible murder rates. That is, the proportion of death-eligible homicides is assumed to be consistent across jurisdictions, which is certainly not the case. Texas defines capital murder according to eight tightly circumscribed statutory criteria. Therefore, the proportion of murders in Texas that may be subjected to capital punishment is more restricted than in most other retentionist jurisdictions, which often include numerous catchall categories among the aggravating factors that make a murder case eligible for the death penalty.[11]

So it is plausible that Texas has experienced reductions in capital murders—those reasonably expected to be deterred by the threat of capital punishment—even as its overall murder rate remains high, relative to the rates in abolitionist states. A more precise analysis would therefore compare only "death-eligible" murders to evaluate capital punishment as a deterrent for those crimes. A test analyzing the rates of a particular type of capital murder across states would be ideal. Such an analysis, because of the statutory differences in the definition of capital murder across jurisdictions, must be limited to a type of murder that is death-eligible in all jurisdictions.[12]

One type of murder that is universally reported and statutorily defined as capital murder in all of the death-penalty jurisdictions is murder of a police officer. A more limited analysis of this particular type of capital murder is especially appropriate considering that the protection of law enforcement personnel from would-be killers is an oft-mentioned objective of deterrence through the use of capital punishment.[13] Further, when Texas was reimplementing capital punishment in 1973, this subtype of capital murder was initially singled out for special consideration in House Bill 229. The methodology from the previous section can be used to test the deterrence hypothesis as it relates to the capital murder of police officers.

The results of this analysis found that police officers were not safer in retentionist jurisdictions, where they were murdered at a rate of 8.124 per 100,000 sworn officers; in abolitionist jurisdictions, the rate was 6.096 per 100,000 sworn officers.[14] With a rate of 17.372, Texas had more police officers murdered per capita than all but five other jurisdictions, even though Texas executed more defendants than any other state during the time period. Once again, the evidence tends to support the abolitionist view that law enforcement officers are not safer in retentionist jurisdictions, but are actually at higher risk of being murdered. These results parallel the findings above on general homicide rates and are consistent with the findings from previous studies on deterrence and the killing of police officers.[15]

While abolitionists may consider the cross-sectional comparisons above as evidence in support of the brutalization hypothesis, there are good reasons to be skeptical of these preliminary findings. The first is an oft-repeated quote in introductory statistics texts: "Correlation does not equal causation." Correlation may be the most obvious component, but it is only the first of three elements necessary to prove causation. The remaining two elements are nonspuriousness and time priority, both of which must be demonstrated to support the brutalization hypothesis. To prove that the correlation between two variables is not spurious, it is necessary to show that extraneous factors do not account for the apparent relationship. In this case, factors other than the retention of capital punishment might account for differences in the homicide rates in retentionist and abolitionist jurisdictions. Although it is impossible to rule out every possible alternative causal factor, most studies attempt to control for factors that have previously been found to influence homicide rates and to test for additional factors that could plausibly account for the observed pattern. The question here is whether there are factors other than the status or use of the death penalty that could account for differences in the homicide rates of retentionist and abolitionist jurisdictions.

At first glance, there are some readily apparent differences between retentionist and abolitionist jurisdictions. Abolitionist jurisdictions are located entirely in the Northeast, Midwest, or noncontinental United States. Southern and western continental jurisdictions all retain the death penalty as a sanction. States that are small in area or in population tend to fall into the abolitionist camp; larger states are generally retentionist. New England and midwestern states also have lower levels of urbanization, less poverty, and less racial diversity than southern and western jurisdictions. This is one reason that Sellin used contiguous states when making his comparisons. He believed that the best way to control for all of the potential extraneous factors that could impinge on homicide rates was to compare neighboring states that were similar in many of these respects, but differed primarily in their death-penalty status. For instance, the death-penalty jurisdiction of New Hampshire could be compared with the abolitionist jurisdictions of Maine, Massachusetts, and Vermont. The homicide rate in New Hampshire is slightly lower, but these states all appear to have similarly low homicide rates, regardless of their death-penalty status, which fails to support the deterrence hypothesis.[16] Abolitionist Michigan, on the other hand, has a higher rate of homicide than the neighboring death-penalty states of Indiana and Ohio, which appears to lend some credence to the deterrence hypothesis.

Using this logic, the most appropriate comparison group for Texas would be the contiguous states of Arkansas, Louisiana, New Mexico, and Oklahoma. One problem with this comparison is readily apparent; all of these states are retentionist. They do, however, differ in their level of use. Texas was by far the most frequent executioner, using raw numbers, with 92 executions during the millennial years. However, one must take into consideration that Texas is also the largest jurisdiction by far, suffers an extraordinary number of murders (1,262 on average), and has the largest number of inmates on death row (over 450). The comparison states have smaller populations and considerably fewer murders, and therefore justifiably fewer inmates sentenced to death and executed. Therefore, it was necessary to standardize the risk of execution before comparing the states. The measure used was the number of executions during 1999–2001 as a percentage of the number of homicides occurring in these jurisdictions. By this measure, the highest risk of execution occurred in Oklahoma (5.8 percent, 35 executions for 598 homicides), followed by Texas (2.4 percent, 92 for 3,787) and Arkansas (1.5 percent, 7 for 459). Murderers in New Mexico and Louisiana were at the lowest risk of execution using this measure: 0.2 percent (1 for 404) and 0.1 percent (2 for 1,529), respectively.[17]

Referring back to Figure 2.1, Louisiana has the highest homicide rate in the United States and New Mexico has the eighth highest; Texas, Oklahoma, and Arkansas are clustered between eighteenth and twentieth. Extending Sellin's logic to the frequency with which capital punishment is actually carried out among neighboring retentionist jurisdictions, the evidence appears to support the deterrence argument rather than the brutalization hypothesis. Among these contiguous states, those with the lowest risk of execution have the highest homicide rates, and those with the highest risk of execution have the lowest homicide rates. Again, however, these findings must be received cautiously. Even though these states share a common border, there are likely to be significant social, cultural, and demographic differences among them, other than their execution rates, that could account for the differences in their homicide rates. This is why the evidence from such contiguous-state comparisons remains speculative.

The design relied on herein is quite simple, yet other studies have employed more sophisticated cross-sectional designs, which used multivariate statistical analyses to control for the effects of several potentially influential factors simultaneously, to examine data across U.S. jurisdictions. These studies have generally failed to support either the deterrence or brutalization hypotheses, finding any apparent relationship between the legal status of the death penalty (or executions) and homicide rates to be spurious. After a thorough review of this evidence, Peterson and Bailey concluded:

> [N]ot a single comparative study conducted in the U.S. dating back to the turn of the century has produced any evidence of a marginal deterrent effect for capital punishment. And, not a single . . . cross-sectional analysis of the U.S. . . . dating back to the early part of the century has produced any evidence of a significant deterrent effect for capital punishment.[18]

The third element that is necessary to demonstrate causation is time priority, meaning that it is necessary to show that the change in the proposed causal variable preceded the change in the proposed response variable. For instance, to support the brutalization hypothesis, the data would have to show that homicide rates increased after the introduction of death-penalty legislation or after an increase in executions, or that homicide rates decreased after the abolition of the death penalty or after a decrease in executions. To support the deterrence hypothesis, it would be necessary to show that homicide rates dropped after the introduction of death-penalty legislation or after increases in executions, or that homicide rates increased after the repeal of the death penalty or after decreases in executions.

Past studies have found that the time ordering of the relationship between homicides and a state's death-penalty status appears to go in the opposite direction from that predicted by the deterrence and brutalization hypotheses.[19] When the murder rate in a particular jurisdiction is low, there is a lower perceived need for the sanction and criticisms of the death penalty are more widely accepted; thus the way is paved for the death penalty to be abolished. The most successful abolitionist movement in the United States came after a period of declining crime rates during the early twentieth century, when reformers were able to sway legislators to abolish capital punishment in nine states.[20] Likewise, reenactment in formerly abolitionist jurisdictions is often related to an increase in homicides or to the occurrence of a particularly heinous or gruesome crime. Of the nine states that abolished capital punishment during the early twentieth century, seven reenacted capital punishment after brief periods, often as the result of a high-profile murder.[21]

Given the nature of a cross-sectional analysis, which compares the relationship between variables within a given time period, it is impossible to use this design to adequately evaluate whether time priority exists between homicide rates and the death penalty. Methodologists refer to the difficulty of determining time sequence when the proposed cause and effect are both measured during the same interval as the problem of simultaneity. An analysis that avoids the problem of simultaneity can be devised using a longitudinal design, which measures changes in the target over an extended period of time. The following section uses a longitudinal approach to analyze changes in Texas homicides during periods of abolition, retention, and varying levels of actual implementation—executions.

Texas Homicide Rates during Periods of Abolition, Retention, and Execution

As with the cross-sectional analysis, the first step in performing a longitudinal analysis is to determine whether there is a correlation between the death penalty and the murder rate, except that the correlation measures the relationship within a jurisdiction over a period of time rather than across jurisdictions during the same time interval. This will test the assertion put forth by Carol Vance, the Harris County district attorney, that the absence of executions during the moratorium led to an increase in the number of murders in Texas. Although it is not possible to measure changes in specific subcategories of murder for which the death penalty is most likely to have a deterrent effect, changes in general homicide rates during this period can be analyzed.[22]

A review of the murder rates in Texas over the past few decades appears to support Vance's observations. After a period of decrease in the early 1960s, homicide rates in Texas stabilized just before the moratorium, when the state performed an average of six executions a year. From 1962 through 1964, when the electrocution of Joseph Johnson was carried out, the homicide rate hovered around 7.5 per 100,000. The homicide rate remained at 7.5 in 1965, but rose to 9.1 in 1966. This rather dramatic increase, signaled, it appears, by the onset of the moratorium in executions, marked the beginning of a dramatic rise in homicide rates, which more than doubled from 1964 to 1982, when Charlie Brooks, Jr., was executed by lethal injection. The peak homicide rate of 16.9 was reached in 1980, and the period of 1979–1982 was a period of stable, historically high homicide rates that stayed above 16 per 100,000.

Even more remarkable was the pattern in homicide rates following the resumption of executions in Texas. Homicide rates decreased fairly steadily throughout the 1980s: sharp downturns of about two points each occurred in 1983, after the first execution, and again in 1987, amid the execution wave of the mid-1980s.[23] Homicide rates stabilized at around 12 per 100,000 during the late 1980s. During 1988–1991, executions averaged only four a year; in 1991 homicides soared to 15.3 per 100,000, their highest rate since executions had

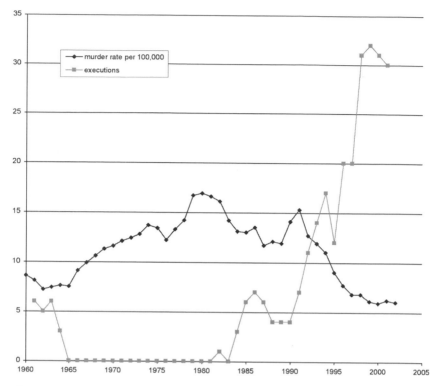

Figure 2.2. Executions and murder rates in Texas, 1960–2002

resumed. The next year ushered in what became a record-setting wave of executions, 214 during 1992–2001. This run of executions made Texas the undisputed leading executioner in the United States. Coincidentally, or perhaps not so coincidentally, homicide rates began falling that year and continued to drop to 6 per 100,000 during 1999–2001. Texas had not experienced homicide rates this low since the experiment with the abolition and reinstatement of the death penalty began, and some have attributed this reduction in homicide rates during the 1990s to the ever-increasing number of executions.[24]

The strength of the relationship between executions and homicide rates pictured in Figure 2.2 can be measured statistically. Using regression analysis, a best-fitting line is plotted between the points for the number of homicides and executions occurring in each year. This yields two useful pieces of information: R^2, which provides a measure of the overall strength of the relationship between executions and homicides, and the regression coefficient, b, which gauges the average effect of each execution on the subsequent number of homicides.[25] After necessary corrections were made that involved restricting the time frame and including a measure of the homicides occurring during each previous year, the regression model yielded an R^2 of .839 and a b for executions of -11.250.[26] The R^2 indicates that nearly 84 percent of the variation in homicides can be predicted by the model. That is, knowing the number of executions and the number of homicides from the previous year allows one to predict the number of homicides in a given year with 84 percent greater accuracy than simply relying on the average number of homicides occurring across all years. Most importantly, the regression coefficient for executions shows that a decrease of 11.25 homicides can be expected on average for each execution carried out. That is, relative to the previous year's number of homicides, each execution decreased the occurrence of homicides in a given year by 11.25. Results from this regression model suggest that each year an average of nearly thirteen executions saved approximately 144 lives during this twenty-year period. Summarily, this measure would suggest that the 256 executions occurring during 1982–2001 saved 2,880 people from being murdered in Texas during those years.

These figures are quite encouraging for those on the pro side of the deterrence argument. The correlation between executions and homicides is certainly too large to be immediately dismissed as purely coincidental, but what about the other requirements needed to prove causation—time priority and a nonspurious relationship? Although changes in executions appear to predate changes in homicides, an empirical test conducted herein was unable to rule out the possibility that changes in homicides and executions occurred simultaneously.[27] To rule out spuriousness, it would be necessary to utilize a multivariate statistical technique to show that the effect of executions on homicides remained even after accounting for the influence of other variables typically found to influence homicides. In a previous study, a correlation was found between monthly executions and homicides or felony homicides in Texas during 1984–1997. However, after multiple regression was used to control for ten variables typically associated with homicide rates, the apparent relationship disappeared.[28]

Unfortunately, this type of examination is impossible in the current situation because the sample size by year (N = 25) is too small to accommodate control variables in a multivariate analysis. An alternative means of gauging whether the trend in Texas homicide rates was a result of its reliance on capital punishment involves comparing homicide trends in Texas to homicide trends elsewhere in the United States. If homicides in Texas were responding to the deterrent effect of capital punishment, then one would expect the trend in Texas homicides to be distinct from the more general trend across states that did not experience the same pattern of executions. If, however, the homicide trend in Texas mirrors that of the United States generally, then the implemen-

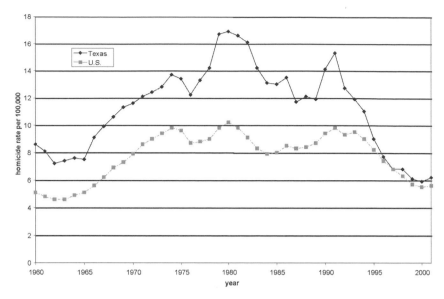

Figure 2.3. Homicide trends in Texas and the U.S., 1960–2001

tation of capital punishment should not be considered key to changes in Texas homicides. This comparison combines the strength of a cross-sectional design, by comparing the rate of homicide in Texas to a reference category, with the strength of a longitudinal design, by making this comparison over a number of years, from the 1960s through the millennial years.

Figure 2.3 provides mixed support for the deterrence hypothesis. From the 1960s through the early 1990s, the Texas homicide rate almost perfectly tracked that of the United States.[29] The fact that Texas trends nearly mirror national ones during the 1960s through the early 1990s, albeit with rates generally higher and changes in rates slightly exaggerated, suggests that there must have been some factor other than executions influencing homicide rates during that period. In fact, this was a period of rising crime rates generally across the United States, not just those expected to increase from a paucity of executions. Although the homicide rate doubled from the early 1960s to the early 1990s, the rate of violent crime increased by more than 4½ times.[30]

The evidence from the mid- to late 1990s, however, presents a different picture. For the first time in recent history, perhaps ever, Texas homicide rates decreased drastically, actually converging with U.S. rates in 1997 at 6.8 per 100,000. This happened as Texas executions reaching a historic high. This finding appears to support the deterrence hypothesis. It seems that something was happening in Texas in the 1990s that was not happening across the entire

United States. Or, rather, something was reducing homicides in Texas more severely than in the United States as a whole. The main question at this point is whether that "something" was an increase in executions.

Perhaps the something that was happening in Texas wasn't happening at the same rate for the United States generally, but crime rates, for homicide in particular, dropped to all-time lows in many parts of the country during the 1990s. And in many ways, Texas is different from the United States as a whole. Recall its overall higher rates of homicides and its more abrupt ascents and declines relative to changes in U.S. rates during the earlier years in the series. One of the most obvious differences between Texas and most other states is that Texas has several large urban centers. Homicide trends in urban areas have shown much more dramatic shifts than those in rural areas. In fact, homicide rates have been fairly stable in rural areas and small cities over the past quarter century. Overall changes in U.S. homicide rates have been disproportionately influenced by changes in urban homicide rates. When homicide rates are disaggregated by city size, the cities that have experienced the most dramatic shifts in rates of homicide during recent decades are those with a population in excess of one million.[31] Texas is home to three of the nine U.S. cities with populations in excess of one million: Houston, with nearly 2 million residents, and Dallas and San Antonio, each with between 1.1 and 1.2 million residents. Combined, these three cities account for just over 20 percent of the state's more than 20 million inhabitants, yet they accounted for 44 percent (546 of 1,238) of the state's homicides in 2000.

If the disproportionate decline in homicides that Texas experienced in the 1990s was due to the wave of executions being carried out in the state, such large reductions in homicide rates would not be expected in other jurisdictions with similar demographics. On the other hand, if Texas was once again merely mimicking a national trend, though one historically without precedent, then similar reductions would be expected in other jurisdictions with demographics similar to Texas's, but without the wave of executions. To test this theory, the two states with the largest population centers in the United States were chosen for comparison: New York and California. New York includes New York City, which, with a population of over eight million, makes up 42.2 percent of the state's population. California includes Los Angeles and San Diego, which, combined, include nearly five million residents, or 14.5 percent of the nearly thirty-four million residents of California. Although both these states currently have enacted capital-punishment statutes, they differ dramatically from Texas in the number of actual executions. New York enacted its death penalty in 1995, by the end of 2002 had sentenced only 9 prisoners to death, and has yet to perform any executions in the post-*Furman* era. California had

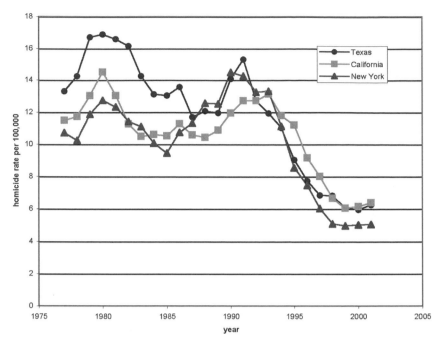

Figure 2.4. Homicide trends in Texas, California, and New York, 1977–2001

sentenced 795 capital defendants to death by the end of 2002, but had executed only 10 prisoners by the end of 2003. Compare this to the situation in Texas, where 954 inmates had been sentenced to death and 313 inmates executed by the end of 2003.

Despite the differences between these three states in their use of the death penalty, Figure 2.4 demonstrates the striking similarity among their homicide trends during the 1990s. Each state experienced historically large drops in the homicide rates in their major urban centers. Consistent with the findings that homicide trends are related to size of urban areas, New York experienced the largest reductions during the 1990s. Texas, second highest in the percentage of its population residing in large cities, had the second-largest reduction in homicide rates during the 1990s. California, lowest among the three in the percentage of its population living in large urban areas, experienced less of a reduction than either Texas or New York. The trends presented in Figure 2.4 suggest that Texas is simply experiencing a reduction in homicide rates that is on par with the reductions enjoyed by other states with large urban centers, and that this reduction is attributable to many of the same shared reasons, which do not include the recent wave of executions in Texas.

Voodoo Economics

Before the 1970s, criminologists relied mainly on evidence from contiguous-state analyses and before-after studies in states that had abolished or reenacted capital punishment. The results from these studies were just as likely to find evidence of a brutalization effect as of a deterrent effect, though more often they found no relationship at all.[32] Criminologists considered the issue closed, and the deterrence hypothesis was relegated to the bin of null findings. However, a study released in the immediate aftermath of *Furman v. Georgia* challenged these assumptions. The study, published by economist Isaac Ehrlich, was the most statistically sophisticated analysis ever performed on the issue.[33] Ehrlich examined the relationship between executions and homicide rates during the years 1933–1969. He used multiple regression to control for the sociodemographic variables commonly related to homicide rates, and used measures of the certainty of imprisonment and execution to distinguish the deterrent effect due to executions from the deterrent and incapacitation effects of imprisonment and other control variables. His conclusion was that, holding all of these factors constant, an inverse relationship existed between executions and homicide rates to the extent that each execution carried out between 1933 and 1969 saved an average of seven to eight lives. This evidence was submitted to the U.S. Supreme Court in the solicitor general's briefs in *Fowler v. North Carolina* and played a role in the Court's willingness to reapprove capital-punishment statutes in a series of cases in 1976.[34]

Among criminologists, Ehrlich's findings were greeted with a high degree of skepticism and confusion. Not only did his findings challenge long-held beliefs about the deterrent effect of capital punishment, but criminologists were further confounded by the complex statistical techniques that Ehrlich had employed and that made it difficult for them to adequately critique and challenge his findings. A panel was commissioned by the National Academy of Sciences for the purpose of reviewing new evidence on deterrence and incapacitation; Ehrlich's work was its primary target. Those commissioned by the panel, as well as independent researchers, soon discovered numerous flaws in Ehrlich's original work.[35] Most of the problems stemmed from his focus on patterns across the United States as a whole. By failing to disaggregate data at the level of jurisdiction, Ehrlich had included abolitionist jurisdictions along with retentionist jurisdictions, ignoring whether a jurisdiction even provided for capital punishment. This made it impossible for him to discern whether retentionist jurisdictions experienced greater decreases in homicides than abolitionist jurisdictions, a necessity for proving a deterrent effect during those years. The other major problem with his research was that the findings hinged on data included from the late 1960s, a period which experienced no executions and a dramatic rise in homicides. When the analysis was restricted to a cut-off point in the mid-1960s, any evidence of a deterrent effect washed out of the results.

In response to this criticism, Ehrlich performed a subsequent analysis using a cross-section of state-level data from the 1940s and 1950s.[36] Using this new design and limiting data under review to the period previous to the moratorium, he again discovered evidence of deterrence, but critics again found serious flaws in his research.[37] In addition to generating critiques, Ehrlich's work spawned a whole new genre of research on deterrence and the death penalty. A cadre of researchers began performing studies using multiple regression to control for numerous variables and the risk of execution. Other than a couple of notable exceptions, these researchers found no support for the deterrence hypothesis. Studies that did find evidence of deterrence were quickly discredited.[38]

Since the initial wave of post-*Furman* studies using multiple regression, an almost endless stream of analyses have varied jurisdictions and time periods, disaggregated data by particular types of homicide, and used various measures of perceived execution risk. Again, with few exceptions, the evidence from these studies (over 100 in all) has overwhelmingly failed to find evidence of a deterrent effect. Those few studies that have found evidence of a deterrent effect have been completed mainly, although not entirely, by economists.[39] The findings from these studies are often stated quite boldly; for example, that each execution saves an average of 18.5 lives or 156 lives, or that executions are responsible for an 8 percent reduction in homicide rates.[40] Although the studies finding evidence of deterrence were sporadic during the 1980s and 1990s, they generally spurred reanalyses and critiques.[41] The vast majority of studies, completed primarily by sociologists, have not met with the same response, but rather have been seen by most criminologists as once again closing the book on deterrence.[42]

Very recently, however, a new wave of econometric deterrence studies surfaced; these analyses employ panel data, which essentially combine the strengths of cross-sectional and longitudinal approaches by using data from several jurisdictions, typically states, over time.[43] As with the econometric studies completed in the early 1970s, these studies consistently find evidence of deterrence using data from the post-*Furman* era. These studies are also more statistically sophisticated than those completed by criminologists.

However, these studies suffer from many of the same methodological and analytical problems as their earlier counterparts. Of greatest concern is that the findings are not robust, but instead change dramatically with the slightest change in model specifications. This weakness fails to inspire confidence in the findings: the studies are vulnerable to the criticism that their statistics are easily manipulated to reach any result desired by their authors. The time is ripe for such studies to be performed. The increase in executions and the decreasing rates of homicide throughout the 1990s gave rise to a situation that was the reverse of what was happening in the late 1960s. So far in these studies, just as in those from the late 1960s, the apparent causal connection between homicide rates and execution rates is proving to be more illusory than real.[44]

The Texas Moratorium Study: A Replication

One such study on the deterrent effect of executions was recently completed by two University of Houston–Clear Lake economists, Dale Cloninger and Roberto Marchesini.[45] As a result of legal challenges to the constitutionality of newly imposed restrictions on subsequent applications for habeas corpus, the Texas Court of Criminal Appeals ordered a moratorium on executions in early 1996, until the issue was resolved.[46] The court ultimately denied relief on this issue, and executions resumed in early 1997. Consequently, there were an average of seventeen executions in Texas yearly during 1993–1995, only three executions in 1996 (two of those executed had voluntarily dropped their appeals), and thirty-seven executions in 1997. Cloninger and Marchesini asserted that the lack of executions in Texas in 1996 had resulted in an increase of some 249 murders in the state.

To test whether this change in the level of executions affected the incidence of homicide, Cloninger and Marchesini used a modeling technique they had previously developed in other studies.[47] This technique, referred to in their previous works as a portfolio approach, borrows from econometric studies of the financial market. Just as financial economists model the relationship between a specific asset and a portfolio of assets, Cloninger applied this approach to model the relationship between particular crimes (i.e., homicide) and a portfolio of crimes (i.e., index offenses). In essence, changes in the portfolio (index crimes) became the standard against which changes in the specific asset (homicides) were measured using the financial (crime) beta.

In financial markets, the beta is a measure of a security's volatility in comparison to some broad market index that is a composite of the returns on an array of securities. Similarly, "crime betas indicate the amounts that individual crimes can be expected to vary as a result of variations in a broad-based or aggregate (multi-community) crime index."[48] The crime beta is derived by regressing the percentage change in a particular crime by the percentage change in the crime index over some period of time. A beta of one indicates that the particular crime and the crime index vary at the same rate. A beta greater than one indicates greater variations in a particular crime relative to the crime index; a beta less than one indicates lesser variations in the particular crime relative to the crime index.[49]

Cloninger and Marchesini used the portfolio approach to study the impact of the brief respite from execution in Texas during 1996 and the wave of executions that followed in 1997. However, rather than measure changes in the occurrence of homicides against the crime index, as they did in their previous study, Cloninger and Marchesini chose to treat the occurrence of homicides across the entire nation as the index against which changes in Texas homicides were to be measured.[50] The authors proceeded using a standard event-study methodology.[51] Financial economists use this methodology to study the impact of a given event on the returns of an individual security. To do so, the portfolio approach is employed: a linear model is constructed for the period just before an event by regressing the returns on the individual security against a broad financial market index. This model provides estimates of the expected returns on a security without the event. These estimates are then compared to the actual performance of the security to determine if the event had a significant impact on the security's expected performance, beyond that which would be expected from changes in the overall market index.

The first event in Cloninger and Marchesini's study consisted of a decrease in scheduled executions to near zero beginning in April 1996. The second event consisted of a return to an extraordinary number of executions beginning around April 1997, when six executions took place, followed by eight in both May and June. To study the impact of these events, Cloninger and Marchesini calculated a baseline equation using twelve-month percentage changes in homicides during 1989–1995 (N = 72) from data supplied by the FBI.[52] They used this equation to estimate the expected twelve-month percentage changes in Texas homicides during 1996 and 1997. The *estimated* percentage change in Texas homicides was then subtracted from the *actual* percentage change in Texas homicides to determine if the monthly numbers of homicides in Texas during 1996–1997 were higher than expected.[53]

Following this procedure, Cloninger and Marchesini found that homicides were 45 percent higher than expected during May 1996, the second month of the moratorium.[54] This month offered the strongest evidence of a deterrent effect, but they also found significant positive differences for five of the twelve months from March 1996 through March 1997, suggesting that the occurrence of homicides was higher than expected during much of the de facto abolition in Texas. They also found a higher-than-expected level of homicides in April 1997, which, although that month technically marked the beginning of the execution wave, they took as evidence of a spillover effect from the period of abolition. Figures from the execution wave of May 1997 through December 1997 did provide some support for the deterrence hypothesis—two months reported fewer than the expected number of homicides—but Cloninger and Marchesini considered the evidence of a deterrent effect during the period of increased executions to be marginal. After converting the percentage difference between actual and expected homicide rates, they found that the cumulative number of additional homicides over that predicted by the model peaked in April 1997 at 249 and decreased only slightly to 221 during the remaining months of 1997. Cloninger and Marchesini interpreted this as evidence that the moratorium cost the state of Texas the loss of 249 innocent lives during its brief imposition, a figure that only marginally decreased during the execution wave that followed.

Their study, like those of other economists, relied on a number of questionable data-analysis choices that are likely to reveal faults under closer examination. To determine the extent to which decisions made during data analysis influenced their findings, a reanalysis of their data is undertaken herein. The following critique does not question the assumptions underlying econometric studies of the deterrent effect of capital punishment, i.e., whether potential offenders are rational and capable of calculating the likelihood of execution for committing a murder at any given point in time. Rather, it is limited to an empirical reanalysis using Cloninger and Marchesini's method and slightly varying the data used to project the number of homicides expected to occur in Texas during 1996–1997, in the absence of any change in the frequency of executions.

In the first exercise, the time period used to measure the relationship between Texas and U.S. homicide rates was expanded to include the thirty-five years before the moratorium. In the second model, national homicide estimates were adjusted for reporting bias. In the final analysis, statewide violent crimes replaced U.S. homicides as the index against which changes in Texas homicides were measured. Such a reanalysis should either provide support for the robustness of the study's findings or illustrate how these authors and others performing similar studies can manipulate their outcomes through choices made during the collection and analysis of data.

Failure to Consider Historical Trends

Cloninger and Marchesini rightly asserted that Texas homicide rates have typically fluctuated more than national rates and in the same direction; however, they failed to consider anomalies in the relationship between Texas and

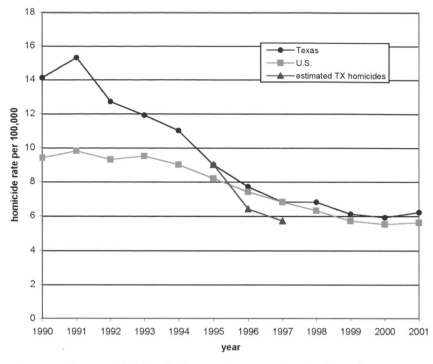

Figure 2.5. Texas and U.S. homicide rates (1990–2001) and estimated Texas homicide rates (1996–1997), based on Cloninger and Marchesini's model

national homicide rates during the 1990s. First, the change in Texas homicide rates relative to national rates was more pronounced in the 1990s than in previous decades. Second, the rate of homicide in Texas actually converged with the national rate in 1997 for the first time in recent history. Third, as shown earlier in Figure 2.3, the Texas homicide rate reached its lowest point in recent history during the late 1990s and essentially bottomed out.

Cloninger and Marchesini's assumption that Texas homicides would continue to decrease at the same rate relative to homicides nationally seems untenable given these facts. According to their model, but using the calendar year to define the moratorium period, Texas should have experienced 254 fewer homicides in 1996 than actually occurred.[55] Had their predictions been correct, the Texas homicide rate in 1996 would have been 6.4 per 100,000 instead of the actual rate of 7.7.[56] According to their model, then, Texas homicide rates were expected to dip well below the national homicide rate of 7.4 for the first time in recent history. If their predictions for homicides in 1997 are not readjusted to take into account the actual 1996 homicide figures, the expected rate for 1997 should have dropped still further to 5.7, rather than converging with the national average at 6.8, as it actually did.[57]

One may reasonably wonder how a longer estimation period would have influenced the number of homicides projected to occur in Texas during 1996–1997. To discover the answer, changes in the annual number of Texas homicides were regressed against changes in U.S. homicides for 1960–1995. Expected changes in Texas homicides during 1996–1997 were derived using Cloninger and Marchesini's formula.[58]

Cloninger and Marchesini found the actual number of Texas homicides in 1996 to be larger than the expected value, but the results from the model calculated herein, using annual data, found the actual number of Texas homicides to closely parallel, and perhaps fall even slightly below, the number of homicides predicted for both years. Actual Texas homicides decreased by nearly 13 percent in 1996 and by 10 percent in 1997; the model predicted decreases of 11 percent and 9 percent, respectively. The conclusion from this exercise is clear: had estimates of the 1996 and 1997 Texas homicide figures been derived from data covering a longer period, the results would not have supported the deterrence hypothesis. In fact, the number of homicides occurring in Texas appears to have been unaffected by either the brief moratorium or the wave of executions that followed.

Failure to Account for Reporting Bias in U.S. Homicide Data

Cloninger and Marchesini relied on raw data reported by agencies to the FBI to calculate twelve-month percentage changes from one year to the next. Reporting, however, is not universal. In any given year, numerous departments fail to respond. Cloninger and Marchesini made no effort to adjust their monthly homicide figures for unreported (missing) data. According to their study, "this methodology does not require zero reporting bias, it requires only that the reporting bias be consistent over the sampled period."[59] The validity of their estimates hinges on the assumption that missing data are distributed evenly across the years, yet the authors presented no test for the alternate possibility of nonsystematic reporting bias across the sampled period.

To check for the potential influence of reporting bias, Cloninger and Marchesini's monthly homicide figures were summed by year and compared to the FBI's estimated total number of homicides for Texas and the entire United States during 1989–1997.[60] For each year, Cloninger and Marchesini's Texas

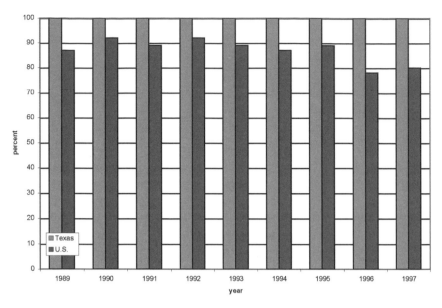

Figure 2.6. Percentage of Texas and U.S. homicides (1989–1997) included in Cloninger and Marchesini's monthly data

homicide figures matched almost identically the FBI's estimated totals, suggesting that Texas had nearly complete reporting during those years. This was not true for the United States; Cloninger and Marchesini's national homicide figures ranged from 78 to 92 percent of the FBI's estimated totals. The reporting bias, then, was not systematic over the reporting period. Cloninger and Marchesini's figures captured about 89 percent of the homicides on average during 1989–1995, but the percentage dropped to 78 percent in 1996 and 80 percent in 1997. Their figures registered a 19.67 percent reduction in homicides nationally (19,197 to 15,241) from 1995 to 1996, when the FBI estimated a 9.07 percent reduction (21,610 to 19,650). Since changes in national homicide rates were used to estimate expected changes in Texas homicide rates, Cloninger and Marchesini's use of an estimated national homicide reduction, during the most critical year of the study, that was more than twice as large as the FBI's estimate had obvious effects on their projected reductions in Texas homicides.

One may reasonably wonder how adjusting the national homicide figures for reporting bias throughout the 1989–1997 series would influence Texas homicide projections for 1996–1997. This is precisely what the FBI does when estimating the total number of homicides that occurred during each of these years. It is therefore possible to take the FBI's estimated number of homicides in the United States and partition them by month according to the distribution of reported murders in a given year.[61] Cloninger and Marchesini's model was recomputed with the new monthly estimated U.S. homicide totals.[62] Figures (from the newly derived model) necessary to reproduce Cloninger and Marchesini's "expected versus actual" changes in Texas homicides are included as Tables A and B in the Appendix.

The figures for 1996 resulting from this newly calculated model diverge dramatically from those presented by Cloninger and Marchesini. In only five of the twelve months did the estimated percentage change (decrease) in Texas homicides in 1996 exceed the actual percentage change in Texas homicides, whereas Cloninger and Marchesini found that the estimated percentage change (decrease) in Texas homicides exceeded the actual percentage change for each of the twelve months in 1996. Further, May was the only month to experience a significant (positive) difference between the estimated and actual change in Texas homicides during 1996, whereas Cloninger and Marchesini found that five of the months experienced significantly lower-than-expected reductions in Texas homicides. These differences reflect Cloninger and Marchesini's failure to consider the effect that uneven reporting across years (89 percent of homicides reported in 1995 versus 78 percent in 1996) would have on the percentage change in U.S. homicides from 1995 to 1996, and by extension, all of the additional figures calculated using this faulty measure.

The figures from 1997 are much more consistent with those reported by Cloninger and Marchesini. This is not surprising, since Cloninger and Marchesini's data for 1997 suffered from reporting bias similar to that from the previous year: 80 percent of homicides reported in 1997 and 78 percent of homicides reported in 1996. (Recall that the disparity in reporting bias from 1995 to 1996—from 89 percent to 78 percent—led to the skewed figures for 1996 in the original model.) The only significant difference between expected and actual changes in Texas homicides in 1997 was during the month of April, when homicides increased. Cloninger and Marchesini argued that this higher-than-expected number of homicides could be considered a "carryover effect" from the period of reduced executions; one could as easily argue that it represented a brutalization effect, an increase in homicides resulting from the state's example that killing is an appropriate response to provocation.[63] For an objective reader, the evidence appears mixed: a higher-than-expected level of homicide during the month after the moratorium was in full force, as well as a higher-than-expected level of homicide one month into the execution wave. Chance variation could as readily explain these findings.

Failure to Utilize a Localized Composite Crime Index

In a previous study of deterrence and the death penalty, Cloninger (1992) used the broad-based measure of crime as the portfolio against which changes in homicides were measured across a jurisdiction.[64] In the study under consideration here, Cloninger and Marchesini used U.S. homicides as the portfolio against which changes in Texas homicides were measured.[65] Conceptually, the prior approach, i.e., using a localized composite measure of crime as the portfolio, appears better suited to the task of estimating changes in one state's homicides. In other words, factors expected to influence changes in homicides in Texas should be similar to those expected to influence changes in crime generally in Texas, with the exception of executions.

One may reasonably wonder how utilizing a broad-based measure of changes in crime in Texas would influence projections of homicides within the state. In his 1992 study, Cloninger used the FBI's crime index as a composite indicator of crime against which changes in homicides were measured. Cloninger and Marchesini's model was recomputed herein using the FBI's violent crime index for Texas as the portfolio against which changes in Texas homicides were estimated. Figures from the newly derived model necessary to reproduce Cloninger and Marchesini's "expected versus actual" changes in Texas homicides are included as Table C in the Appendix.[66]

Figures based on this newly calculated model suggest an altogether different interpretation of changes in Texas homicides during 1996–1997. The beta is much smaller than that found in the previous model, suggesting that Texas homicides fluctuated less in relation to Texas violent crimes than they did in relation to U.S. homicides during 1989–1995. Based on the relationship between violent crime generally and homicide specifically in Texas during 1989–1995, and the change in violent crimes during 1996, one would expect less of a reduction in Texas homicides than actually occurred. Also, unlike the results from the previous model, the difference between the actual change and the expected change was negative for nine of the twelve months during 1996. In fact, the cumulative number of additional homicides occurring in 1996 was -128.95, suggesting that 129 fewer homicides occurred in the state than were expected, given the overall reduction in violent crime during that year.

These findings are completely contrary to those of Cloninger and Marchesini, who found that, according to their predictions, additional homicides occurred during the moratorium period. They found significant positive differences for five of the twelve months during 1996; in the recalculated model, April was the only month to produce a significant difference, though negative.

Alternately, in the recalculated model only one month during 1997 produced a significant difference, again April, but this time positive. The remaining months in 1997, though not statistically significant, were more positive than negative.

So, it appears from the recalculated figures that the advent of the moratorium in 1996 coincided with greater decreases in homicides than expected, and the reimplementation of executions in 1997 actually coincided with higher-than-expected occurrences of homicide. The cumulative homicide total finished out at -121.96, which suggests that, according to Cloninger and Marchesini's interpretation, the moratorium of 1996 saved 129 lives, while the execution wave of 1997 cost the state of Texas 7 innocent lives.

Conclusion

Though deterrence is often cited as one of the most compelling justifications for the retention of capital punishment, isolating the deterrent effect of the death penalty has proven to be as problematic as it is controversial. In the House debates over capital punishment, attorney Fred A. Semaan noted the difficulty in measuring a phenomenon that does not occur:

> Now, I've heard statistics of all kinds for years and years and years. The gentleman on my right [Rep. Baker] here has asked every speaker about statistics concerning whether or not the death penalty is a deterrent. I don't think there are any statistics on that, and I'll tell you why. Let's assume that I am going to kill you, and I get a gun and look you up and decide to blow your head off. And at the last minute I get to thinking about the death penalty and I decide, no, I better not do that or I might be executed myself, and I change my mind. Nobody knows about that. I am certainly not going to a statistician and say, "Put that down as a statistic." I was gonna commit murder but the death penalty deterred me.[67]

However, one can measure the changes in actual homicides that are not prevented by the death penalty. If the death penalty actually deters murders, then one should be able to gauge this through lower murder rates after the implementation or actual use of the death penalty. The analyses in this chapter support the bulk of previous studies that failed to find a causal connection between homicide rates and either the legal status of the death penalty or executions. Like other states with large urban areas, Texas experienced large reductions in the rates of violent crime and homicide throughout the mid- to late 1990s. The decrease in homicide rates in Texas, therefore, is not the result of increases in the number of executions.

It is beyond the scope of this analysis to determine exactly what led to these decreases in homicides or in violent crimes more generally; however, several variables have been suggested. These include changes in the age structure of the population, drug markets, the availability of weapons, police presence and practice, and the use of incarceration.[68] The possibility that the increased use of incarceration accounted for some of the decrease in homicides during the 1990s holds the most interest herein, as the other major teleological justification for the death penalty is its value in preventing convicted murderers from committing additional violent crimes.

CHAPTER 3

Incapacitation:
Does It Keep Them from Killing Again?

It is, of course, not easy to predict future behavior. The fact that such a determination is difficult, however, does not mean that it cannot be made. Indeed, prediction of future criminal conduct is an essential element in many of the decisions rendered throughout our criminal justice system. The decision whether to admit a defendant to bail, for instance, must often turn on a judge's prediction of the defendant's future conduct. Any sentencing authority must predict a convicted person's probable future conduct when it engages in the process of determining what punishment to impose. For those sentenced to prison, these same predictions must be made by parole authorities. The task that a Texas jury must perform [during the sentencing phase of a capital murder trial] in answering the statutory question [whether there is a probability that the defendant would commit criminal acts of violence that would constitute a continuing threat to society] is thus basically no different from the task performed countless times each day throughout the American system of criminal justice. What is essential is that the jury have before it all possible relevant information about the individual defendant whose fate it must determine.

JUSTICE STEWART IN *JUREK V. TEXAS*

During a public hearing in the Texas House of Representatives concerning the reimplementation of capital punishment in 1973, justifications offered in support of the death penalty most often focused on its efficacy in preventing similar crimes from being committed by someone other than a particular defendant. Some of this debate, however, spilled over into the related issue of preventing those convicted of crimes from committing additional offenses. The exchange between Tom Hanna, the district attorney of Jefferson County, and Representative Baker shows that those supporting the bill did not always draw a clear distinction between the two related goals, both of which focus on protecting society from further criminal acts:

REP. BAKER: I take it that you and the District and County Attorneys Association advocate the death penalty strictly as a deterrent?

DA HANNA: Yes.

REP. BAKER: And not because you think these people ought to just be put out of the way—put away?

DA HANNA: Mr. Baker, in whichever way we can come to it, be it speaking about the death penalty or life without parole, we are speaking about the concept of putting them away, forever, out of society.[1]

The commingling of these two "deterrent" goals of capital punishment by Hanna is understandable, given that deterrence itself has two meanings. The first, discussed in the previous chapter, is general deterrence. General deterrence is concerned with whether the punishment of a convicted criminal for a particular crime will prevent others from committing a similar crime because they fear suffering the same punishment. The other form of deterrence is known as special or specific deterrence. It is concerned with whether the punishment of convicted criminals will prevent recidivism, i.e., prevent them from committing further crimes. Because the death penalty is a final punishment, it is more appropriate to refer to the prevention of recidivism by capital offenders as incapacitation rather than deterrence. Incapacitation does not rely on a fear of consequences for its effectiveness, but simply removes any opportunity or ability of offenders to commit further criminal acts.

John Green, district attorney of Ector County, also commingled the two issues in an illustration he used to support the reimplementation of capital punishment. He discussed the case of Johnny Meadows, a serial killer who confessed to murdering six women, many of whom were raped and either stabbed or strangled to death. When Meadows was arrested for these murders, a background search revealed a lengthy criminal history, including two rape prosecutions that had resulted in acquittals. A colorful character, Meadows had terrified Odessa residents from his first strike in November 1968 through his capture in December 1971. He later concocted stories of multiple personality disorder, lunged at media representatives, and falsely accused investigators of abuse during their interrogation. During a courtroom appearance in Dallas, Meadows stripped off his shirt to display brand marks allegedly received during interrogation; it was later discovered that the marks were inflicted by his cellmates at his request.[2]

In a filmed interview played for the House, Meadows explained that as he was carrying out his crimes he was aware that the death penalty had not been carried out in some time. While in custody, he followed the case of *Furman v. Georgia* in the Supreme Court, and to avoid the death penalty he decided to plead guilty a week after the decision was handed down.[3] Although he would not have been eligible for a death sentence under any legislation passed after his crimes were committed, Meadows proved to be quite savvy in manipulating the system, including getting three of his murder confessions permanently banned through his abuse ruse. When asked what he was looking forward to in the future, Meadows stated in the interview that he looked forward to life on the outside after his "life" sentence, from which he figured he would be paroled in about twelve years.

Green used Meadows not only as an example of a sophisticated criminal who could have been deterred by the death penalty had it been in use at the time, but also as an example of why, if it failed to deter crimes of this sort in the first place, the death penalty would be necessary to keep an individual like Meadows from committing further crimes once caught. Recapping the filmed interview for the House, Green stated:

> That particular individual sitting there killed three innocent women by taking them out, raping them, and strangling them—picked them up out of laundries, out of places of business, and out of places they worked. This is the type of case that we feel—or where I believe—the death penalty should be put into effect; or [we should] remove him from society by whatever means we can to keep him away from other stores and other people.[4]

Although Green commented favorably on the prospect of a mandatory life sentence, he did not have faith in the current system, which allowed the parole board the discretion to release a murderer sentenced to life after having served a relatively short sentence. He offered the example of a recently paroled murderer who, after having served only eight years of a life sentence, killed two other people in West Texas. And though most of the representatives considered Meadow's own estimate of twelve years preposterous, he actually was paroled in 1990, after serving less than twenty years for his string of horrific killings. And though he did not kill again, two and a half years later Meadows, posing as an attorney, lured a woman into an office where he raped her at knifepoint. Meadows is currently back in prison, serving time for this aggravated sexual assault. He will be up for parole again in 2008.

Given estimates that those sentenced to life would serve from eight to ten years, with a likely maximum of twenty years, few representatives supported the system in place at the time as a workable alternative to the death penalty. Those opposed to the death penalty, however, were also opposed to mandatory life sentences. They wanted a system in which the length of the sentence would be tailored to the circumstances of the individual offender; such a system would ensure the protection of society. Proponents of the death penalty did not believe that such a system could be trusted, probably because, although it was not stated outright, this was how the current system was supposed to operate.

Further, many death-penalty supporters were not optimistic that mandatory life would provide the level of protection afforded by the death penalty. Although outside society may be protected if such murderers were actually kept in prison without being paroled, a prospect beyond the realm of these lawyers' experiences, many representatives and other supporters of the bill voiced concerns that prisoners would still have opportunities to kill again while incarcerated. Without the death penalty, they asked, what would keep individual inmates from killing guards, or deter collectivities of inmates from rising up and taking over the prison, as they had done a year earlier at Attica?

The Statutory Imperative That Jurors Consider Future Dangerousness in Sentencing

The goal of incapacitation is implicit in many of the aggravating circumstances listed in the guided-discretion statutes enacted in the wake of *Furman v. Georgia*, as well as in the types of murder that are considered capital murder. For example, offenders who commit murder for hire and murder of a potential witness are generally considered to present a continuing threat to the community because of the level of premeditation involved in the crime and because of the likelihood that they will repeat the same type of offense. Additionally, jurors are almost always instructed to consider a defendant's previous criminal history, or lack thereof, in their sentencing decisions. If a defendant has a prior history of criminal acts, particularly violent ones, that history becomes an aggravating circumstance in the jury's considerations. If a defendant has no prior history of criminal acts, that absence serves as a mitigating circumstance. Having held that information relevant to individualized consideration could not be excluded from jury deliberations, the Supreme Court also ruled in *Skipper v. South Carolina* that states must allow defendants to present evidence of nondangerousness as a mitigating factor in the punishment phase of capital trials.[5]

Consideration of the presence or lack of a prior criminal record has an explicitly teleological dimension. Rather than simply bearing on whether a defendant deserves a death sentence for the current offense, these circumstances allow sentencing authorities to determine punishment based on the likelihood that the defendant will commit another assaultive offense, possibly a homicide, in the future. In fact, the goal of incapacitating dangerous offenders prompted twenty-one states to explicitly include a defendant's potential for future violence among the aggravating circumstances jurors may be directed to consider before reaching a punishment decision.[6] Texas is one of only two states, however, that *require* jurors to make a prediction about the future conduct of a defendant before imposing a death sentence.[7] The first question jurors must answer in deciding whether to sentence a defendant to death is "whether there is a probability that the defendant would commit criminal acts of violence that would constitute a continuing threat to society."[8]

The significance of focusing sentencing deliberations on future dangerousness cannot be overlooked. In a survey of twenty-seven jurors who sat on nine capital cases in Oregon, the only state sharing Texas's special-issues format, researchers found that in each case resulting in a life verdict, jurors had failed to reach agreement on future dangerousness. The authors concluded that under the Oregon statute, "the issue of future dangerousness plays a prominent, if not central, role. Virtually all disagreements and prolonged discussion concerned only the [special issue] of future dangerousness. Jurors clearly perceived the penalty decision as hinging on this issue."[9]

Research has also shown that the issue of future dangerousness plays a central role when capital defendants receive death sentences in Texas. Among the 126 capital cases resulting in life sentences in Texas during 1974–1988, under the old special-issues sentencing format, juries answered the special issue related to deliberateness affirmatively in 76 percent of the cases, and, when raised, the special issue related to lack of provocation affirmatively in 91 percent of the cases.[10] The future-dangerousness special issue, on the other hand, was answered affirmatively in only 15 percent of the life-sentence cases. Thus, in 85 percent of the cases (107 of 126) in which jurors returned a life sentence in the penalty phase of a capital trial in Texas during 1974–1988, a prediction about the future dangerousness of the individual resulted in this leniency. A study completed on cases decided during the 1990s in Texas, under the current special-issues framework that explicitly inquires about mitigating evidence, has concluded that the level of future dangerousness posed by defendants remains a strong determinant of jurors' sentencing decisions.[11]

The future-dangerousness provision of the Texas death-penalty statute raises two major types of concerns. The first is whether it is fair to sentence someone to death on the basis of a prediction about future actions, rather than simply punishing the current offense. Even though the Texas statute has explicitly adopted this utilitarian position, the U.S. Supreme Court still evaluates the statute on its provisions allowing jurors to distinguish between those who do or do not deserve a death sentence.[12] In fact, the only major change to the Texas statute resulted from this premise: sentencers must be allowed to consider as mitigating evidence any factors that may make the person less deserving of a death sentence, even if that evidence suggests the offender will be a greater threat to the community in the future. This broader philosophical question of fairness in relation to such a utilitarian position requires a value judgment that is outside the realm of an empirical inquiry. The second and more pragmatic concern about the future-dangerousness provision is twofold: 1) whether a death sentence is a more effective and efficient means of incapacitating capital murderers, compared to alternative sentences, and 2) how accurately sentencers can predict which defendants will continue to commit criminal acts in the future.

How Dangerous Are They?

There used to be a common perspective in corrections that murderers typically made the best prisoners, often behaving as model inmates.[13] Wardens would frequently select murderers for the most sensitive positions in the prisoner work hierarchy, choosing them to serve as their own houseboys, as clerks, and even as inmate guards. Most of those currently serving prison terms for murder and capital murder appear to adhere to this same pattern, falling into the perspective of the lifer, which is to dig in, make the prison their home, and try to make things better for themselves and their fellow inhabitants.[14] Capital inmates and other long-term inmates have been found to have a stabilizing effect on the prison population by maintaining the positive aspects of the prisoner subculture, which tends to deteriorate in places where there is a great deal of turnover with younger, short-term prisoners.

Being in prison for such long stretches, however, also makes it a certainty that some of these inmates will adapt in less positive ways: becoming immersed in the negative side of the prisoner subculture, using drugs, and joining inmate gangs. This type of behavior and the affiliation with these groups can lead to trouble. When extreme violence erupts in the prison community and a homicide occurs, murderers, and capital murderers in particular, are often found to be disproportionately involved. For example, a member of the Texas Department of Criminal Justice (TDCJ) Special Prosecution Unit, A. P. Merillat, noted that three of the eight prison murders occurring in 1999 were committed by inmates serving life sentences for capital murder.[15] He describes two of these murders in particular. The first was committed by Carey Money, who attacked and killed fellow inmate William Smith on September 27, 1999. Money used a box-cutter blade attached to Popsicle sticks to cut Smith's throat, nearly decapitating him. The second murder Merillat describes was committed by Robert Pruett on December 17, 1999. Pruett was purportedly angry because Officer

Danny Nagle had written him up for taking a sandwich into the "rec" yard, a minor offense. Nagle had a reputation among the inmates for being very strict, and Pruett was facing transfer to a higher-security unit for the violation. Nagle apparently changed his mind about submitting the infraction against Pruett, but Pruett's anger had been escalating. When Nagle went into the television room to tell Pruett about his change of heart, and started to tear up the paperwork, Pruett allegedly told the officer that it was too late and stabbed him with a metal shank. Nagle died before help could reach him.

Although these cases are tragic, Merillat unwittingly provided evidence that undermined his argument that the death penalty is necessary to incapacitate capital murderers. First, the death penalty was in effect when these murders took place, yet was not successful at preventing them. Second, Merillat states that Nagle was the first prison guard to be murdered by a Texas prison inmate in sixteen years. Although Nagle's murder was senseless and tragic, it illustrates the actual rarity of murders of prison guards by inmates.

To determine the true efficacy of the death penalty in incapacitating capital murderers, the first step is to estimate how much crime executions prevent. This is no easy task, however. Much like measuring deterrence, this is an attempt to determine the quantity of acts that did not occur because of the defendants' executions. It is true that at the moment the sanction is carried out those executed are completely and forever incapacitated, but the issue then becomes how much crime they would have been responsible for if they had not been executed. One way to calculate this figure is to look at the behavior of death-sentenced inmates who have been spared.

When the U.S. Supreme Court overturned the death penalty in *Furman v. Georgia*, it created just such an opportunity: over 600 inmates were released from death rows across the United States. A nationwide follow-up of their behavior in the fifteen years since their release from death row provides an indication of their propensity for additional violence.[16] Of the 558 inmates for whom data were obtained, 6 killed again in prison: 4 killed other inmates and 2 killed guards. As a group, they committed 325 serious rule violations. Nearly half of these inmates (243) had been released from prison back into the community by the time of the follow-up study, spending an average time of 5.3 years free; 20 had committed new felony offenses and 1 had killed again. Forty-seven of these inmates were released from death row in Texas.[17] The Texas inmates were responsible for 21 of 325 serious rule violations in prison, but none of the prison killings. Of those released from prison, records show that 4 had committed new felonies. The *Furman*-released inmate who killed again, Kenneth McDuff, was from Texas.

Kenneth McDuff is the poster child for those supporting capital punishment for its potential to incapacitate. McDuff's criminal record began in February 1965, when he was convicted on twelve counts of burglary and attempted burglary. He received twelve concurrent four-year sentences for these crimes, but was paroled in December 1965. Several months later he got into a fight, and his parole was revoked. He was released again in 1966, and shortly thereafter committed his first capital murder. In 1968 McDuff received his first three death sentences for the brutal murders of three teens, including the rape-murder of sixteen-year-old Edna Sullivan, committed in August 1966.[18]

McDuff and his accomplice, Roy Dale Green, happened upon the three teens parked near a baseball field in Guadalupe County. McDuff forced the teens into the trunk of their own car at gunpoint. He drove their car to a deserted field while Green followed in McDuff's car. McDuff pulled the girl out of the victims' trunk and forced her into his own trunk, then shot the two boys in the head. McDuff and Green then wiped the car clean of fingerprints, wiped out the tire tracks, got into McDuff's car, and drove about a mile to another secluded road. McDuff forced Edna Sullivan from the trunk into the backseat, told her to undress, and raped her. Green and McDuff took turns repeatedly raping Edna Sullivan, and finally drove to yet another location. McDuff told the girl to get out of the car and sit on the gravel road. He took a three-foot piece of broomstick and choked her with it. As he forced the broomstick against her neck, she started waving her arms and kicking her legs, so Green held her body down until she stopped struggling. McDuff and Green then threw her body over a nearby fence, which they also crossed. After dragging her a short distance, McDuff choked her some more and then left her in some bushes. McDuff was caught because Green turned himself over to the police and testified about the entire ordeal.

McDuff received two last-minute stays of execution before the United States Supreme Court deemed capital punishment unconstitutional in 1972; his sentences were commuted to life. After serving seventeen years on his life sentence, McDuff was paroled in October 1989 to Milam County, where within days of his parole he murdered Sarafina Parker. His role in this murder as yet undiscovered, McDuff was returned to prison as a parole violator without new charges in October 1990, after he made death threats against a youth in Rosebud. He was again paroled in December 1990.[19]

He remained out of the eyes of the law for almost a year. In October 1991, McDuff committed the first of another series of brutal murders. After abducting Brenda Thompson, McDuff was stopped at a Waco Police Department vehicle checkpoint. McDuff stopped his truck about fifty feet from the checkpoint, and an officer, shining his flashlight up so as to identify himself to McDuff, approached the vehicle. Suddenly, Thompson started screaming and kicking desperately; she shattered the windshield on the passenger side, attempting to escape. The officer noted that her arms appeared to be bound behind her. McDuff gunned the accelerator and tried to run down the officers. A chase ensued, but McDuff eluded the officers' attempts to catch him. Furious with Thompson over the commotion and the damage to his truck, he slowly tortured her to death. Thompson's body was not discovered until October 1998, about a month before McDuff's execution.

About five days later, McDuff had an argument with his girlfriend, a seventeen-year-old prostitute named Regenia Moore. The last anyone saw of her alive was a witness who stated he saw them drive away in a pickup truck. Her body was found in September 1998 in a sinkhole near Tehuacana Creek. Her hands were bound behind her. Her ankles were bound with stockings and tied in such a way as to allow her to walk. The remains of her dress were wrapped around her pelvic area.

In late December 1991, McDuff and his accomplice, Hank Worley, abducted twenty-eight-year-old Colleen Reed from a car wash in Austin. McDuff threw her, bound, in the backseat of his Thunderbird, and they headed for Round Rock. McDuff then pulled the car over and climbed into the backseat with Colleen, as Worley drove the car. McDuff forced Reed to perform oral sex on him, then raped her. Worley exited at Stillhouse Hollow and pulled over in a secluded area near some trailer houses. Both Worley and McDuff repeatedly raped Reed. McDuff tortured her with lighted cigarettes, burning her all over her body, including her vagina. He then snapped her neck, killing her. Worley confessed to the murder after being pulled into the Bell County Sheriff's Department for questioning in April 1992. Reed's body wasn't found until October 1998, when McDuff told police the location of her grave.

In February 1992, McDuff committed his second-to-last murder, strangling to death Valencia Joshua. In early March of that year, McDuff targeted Melissa Northrup, who would become his last victim. Melissa was married and two months pregnant. When she failed to return home after work, her husband went looking for her and found that the store she worked in had been robbed. He dialed 911 and a search ensued. Though there were no witnesses to Melissa's abduction, McDuff's Thunderbird was found close by, and within hours he was placed on the FBI's Top Ten Most Wanted List. Appeals for information about his whereabouts were placed in newspapers and on television. A fisherman found Northrup's body floating in a flooded gravel pit in southeast Dallas County on April 26, 1992. She had been strangled with a rope. She was partially dressed, her hands tied behind her back; part of her lower torso was missing.

McDuff was not caught until May 1992, when Gary Smithee, an employee of a Kansas City refuse company, noted a striking resemblance between his coworker, Richard Fowler, and the pictures of Kenneth McDuff that were displayed on the television show, *America's Most Wanted*. He phoned the Kansas City police, who ran a cross-check of Fowler and McDuff and discovered that their fingerprints were identical. The following morning, the police followed McDuff's trash route and created a checkpoint. After a brief attempt to escape, McDuff surrendered.

McDuff received his final death sentence for the murder of Melissa Northrup. He confessed to all of his crimes, but refused to disclose the locations of the bodies unless he was paid $700 a body. He was finally executed on November 17, 1998.

Although the details of McDuff's crimes are shocking, the actual level of dangerousness (the base rate of violence) presented by the group of forty-seven *Furman*-commuted capital murderers in Texas was quite low overall. Spending an average of ten years in the prison population, these inmates incurred 4.5 serious violations per 100 inmates per year.[20] This rate of violence was consistent with those found in other studies that looked at the rate of violence among capital murderers, and was also similar to that of a control group of Texas murderers who had been sentenced to life terms in the year following *Furman*.[21] With the obvious exception of McDuff, the remaining forty-six *Furman*-released Texas inmates did not present an extraordinary threat to fellow inmates, prison staff, or members of the community.

Inmates released by the *Furman* decision, however, were somewhat different from those being sentenced to death during the modern era. For example, the forty-seven *Furman*-released inmates from Texas included seven rapists and three armed robbers. Inmates currently convicted of such crimes are not eligible for the death penalty. Some of the remaining thirty-seven murderers would not have been eligible for the death penalty under the more restrictive definition of capital murder in the current statute. A better test of how well the current capital-punishment scheme fosters incapacitation would involve an analysis of the behavior of those sentenced to death, but released from this sentence, during the era of lethal injection.

A follow-up of ninety-two inmates sentenced to death, but released from death row by commutation or reversal during 1974–1988, was conducted to see if their behavior was worse than that of the *Furman*-commuted inmates.[22] Of the ninety inmates serving time in the general prisoner population because their sentences were reduced from death to life imprisonment, nine committed serious violent rule infractions. Since these inmates had spent an average of 6.3 years in the prison population, the rate of serious violent activity was 1.6 per 100 inmates per year.[23] For a control group of inmates sentenced to life in prison for capital murder during the same period, the rate of violence was 2.6 per 100 inmates per year.

A more recent follow-up of offenders commuted during the era of lethal injection was conducted by Special Prosecutions Unit member A. P. Merillat, and expanded through March 1, 2000.[24] The author found that the former death-row inmates, by then numbering 149, had assaulted 62 correctional officers and 51 inmates during their time in the general prisoner population. Although it is not clear from the study, it appears that the author used a more inclusive definition of assault than previous researchers', tracking simple assaults in addition to aggravated assaults, for example.[25] Even so, the author still noted that many of the former death-row inmates did not present a continuing threat to the prison community: 110 of the 149 committed less than ten disciplinary infractions of any type, and nearly half (70) attained the highest allowable classification, entitling them to the least restrictive level of monitoring within the prison environment.

The overall level of threat may not have been as high as expected from these former death-row inmates, but one of the former death row inmates committed murder. Noe Beltran had been sentenced to death for the capital murder of an elderly woman in 1981. In 1987, the Texas Court of Criminal Appeals overturned Beltran's sentence, finding that the evidence was insufficient to support a finding of future dangerousness, and his death sentence was commuted to life.[26] On July 17, 1988, Beltran and another inmate, both members of the Mexican Mafia, stabbed another inmate to death. The murder was a hit ordered by the gang. Because of this crime, Beltran gained the distinction of being the second death-row inmate in the history of the state, Kenneth McDuff being the first, to be released from death row and then returned to it for a crime committed after his release.

The death-penalty statute at that time did not include a provision for inmates who murdered other inmates, only those who killed prison staff or killed during the course of an escape.[27] The Special Prosecutions Unit found an inventive way of construing the case as capital murder by arguing that the gain in gang status that Beltran would experience as a necessary result of the killing was a form of remuneration, and the crime was therefore chargeable as capital murder under the remuneration provisions of the statute.[28] The Court of Criminal Appeals disagreed with this theory of remuneration, however, and overturned his conviction.[29] Beltran thus became the first inmate in the history of the state, or perhaps anywhere, to be sentenced to death, commuted, sentenced to death for an ensuing crime, and then commuted again.

Nor was his the only murder committed by the original ninety-two commuted inmates. At the time of the first follow-up in 1989, eleven of these inmates had been released into the community, where they had lived for an average of four and a half years. One of these inmates, Kenneth Stogsdill, killed again after his release from prison. In 1976, Stogsdill was sentenced to death for a dismemberment slaying. His capital-murder conviction was overturned by the Texas Court of Criminal Appeals in 1977 for lack of evidence, but he was sentenced to ten years for burglary and sexual assault connected to the same crime.[30] He was released from prison in 1980 and moved to California, where in 1985 he was convicted of first-degree murder for another dismemberment slaying and sentenced to twenty-five years to life. He had chopped up the body of a man he met in a San Diego bar, thrown some parts in a trash container near his apartment, and tossed the rest into the bay—he was caught after the victim's head washed ashore.[31]

Although the overall odds of violence being committed by those whose death sentences were commuted may seem low, considering their previous status, the commission of seven additional murders by three former death-row inmates from one state would certainly cause any neutral observer to pause. Murders by one of the forty-seven *Furman*-commuted inmates and two of the ninety-two post-*Furman*-commuted inmates works out to a recidivism rate of about 2 percent. Considering that seven victims were murdered, the rate actually turns out to be 5 murders per 100 former death-row inmates. If it is assumed that this rate could be used to forecast the likelihood of recidivism for those who have been executed during the modern era, the execution of three hundred inmates by the state has saved at least fifteen innocent lives. Given this recidivism rate, executing rather than releasing the 450 current death row inmates could save twenty-three innocent lives. That is a total of thirty-seven lives that may have been saved up to this point by the incapacitation effect of the death penalty in Texas.

Some would argue that this estimation is incorrect. First, the death penalty, while it has been in force, has done nothing to prevent some former death-row inmates from killing again after their release from death row. This raises the point that death sentences are effective only once they are actually carried out. From sentencing to execution, death-sentenced inmates have been responsible for many violent acts and a number of deaths. One may ask how an inmate on death row has any opportunity to commit such acts of violence. After all, death row is supposed to be a place with security measures so tight that death-sentenced inmates have little or no opportunity to hurt fellow inmates or staff. A short description of just some of the incidents on death row should be enough to convince readers that the death penalty cannot completely prevent acts of violence by the inhabitants of death row while awaiting their demise:[32]

- Anthony Leroy Pierce was convicted of the stabbing death of fellow death-row inmate Edward King in August 1979.
- In August 1983, James Demouchette murdered fellow death-row inmate Johnny Swift by stabbing him sixteen times in the chest while they were inside the prison dayroom.
- Jay Kelly Pinkerton stabbed fellow death-row inmate Charles Rector in October 1983. Rector survived the attack.
- In a gang-ordered hit, Warren Bridge firebombed the cell of Calvin Williams in September 1984. Williams survived by pulling a mattress over himself. Bridge also stabbed another inmate in March 1985.
- In 1990, David Gibbs succeeded where Warren Bridge had failed, strangling Calvin Williams to death with a jump rope.
- Jemarr Arnold fatally stabbed to death Maurice Andrews in April 1995 while they were on the death-row rec yard. Arnold's final blow was to ram a ten-inch, all-thread bolt through Andrews's temple until it nearly protruded from his head; he then jumped on Andrews's body. Most of Arnold's actions were caught on video.
- In November 1998, a death-row inmate slipped into Robert Anderson's cell during their "in and out" period (a time when inmates are free to go in and out of their cells as they please) and stabbed Anderson sixty times with an eight-and-a-half-inch shank, yet Anderson somehow managed to survive the attack.

Most of these incidents took place at the Ellis I Unit in Huntsville, before death row was moved to the Terrell Unit, later renamed the Polunsky Unit, in Livingston in 1999. The inmates, many of whom worked in a garment factory and spent much of their time out of their cells at Ellis, certainly had more opportunities to commit violent acts.[33] The security has been increased at Polunsky, and inmates are now restricted to single cells and recreated separately.[34] However, as Merillat describes, there are still opportunities for violence, and these opportunities extend not only to fellow prisoners, but to guards and other "freeworlders" as well. On February 21, 2000, two death-row inmates overpowered a female guard and held her hostage for thirteen hours. On June 9, 2000, Juan Soria trapped the arm of a seventy-eight-year-old chaplain, pulled it through the food tray slot of his solid-metal door, and wrapped a bedsheet around it. Then, using two razor blades, Soria attempted to saw the chaplain's arm off, exposing four inches of the chaplain's arm bone and severing major arteries and vessels before guards saved the chaplain.

Although the heightened security on death row does largely offset the likelihood of violence, death-sentenced inmates have fewer restrictions on their movement when moved from death row, such as when they are escorted to court proceedings. During these postconviction proceedings, death-sentenced inmates typically are held in local jails, which are generally much less secure than death row. For instance, in June 1983 Ovide Dugas attempted to escape while on a bench warrant in Jefferson County, but was killed by authorities.[35] Perhaps the most dramatic incident involving a death-sentenced inmate out on a bench warrant to a county jail was that of Jerry McFadden. McFadden was convicted in the abduction, rape, and strangulation death of 18-year-old Suzanne Harrison in May 1986. Harrison and her two friends, Gena Turner and Bryan Boone, were abducted during a trip to a local lake. McFadden raped and sodomized Harrison, then strangled her with her panties. The bodies of Turner and Boone were found five days after Harrison's. Both had been shot, execution-style, with a .38-caliber pistol. On July 9, 1986, while being held in the Upshur County jail, McFadden overpowered a male jailer and escaped in the car of a female jailer, whom he took hostage. McFadden held her in an abandoned railroad boxcar in Big Sandy, but she escaped after twenty-eight hours. He was captured after an extensive, three-day manhunt.

Although escape is much likelier from county jails, inmates have escaped from death row. The first death-row escape dates back to 1934, when three death-row inmates escaped from the Walls Unit with the help of general-population prisoners who had smuggled in a gun. What made this story even more newsworthy was that one of the escapees, Raymond Hamilton, had been sentenced to death for his role in the killing of a guard a year earlier during an escape from another Texas prison unit, aided by the infamous Bonnie Parker and Clyde Barrow. One of the three 1934 escapees was killed by police in Amarillo six months later; Raymond Hamilton and the other escapee were returned to the Walls Unit and executed there in 1935.

More recently, seven inmates attempted to escape from death row at the Ellis Unit. All seven managed to escape their housing areas and hide on the roof for four hours during the Thanksgiving holidays in 1998. Martin Gurule, outfitted with a suit fashioned from cardboard, was the only one to successfully navigate the razor wire. A wound inflicted by guards during his escape exacerbated the trouble Gurule later had with his cardboard suit: it soaked up water and took on weight during his trek through the backwaters of the Trinity River, causing him to drown.

A dramatic escape in 2000 did not involve death-row inmates, but did include a capital-murder defendant and others convicted of violent crimes. This case raised the possibility of escape by a capital murderer sentenced to life in prison rather than to death. On December 13, 2000, the "Texas 7" escaped from the John Connally Unit, a maximum-security prison just outside of Kenedy, Texas. Led by George Rivas, a trustee serving eighteen life sentences for aggravated kidnapping and robbery, the seven inmates systematically incapacitated a series of guards over a two-hour period, tying them up and locking them in a storage room. They then impersonated guards and servicemen, tricking other guards into letting them out.[36]

The seven men were in the Connally Unit for a variety of crimes. As previously mentioned, George Rivas, thirty, was serving eighteen life sentences, seventeen to run consecutively, for aggravated kidnapping and robbery. Patrick Henry Murphy, thirty-nine, was serving fifty years for burglary and aggravated sexual assault with a deadly weapon. Donald Keith Newbury, thirty-eight, was serving time for armed robbery. Joseph C. Garcia, twenty-nine, was serving fifty years for murder. Randy Ethan Halprin, twenty-three, pleaded guilty to causing serious bodily injury to a child rather than face capital-murder charges for the beating death of his girlfriend's baby boy. When the paramedics found the boy, both of his arms and both of his legs were broken, he had multiple skull fractures, and one eardrum was ruptured. Halprin was sentenced to thirty years by a judge. Larry James Harper, thirty-seven, was serving fifty years for a series of rapes. Michael Anthony Rodriguez was serving a life sentence for capital murder: he had hired an assassin to murder his wife so that he could collect on two $150,000 insurance policies on her life.

After their escape, the Texas 7 committed a series of robberies to fund their newfound freedom. They avoided violence, other than the robberies, and everything was going according to their plans when George Rivas decided to rob an Oshman's sporting-goods store. An off-duty employee who witnessed the robbery telephoned the police. Officer Aubrey Hawkins arrived on the scene as the group was making its escape. Before Hawkins was able to get out of his car, pull a weapon, or attempt to flee, the escapees rained bullets into his car. After shooting at Hawkins, they pulled him from his car, shot him a few more times, and then ran over his head three times with their Explorer. Hawkins sustained six shots to the head, one to the back, and four to the left arm; his bulletproof vest protected him from two additional shots. Ironically, this was the same Oshman's that Rivas had attempted to rob previously, the crime that had resulted in his incarceration.

The Texas 7 found themselves on *America's Most Wanted*. The owner of the Coachlight RV Park in Woodland Park, Colorado, saw the program, which promised a $500,000 reward for information leading to their capture. He recognized the Texas 7 as the group of men who had recently rented space from him. He telephoned the police, who set up an elaborate plan to capture the fugitives. The first to be caught in a roadblock were Rodriguez, Garcia, and Rivas.

Soon thereafter Halprin surrendered in the RV; Harper committed suicide rather than return to prison. Murphy and Newbury were found a short while later, hiding at a Holiday Inn. Each man was charged with capital murder in the death of Officer Hawkins. Patsy Gomez and Raul Rodriguez were arrested and charged with seven counts of assisting escape. Rivas, the first tried for the death of Hawkins, received the death penalty, as did the five other escapees.

Dramatic anecdotes like those just outlined can inflate popular estimates of the likelihood of a successful escape. In reality, successful escapes are extremely uncommon. In the forty jurisdictions responding to a survey conducted by the American Correctional Association, 577 inmates escaped from custody during 2000.[37] Considering that these jurisdictions housed over 1 million prisoners that year, the actual likelihood of an inmate escaping was less than 6 in 10,000. Furthermore, over 87 percent of these inmates were successfully returned to custody.

It is clear that some death-sentenced inmates, if given any opportunity, will continue to commit violent criminal acts. However, the vast majority of capital offenders, including those on death row and those released from death row, have not presented a threat to fellow prisoners or guards. Since capital murderers in Texas who receive a life sentence must now serve forty years before becoming eligible for parole, the prison population is the one most at risk until the offender becomes aged. There is always a chance of a prisoner escaping, but this chance is remote. Additionally, though the death penalty does protect society from further acts of violence by a person after that person has been executed, it was not able to prevent a few former death-row inmates and other capital offenders from committing additional violent crimes. If the death penalty is to successfully incapacitate dangerous offenders, capital murderers who present a threat of danger in the future must be identified and targeted for capital punishment, then carefully guarded until their execution.

Which Ones Will Be Dangerous in the Future?

As previously mentioned, future dangerousness plays a central role in the Texas death-penalty process, but exactly how do jurors make such predictions? The capital trial is a unique and strange experience for jurors. They must determine the ultimate fate of another person, perhaps for the first and only time in their lives. The prediction that jurors are charged with making is nearly impossible: whether the person sitting in front of them will be dangerous in the future. Jurors often lack any sort of objective information with which to perform this task. What follows is a discussion of the sorts of materials typically available to jurors making these determinations, as well as other information that may be useful for predicting who will be violent in prison.

When determining a defendant's propensity for future dangerousness, jurors may rely on three types of predictions: clinical, anamnestic, and actuarial. Psychiatrists or psychologists are often called upon to assist jurors with their deliberations concerning future dangerousness. These clinical predictions are primarily intuitive and subjective. Psychologists and psychiatrists form hypotheses about the structure and dynamics of a defendant's personality from their clinical impressions of personality factors and the interaction of these factors, both of which they evaluate on the basis of the offender's personal history, the results of psychometric tests, and the clinician's past experience and expertise. Any evidence consistent with previous observations of violent behavior among other offenders can be used to support a prediction of future dangerousness. Therefore, clinicians are prone to overestimate dangerousness, resulting in an extremely high number of erroneous predictions.[38] (In statistics, these are known as false positives: assertions that a phenomenon exists when it is actually absent.) The extent to which clinicians are able to provide accurate assessments of future dangerousness coincides with their use of base rates and actuarial data (to be discussed in the next section), still a rarity among clinicians on the death-penalty circuit.[39]

Although clinical assessment is the least accurate basis for prediction, it is commonly used in capital trials in the post-*Furman* era. Additionally, jurors tend to respect the clinicians who make the assessments and predictions, so their testimony often carries great weight in jury deliberations. One psychiatrist represents many of the dangers inherent in utilizing only clinical predictions when assessing a defendant's propensity toward future dangerousness. Dubbed "Dr. Death" because of his unequivocal testimony for the prosecution, James Grigson has testified with "absolute" certainty about the future dangerousness of several defendants. The pattern of his testimony has been similar from one trial to the next. After listening to the prosecutor give a lengthy narrative about a hypothetical person (aka the defendant), Grigson begins by classifying the defendant as a sociopath.[40] He then discusses the characteristics of a sociopath: a highly skilled manipulator who, lacking a conscience, kills without remorse. The prosecutor then asks what type of medical treatment is available for such a condition. After indicating that there is no known cure for sociopathy, Grigson testifies with absolute certainty that the defendant will kill again. Consider the following typical exchanges from three cases:

PROSECUTOR: In your opinion will he kill again?
GRIGSON: Yes, he certainly will if there is any way at all he was given the

opportunity to, he certainly will. . . . Well, society can restrict him, confine him; yet even in areas of confinement, this behavior [killing people] will continue.[41]

PROSECUTOR: Can you tell us whether or not, in your opinion, having killed in the past, he is likely to kill in the future, given the opportunity?

GRIGSON: He absolutely will, regardless of whether he's inside an institutional-type setting or whether he is outside. No matter where he is, he will kill again.

PROSECUTOR: Are you telling me, then, that even if he were institutionalized, put in a penitentiary for a life sentence—would he still be a danger to guards, prisoners, and other people around him?

GRIGSON: Yes. He would be a danger in any type of setting, and especially to guards or to other inmates. No matter where he might be, he is a danger.[42]

PROSECUTOR: Doctor, based upon that hypothetical, those facts that I explained to you, do you have an opinion within reasonable medical probability as to whether the defendant will commit criminal acts of violence that will constitute a continuing threat to society?

GRIGSON: Yes sir, I most certainly do have an opinion with regard to that.

PROSECUTOR: What is your opinion, please, sir?

GRIGSON: That absolutely there is no question, no doubt whatsoever, that the individual you described, that has been involved in repeated escalating behavior of violence, will commit acts of violence in the future, and represents a very serious threat to any society which he finds himself in.

PROSECUTOR: Do you mean that he will be a threat in any society, even the prison society?

GRIGSON: Absolutely, yes sir. He will do the same thing that he will do outside.[43]

Anamnestic predictions, based on an individual's previous pattern of behavior, are the best means of forecasting future dangerousness. The drawback to this method is that it is dependent on context. Most capital defendants, even if they would be a threat to the outside community, are not likely to commit violent acts in prison. A defendant's behavior during a previous incarceration or while in jail awaiting trial is the most telling indicator of his or her violence potential in prison. Rather than considering the environment into which the defendant will be placed, however, most jurors, when weighing the evidence, view the defendant as a permanent threat to society because of the horrible details of the current offense.

Prosecutors often capitalize on the most egregious elements of a particular homicide to prove that a defendant poses a continuing threat to society. Prosecutors also rely on psychiatrists to confirm jurors' initial emotional reactions to these gory details: these clinicians often testify that a defendant is antisocial and unlikely to reform. Such evidence and testimony appeals to jurors' stereotypical images of the violent recidivist, i.e., the psychopathic serial killer disproportionately portrayed in the media and the new "true crime" genre of television show.[44]

A much more effective and accurate means of computing the violence risk presented by a defendant is through an actuarial assessment. In an actuarial prediction, a social scientist estimates the future dangerousness of a particular offender from the behavior of groups of similar offenders. An actuarial prediction, or risk assessment, is derived from a formula based on membership in a group for which a consistent and tested pattern of conduct has been shown. Perhaps the best-known type of actuarial prediction is that used by the insurance industry. Insurance agencies set premiums based on an applicant's level of risk. The auto-insurance industry, for example, does this by comparing an applicant to others in the larger group of all those insured who share characteristics that influence driving performance (number of speeding tickets, accidents, etc.). Based on the past driving records of insured motorists with similar personal characteristics (such as age, gender, and marital status), automobile insurers estimate the likelihood that an applicant will have an accident, and then set the premiums accordingly.

Mental-health researchers have recently begun to show that violence is most accurately predicted by objective actuarial methods.[45] These studies typically include a broad array of predictor variables and carefully specify the probability that particular types of violence are likely to recur.[46] Paul Meehl first distinguished actuarial from clinical predictions, defining the latter as a "psychological hypothesis regarding the structure and the dynamics of [a] particular individual" and characterizing the former as a "mechanical combining of information for classification purposes, and the resultant probability figure which is an empirically determined relative frequency."[47] Individuals responsible for making housing and security decisions in prisons have now turned to objective classification models constructed from actuarial data.[48] This method of decision making has permeated the correctional system during the past two decades because of legal challenges to existing classification procedures.[49] The development and testing of these models have revealed a number of consistent correlates of prison misbehavior and adjustment problems.[50]

To make an accurate actuarial prediction of a defendant's potential for committing future violent acts against "society," one must know which society is being referring to and for what length of time. Historically, in order to protect defendants, states have not allowed juries to be informed of parole-eligibility dates. In the 1970s, a sentence of "life" in many states carried a relatively short term of imprisonment before parole eligibility. Under the post-*Furman* death-penalty statute in Texas, a capital murderer sentenced to life imprisonment could be released on parole after serving only twenty years.[51] Jurors have often heard anecdotes about prisoners being given life sentences yet serving very little time, as happened in many places during the 1970s, or about noncapital murderers serving relatively short terms. For these and similar reasons, jurors are still prone to underestimate the minimum length of time to be served by capital defendants given a life sentence.

An ongoing nationwide study found that among the various issues discussed by jurors in the punishment phase of capital trials, the possibility of early release for offenders sentenced to life has had the most pernicious influence on jury deliberations.[52] The researchers found that among jurors who considered life in the early stages of deliberation, but eventually returned a death sentence, the key to changing their minds was nearly always the mistaken belief that those sentenced to life would be released early. An investigation in California found that the possibility of early release for those sentenced to life influenced the deliberations of eight of the ten juries studied.[53] Twenty-three of twenty-seven jurors interviewed in Oregon felt that the possibility of parole was an important factor when considering the defendant's sentence.[54]

Whereas the alternative sanction in many states is life without the possibility of parole (LWOP), capital murderers currently sentenced to life in Texas become eligible for parole after serving a minimum of forty years.[55] Senate Bill 85, passed by the Senate in 2001, would have given jurors the option of sentencing defendants to LWOP as an alternative to death. Under the proposed scheme, if jurors answered no to the future-dangerousness inquiry, a prisoner would continue to receive the forty-year minimum sentence; yes to the question of future dangerousness would result in LWOP or death, depending on the jury's answer to the mitigating question. This statute would have allowed jurors to grant a defendant mercy, even if the defendant was perceived as dangerous to the outside community. The bill, however, died in committee.[56]

Recently, the U.S. Supreme Court has recognized the importance of supplying parole-eligibility information to jurors when they are asked to assess the likelihood of future dangerousness posed by a defendant. In *Simmons v. South Carolina,* the Court held that

[i]n assessing future dangerousness, the actual duration of the defendant's prison sentence is indisputably relevant. Holding all other factors constant, it is entirely reasonable for a sentencing jury to view a defendant who is eligible

for parole as a greater threat to society than a defendant who is not. Indeed, there may be no greater assurance of a defendant's future nondangerousness to the public than the fact that he never will be released on parole. The trial court's refusal to apprise the jury of information so crucial to its sentencing determination, particularly when the prosecution alluded to the defendant's future dangerousness in its argument to the jury, cannot be reconciled with our well-established precedents interpreting the Due Process Clause.[57]

In a dissent from a denial of certiorari in *Brown v. Texas,* Justice Stevens noted the inconsistency in Texas's practice of instructing jurors about parole eligibility in all but capital cases, and the obvious tension between that practice and their ruling in *Simmons,* given that Brown, at that time, would have had to serve thirty-five years without the possibility of parole.[58] The Texas legislature responded to the perceived need, despite the fact that *Brown* had been denied certiorari, and provided for a jury instruction on parole eligibility, when requested, in capital cases.[59] Therefore, the current practice in Texas capital murder cases is to instruct jurors on the meaning of a "life sentence" in order to assist them in their deliberations.

Besides being presented with evidence of a defendant's risk of violence while incarcerated, jurors should also be presented with accurate information about the level of violence in prisons. Most jurors are unaware that the constraints of prison reduce the violence potential among inmates; for example, rates of homicide in prison are far lower than rates in society.[60] Respondents to the aforementioned American Correctional Association national survey reported only forty-two inmate deaths at the hands of other inmates in 2000.[61] This translates into a homicide rate in prison of 4.2 per 100,000 inmates, compared to a rate in the outside community of 5.5 per 100,000 members of the general public.[62] Even rarer than the killing of an inmate is the killing of a correctional officer. In 2000, no correctional officers were killed in any jurisdiction reporting. In comparison, fifty-one police officers were feloniously slain in the line of duty that year.[63]

Research has shown that even among capital murderers specifically, levels of homicide and other assaultive behaviors are surprisingly low in the prison setting. Convicted murderers—whether murderers serving a term of imprisonment, capital murderers serving life without parole, or capital murderers commuted from a death sentence—commit homicides in prison at a rate of about 2 per 1,000 inmates per year or less.[64] The rate of violent behavior among these same inmates was found to be less than 6 acts per 100 inmates per year.

Reliance on those studies, however, would likely result in an overestimation of the violence potential of current capital defendants. First, the studies included data from previous decades, when overall rates of violence in prison were higher. Advances in classification procedures, along with the proliferation of lockdown units, have reduced overall rates of prison violence in recent years. Second, the data in those studies were drawn disproportionately from the initial stages of the inmates' terms of incarceration. Rates of violence in prison decrease with the length of time served.[65]

An Actuarial Risk Assessment of Violence Posed by Capital-Murder Defendants

What is the threat level posed by Texas capital defendants and others who share their characteristics? Because of the rarity of repeat violence among incarcerated murderers, drawing a study sample large enough to ensure that the base rates of violence and the effects of their correlates could be accurately estimated meant that the entire population of cases for which information was available was included. That is, the population of cases was drawn from the records of murderers currently incarcerated in Texas prisons. To ensure the reliability of these estimates, however, data were restricted to cases as similar as possible to the cases that would be predicted.[66] The final study population consisted of 6,390 murderers who had served an average of 4.55 years during the period January 1990 through March 1999.

Violent acts were defined as assaultive or dangerous acts that either do cause, or have the imminent potential to cause, serious bodily injury. This definition includes homicides and major assaults committed against guards and inmates. Indicators of institutional violence and variables useful in predicting violence in the prison system were gleaned from official records maintained by the TDCJ. Homicide logbooks were consulted to determine which inmates had been involved in homicides during the period studied. Level 1 rule violations by inmates were extracted from computerized records and relied upon as the primary measure of violent acts against other inmates, including assaults with a weapon, fighting with a weapon, and other violent acts.[67] Additional potential predictors identified in previous studies were also retrieved. These variables include information specifically related to the inmates' personal characteristics, their criminal histories, and the offenses that resulted in their incarceration.[68]

The first step was to determine the base rate of violence that can be expected from capital defendants. The table below shows the type and number of violent acts committed by the 6,390 incarcerated murderers, who at that time had served an average of 4.55 years, and the percentage of the group involved in each type of act. Only seven homicides were committed by inmates during

Table 3.1 Violence committed by incarcerated murderers in Texas, January 1990–March 1999

Targets and types of violence	No. of acts	Inmates involved, %
Against guards		
Aggravated assault	33	0.5
Against inmates		
Homicide	7	0.1
Assault with a weapon	352	4.4
Fight with a weapon	307	4.2
Other violence	12	0.2
Total	711	8.4

Note: For murderers, $N = 6,390$.

their cumulative 29,074.5 years served. Not one guard was murdered during the sample period, although thirty-three aggravated assaults were committed against guards. One-half of 1 percent of the incarcerated murderers were responsible for these assaults. The total rate of violence was about 2 acts per 100 inmates per year, involving 8.4 percent of the inmates.[69]

Table 3.1 shows the actual levels of violence among inmates incarcerated during the 1990s. To make these analyses applicable to life-sentenced capital murderers, the likelihood of violence must be estimated for their minimum forty-year term. Estimating this likelihood of violence is more complicated than simply multiplying the observed levels of yearly violence by the number of years to be served; most inmates who commit violent acts do so in their initial stages of incarceration. Institutional control mechanisms, aging, and adjustments to the prison environment make it extremely rare for an inmate to become involved in an initial act of violence after being incarcerated beyond ten or fifteen years. Figure 3.1 shows the projected proportion of incarcerated murderers "surviving," that is, not committing any violent acts, over 111 months.[70]

As shown, the estimated rate of failure (committing a violent act) over the first 111 months of incarceration is approximately 11 percent, with about 89 percent of the inmates surviving over the 9+ years without committing an act of violence. Figure 3.1 also captures the trend in offending. Half of those who committed a violent act did so within the first two years of incarceration. Survival becomes much more common during the middle and latter months in the series; by the ninth year of incarceration, initial acts of violence are rare.

Holding all institutional factors constant, the estimated likelihood of vio-

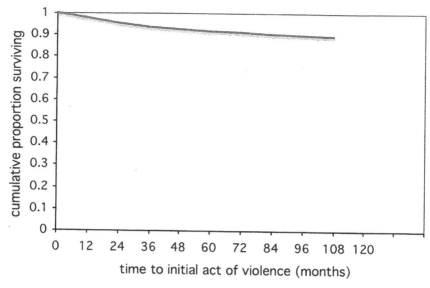

Figure 3.1. Time before incarcerated murderers in Texas first commit a violent act (survival model)

lence being committed by a newly received capital murderer over the next forty years in a Texas prison is 16.4 percent.[71] The approximate risk of a given capital murderer committing any of the offenses catalogued in Table 3.1 over the entire period of incarceration is essentially double the observed estimates. For example, the probability that an incarcerated capital defendant will kill again during a forty-year term is 0.2 percent, or about 2 in 1000.

The expected baseline rate of violent threat posed by capital murderers having been established, the next step was to find factors that would help predict violence. From the entire inventory of potential predictor variables available, six were found significantly related to violence among the incarcerated murderers, controlling for the number of years at risk. Three predictors were related to the circumstances of the offense: involvement in a contemporaneous robbery or burglary, the presence of multiple victims, and additional murder attempts or assaults. Three predictors related to the characteristics of the offender: gang membership, having served a prior prison term, and age.

As shown in Table 3.2, not all murderers have the same propensity toward violence.[72] It is possible to match the characteristics of a particular capital defendant to those of a similar group of incarcerated murderers, thus producing an individualized prediction. To calculate the likelihood of violence for any given case, combine the values of the predictor variables with the base rate of 16.4 percent. For example, involvement in a robbery or burglary during

Table 3.2 Predictors of violence among incarcerated murderers in Texas

Predictor variable	Percentage point increase/decrease
Robbery/burglary	7.4
Multiple victims	5.6
Attempted murder/assault	4.0
Gang membership	10.4
Prior prison term	5.3
Age less than 21	5.5
Age 26–30	-7.2
Age 31–35	-12.3
Age over 35	-14.4

Note: For murderers, N = 6,390; "Age 21–25" is the excluded reference category.

the commission of a murder increases the likelihood of later violence by 7.4 percentage points above 16.4 percent, i.e., the likelihood of violence during a forty-year term of incarceration by those involved in a robbery-murder or burglary-murder is 23.8 percent. Hypothetically, the likelihood of violent risk posed by an incarcerated murderer over a forty-year term ranges from 2 percent, for those over thirty-five with no other aggravating case features, to 54.6 percent, for youths under twenty-one whose personal and offense characteristics include all other predictor variables.

A scale was constructed by first calculating the overall risk score for each of the capital murderers. Then, cases were grouped in rounded intervals of 8 percent into risk categories based on the predicted likelihood of committing violent acts. The first interval includes cases with a violence potential of 7.4 percent and under, the second interval includes those with potentials of 7.5 to 15.4 percent, and so on. The highest category includes cases with a predicted likelihood of violence of 31.5 percent or higher. A test of validity was performed by applying the scale to a group of inmates incarcerated for manslaughter during the same period. Although these inmates differ somewhat from murderers, the results presented in Figure 3.2 show that the scale successfully grouped manslaughter defendants by levels of risk. Projected probabilities of becoming involved in violence over a forty-year term ranged from 2.7 percent in the lowest risk category to 43.3 percent of those in the highest risk category.[73]

Although actuarial measures best predict how a defendant will behave in prison in the future, they are most useful in providing jurors with a relative

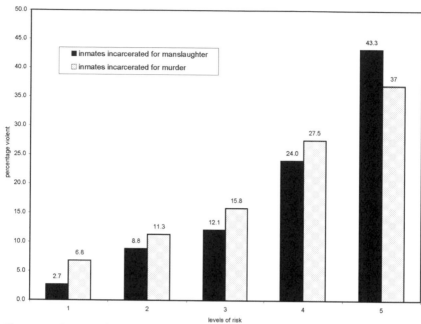

Figure 3.2. Projected probabilities of engaging in violent acts: Texas inmates convicted of manslaughter or murder

likelihood of violence occurring, as opposed to a simple yes or no to the question of future dangerousness. This is because of the low base rate of violent recidivism. Even if a defendant is linked to a factor that doubles the likelihood of the defendant committing a violent act in prison, the odds will still favor a prediction of nondangerousness. Actuarial predictions are therefore best suited to predict nondangerousness when a defendant shares none or very few of the characteristics of those who in the past have repeated their offense.[74]

Conclusion

The possibility that a capital murderer will reoffend has always been one of the primary justifications for the death penalty. Nowhere is this justification given more priority than in Texas. Under the Texas death penalty statute, the question of a defendant's potential for future violence takes center stage in jurors' deliberations, being the first special issue asked of them and the one that often means the difference between life and death. Studies discussed herein have found that in states using this special-issues format, jurors spend most of their time discussing the issue of future dangerousness. By comparison, in states that emphasize the weighing of aggravating and mitigating factors, jurors spend much more time discussing such factors, which go more to the deservedness of the sentence.

While the first special issue in the Texas statute may focus jurors' deliberation on future dangerousness, the second, relating to mitigating circumstances, certainly encourages them to consider the deservedness of punishment, given the characteristics of the defendant and circumstances of the crime. The data on base rates and the actuarial analysis above demonstrate how difficult it is for any person to make a prediction about a defendant's likelihood of future dangerousness with any degree of confidence. The circumstances of the offense have only a small predictive effect on how an inmate will behave in prison. In fact, defendants involved in some of the worst possible crimes, such as the rape and murder of a child, are less likely than others to be involved in violence in the institution, since their victim pool is restricted. As seen in the next chapter, however, it is in these cases, involving these types of crimes, that jurors are most likely to answer affirmatively the special issue related to the future dangerousness of the defendant.

Researchers and commentators often assume that jurors are unaware of their inability to accurately forecast future violence. It could be that, compared to attorneys or statisticians, jurors simply view the probability of future dangerousness differently, believing that any possibility of a defendant repeating the same type of offense warrants a death sentence. That is, jurors may be willing to answer affirmatively the question regarding future dangerousness, even if they are unsure, because of the heinousness of the crime. If so, jurors may be sentencing defendants to death out of retribution rather than in hopes of incapacitating them. Jurors may be behaving much like the U.S. Supreme Court, which has tolerated the Texas death-penalty statute, but still evaluates it on the basis of its ability to achieve consistency in sentencing, a retributive concern. It is this possibility that is addressed in the next chapter.

Addendum

On June 17, 2005, Texas governor Rick Perry signed a life without parole bill into law. Effective September 1, 2005, convicted capital murderers spared the death penalty will serve a sentence of life without the possibility of parole.

CHAPTER 4

Retribution: Do They Deserve to Die?

I represent 65 percent of the American people . . . that favor the death penalty. I believe in the sanctity of human life. . . . We have heard about how cruel and inhumane the death penalty is. What about Jerry Lane Jurek? He kidnapped a girl from the streets of Cuero. When she refused to be raped, he strangled her [pause] he strangled her and threw her in the river. We have heard about the criminal. We have not heard about the victim.

KENNETH WAYNE ROBERTS, A TEXAS CITIZEN SPEAKING AGAINST THE
PROPOSED ABOLITION OF THE DEATH PENALTY, IN A PUBLIC HEARING
BEFORE THE TEXAS HOUSE OF REPRESENTATIVES IN 1977

In the spring of 1977, several death-penalty bills were introduced in the Texas legislature. House Bill 945, which changed the method of execution from electrocution to lethal injection, was the only one that passed, but did so without much debate or fanfare. House Bill 563, introduced by Representative Sam Hudson, called for the abolition of capital punishment, and was the most controversial among the death-penalty bills. In a public hearing on the House floor on March 1, 1977, only two witnesses testified specifically in relation to the lethal-injection bill. In comparison, twenty witnesses were recognized to testify on HB 563. All but three witnesses testified in favor of the bill to abolish capital punishment. Supporters of the bill included an array of religious leaders, civil libertarians, death-penalty activists, law students, the parents of a death-row inmate, a former prison inmate, and other concerned citizens.

As during the debate over the reimplementation of capital punishment in 1973, the supporters of abolition again included references to the failure of the death penalty to deter crime. Rather than dwelling on the failure of the death penalty as a form of social defense, however, most of the participants expressed moral reservations about its use. The core position among the abolitionists was that the death penalty was not warranted under any circumstances. Representative Hudson remarked in closing that he failed to see "how anyone has a right to take anyone's life, whether it be the person who committed the crime or whether it [is] us as organs of the state."[1]

The question of whether the death penalty is an appropriate punishment for any crime relates to the concept of retribution. Retribution is the idea that an individual who commits a crime deserves to be punished for upsetting the moral order; responsibility for restoring balance is upon the offender. To determine how to correct the wrong, retribution looks only at the crime. Therefore, the only relevant issue is what the offender has already done, not what he or she might do in the future or whether a particular sanction may deter other potential offenders.

In *Furman*, Justice Marshall equated retribution with revenge, and concluded that as such it was an inappropriate justification for punishment. He reiterated this position in *Gregg v. Georgia*, finding the taking of a life solely "because the wrongdoer deserves it" to be at odds with the Eighth Amendment's command that the imposition of punishment must be consistent "with our respect for the dignity of [other] men."[2] After reviewing the failings of the death penalty as a criminal sanction, Marshall concluded that if Americans were aware of all of the "facts" concerning the implementation of capital punishment and its failure to deter or incapacitate, they would no longer support its use. Of the only remaining rationale, retribution, Marshall stated, "I cannot believe that at this stage in our history, the American people would ever knowingly support purposeless vengeance."[3]

At the time of *Furman*, public opinion on the death penalty was just beginning to rebound from an all-time low. Gallup poll results in 1972 indicated that 50 percent of Americans answered "yes, in favor" to the question "Are you in favor of the death penalty for a person convicted of murder?" up from 42 percent in 1966.[4] As the civil rights era drew to a close, support for the rehabilitation of criminals was also declining. America was on the verge of a law-and-order movement that would increase support for the death penalty along with other "get tough on crime" measures. Public support for the death penalty had increased to nearly 70 percent by the close of the decade, and remains at that level today. In Texas, the level of support in recent years is even higher, hovering around 80 percent.[5] What might have come as the biggest surprise to Marshall is the reason cited by supporters for favoring the death penalty: its retributive properties. Nearly two-thirds of the death-penalty supporters responding to the 2003 Gallup poll mentioned a retributive reason for supporting the death penalty (i.e., "they deserve it," "an eye for an eye," "serves justice"). In comparison, 11 percent mentioned its deterrent value, another 11 percent mentioned cost, and 7 percent referred to its ability to incapacitate offenders.[6]

Although the broader philosophical issue of whether the state has a right to take a life can never be definitively answered, public opinion polls suggest that most Americans support the use of capital punishment. Even though most Americans in general, and Texans in particular, do not believe that the death penalty is an inappropriate response to murder, they are not willing to employ it in all situations. That some eligible offenders are subject to the death penalty while others are not raises more pragmatic concerns. To serve as retribution, and not mere vengeance, the death penalty must be applied in a manner that is fair and consistent. Only through the consistent application of punishment can offenders receive their just deserts.

This was the main concern of the Supreme Court in *Furman*. Only Brennan and Marshall believed that the death penalty was unconstitutional per se. The other three justices in the plurality held that the death penalty was cruel and unusual because of the manner in which it was applied. Justices Douglas, Stewart, and White focused their criticisms on the perception that the death penalty was administered arbitrarily. Stewart concluded that "the Eighth and Fourteenth Amendments cannot tolerate the infliction of a sentence of death under legal systems that permit this unique penalty to be so wantonly and so freakishly imposed."[7] Douglas echoed this sentiment, stating, "Under these laws, no standards govern the selection of the penalty."[8] White expressed concern that juries were given the responsibility of deciding when to impose the punishment without any guidance as to how to make that determination.

To allot defendants their just deserts and avoid running afoul of the Constitution, the process must consistently mete out the death penalty to the most culpable offenders who have committed the most egregious offenses. Post-*Furman* capital-sentencing procedures were designed to meet this goal by sparing those offenders whose character, background, and personal moral culpability—or the circumstances of whose offense—suggested that they were not deserving of a death sentence.[9] For example, many capital-punishment statutes enacted in the modern era included a provision for proportionality review, in which state appellate courts were charged with determining whether each death sentence imposed was disproportionate compared to sentences imposed in similar cases.[10] The concern was that "equal justice," a necessary prerequisite for any rational retributive system of punishment, would be served.[11] This concern for fairness in the imposition of the death penalty has been the cornerstone of death-penalty jurisprudence since *Furman*.[12]

Empirical methods can never answer the ultimate question of whether a person deserves to die. This is an issue more appropriate for philosophers, ethicists, and religious leaders. However, empirical research can provide a clearer picture of how the death penalty is distributed among capital murder cases. Proportionality, both in the legal and philosophical sense, demands that those eligible for capital punishment are sentenced to death with a degree of regularity. The first issue analyzed in this chapter is the level of proportionality among death-sentenced cases. The remainder of the chapter is devoted to an examination of two particular categories of capital-murder defendants having lessened culpability, which has raised concerns about the appropriateness of the death penalty in their cases: mentally retarded defendants and juveniles.

Proportionality among Death-Sentenced Cases

Of the more than 50,000 homicides occurring in Texas during the modern era, only 955 had resulted in death sentences by the end of 2003. Considering those cases solved by arrest, only 2–3 percent of all homicides during this period resulted in death sentences. This initial evaluation seems to support Justice Douglas's view in *Furman* that the probability of receiving a death sentence is rare, akin to being struck by lightning. Ending the inquiry at this point, however, would be misleading and would not help determine whether the death sentences were arbitrarily imposed in this small portion of cases. First, it is inappropriate to calculate a death-sentencing rate for all homicides; many do not include the requisite level of intent to be considered murder. Further, under the current statute only a few types of murder are considered capital murder, and thus eligible for capital punishment. Additionally, it is possible that whereas a sentence of death is rarely imposed for murders generally, homicides with specific aggravating characteristics may more regularly incur death sentences. In fact, the justices in *Furman* were mostly concerned with the lack of structure that resulted in the seemingly arbitrary imposition of death sentences. If statutory restrictions on capital punishment resulted in a discernible pattern of sentencing, in which certain types of murders were consistently punished with death sentences, concerns regarding arbitrariness would be largely addressed.

Two types of methodology are commonly used to determine the level of proportionality among death-sentenced cases. The first, pioneered by Samuel Gross and Robert Mauro, compares the characteristics of death-row cases to the statewide homicide arrests reported in the Supplemental Homicide Reports (SHR).[13] Gross and Mauro determined which characteristics were commoner among death-row cases vis-à-vis the homicides reported in the SHR, and they used these characteristics to create a scale of case aggravation for homicides occurring in eight states during 1976–1980. They then calculated the odds that a defendant would receive a death sentence at each level of case aggravation. They used this information to draw various conclusions about the likelihood of death sentences being imposed in particular cases, according to their level of aggravation.

Following this approach, a similar analysis for recent death-sentenced cases in Texas is outlined below. Some homicide cases contained in the SHR are obviously not statutorily eligible for the death penalty, and they should be excluded from the comparison pool when possible. Therefore, the first step in the analysis was to limit the pool of cases as closely as possible to only those murders that were eligible for capital punishment. This was done through a series of steps that included restricting the analysis to cases occurring during 1994–2000, eliminating cases involving manslaughter or justifiable homicide, and eliminating those involving defendants who were younger than seventeen at the time of the offense.[14] This process resulted in a total sample pool of 9,395 incidents of murder.

The next step involved matching the death-sentenced cases with their arrest records in the SHR pool. After the records were matched, it was found that 226 of the homicide incidents in the SHR resulted in 242 death sentences.[15] Since only those cases that were solved could result in death sentences, cases that were not cleared by arrest were excluded from the SHR comparison pool. Finally, only those case files that contained complete information on all of the characteristics used to create the measure of case aggravation were retained in the analysis, resulting in a final death-sentencing rate of 3.9 percent (226/5,839).

To find those characteristics that were predictive of a death sentence throughout the state, the likelihood of a death sentence being imposed was calculated for each of the variables available in the SHR. As expected, given the statutory definition of capital murder, the presence of a contemporaneous felony was the best predictor of a death sentence. Cases involving sexual assaults in addition to murder had the highest death-sentencing rate, nearly 58 percent, which was fifteen times the average death-sentencing rate of 3.9 percent. Although cases involving other types of contemporaneous felonies were not as strongly related to death-sentence outcomes, they were all more likely to result in death.

The cause of death was also consistently related to a sentence of death. Gun-related murders were the least likely to result in death sentences; cases involving strangulation were the most likely. Bludgeoning and other causes were also more likely to result in death than murder by gunshot. The weapon used in the crime appears to be an indicator of the perceived brutality of the offense.

Crimes committed by strangers and men were more common among death

Table 4.1 Case characteristics of murder arrests in Texas and the likelihood of receiving a death sentence, 1994–2000

	Total arrests	Cases resulting in a death sentence	
		Number	Percentage
All cases	5,839	226	3.9
Felony type			
Robbery/burglary	845	143	16.9
Sexual assault	78	45	57.7
Other*	373	32	8.6
Cause of death			
Gunshot	3,917	137	3.5
Stabbing	977	38	3.9
Strangulation	120	38	31.7
Bludgeoning	840	44	5.2
Other	42	6	14.3
Defendant characteristics			
Stranger to victim	1,167	99	8.5
Multiple offenders	1,193	103	8.6
Female defendant	715	4	0.6
Defendant youth (17)	348	21	6.0
Victim characteristics			
Multiple victims	290	71	24.5
Female victim	1,555	123	7.9
Child victim (under 6)	296	20	6.8
Youthful victim (under 18)	691	48	6.9
Elderly victim (over 64)	252	23	9.1

*Among others, this category includes murders involving kidnapping, arson, remuneration, police officers, jail inmates, and jail escapees.

sentences, as were those involving multiple offenders and multiple victims. These characteristics point to a more premeditated or instrumental form of homicide. Victim traits indicative of innocence or physical weakness were also more likely to result in death sentences: offenses perpetrated against females, children, youths, and the elderly were overrepresented among those sentenced to death.

The simple bivariate relationships presented in Table 4.1 do not tell the whole story. It is possible that some of the variables are related to death sentences only because of their relationship to other factors. For instance, although those who kill strangers receive the death penalty at a rate higher than the

Table 4.2 Case characteristics of murder arrests in Texas and associated multipliers for the likelihood of receiving a death sentence, 1994–2000

Predictor variable	Multiplier for likelihood of receiving a death sentence
Robbery/burglary	25.503**
Sexual assault	50.117**
Other felony type	6.261**
Stabbing	1.595*
Strangulation	6.554**
Bludgeoning	1.604*
Other cause of death	2.306
Multiple victims	11.961**
Multiple offenders	1.846**
Female victim	1.943**

*p < .05; **p < .001

overall death-penalty sentencing rate (8.5 percent vs. 3.9 percent), this relationship could be due to strangers' being killed more often in felony circumstances than acquaintances or family members. To test the possibility that some of the relationships were spurious, logistic regression was used to model sentencing decisions while simultaneously controlling for the case characteristics included in Table 4.1. As predicted, the category "stranger" was not significant in the subsequent model, because of its relationship with felony type. After all other case characteristics available in the SHR were controlled for, the age of the victim also became insignificant. Statistically significant factors remaining in the reduced model are presented above.[16]

The logistic regression coefficients from the model were simplified for ease of interpretation.[17] The figures presented in Table 4.2 show how many times more likely a homicide case is to result in a death sentence when a particular case characteristic is present, holding the effect of all other factors in the model constant. For example, a case involving a robbery or burglary is twenty-five times more likely to receive a death sentence than cases that do not, all other factors held constant. The presence of a contemporaneous sexual assault increases the likelihood of a death sentence by over fifty times. Aside from felony type, the case characteristic that most influenced the likelihood of a death sentence was the presence of multiple victims, making a death sentence nearly twelve times more likely. An offender who strangled a victim was six and a half times more likely to receive a death sentence.

Based on the strength of the relationships discovered in Table 4.2, a simple additive scale of case seriousness was constructed. For each circumstance present in a given case, a weight derived from the unstandardized logistic regression coefficients was assigned.[18] The final score for each case was the sum of the weights assigned when a particular characteristic was present. These overall case weightings were then used to sort cases into various levels of case seriousness: those having the lowest score were the least likely to result in death sentences, and those with the highest scores were the most likely. Cumulatively, this score should be considered an indicator of the legitimate influence of the seriousness of a case on its ultimate outcome.

The extent to which cases can be successfully sorted into those categories likely to lead to death and those categories likely to result in a life sentence is a measure of the rationality of the system, a measure of its retributive potential. If the measure could sort cases into categories in which the likelihood of death was 0 percent for those cases without any characteristic predictive of a death sentence, or 100 percent for cases with all the characteristics predictive of a death sentence, all of the death sentences in the system would be considered proportionate. That is, all offenders would have received the appropriate sentence, their just deserts. In a system in which death was imposed completely arbitrarily, all cases would have the same likelihood of resulting in a death sentence, the mean of 3.9 percent, regardless of their particular characteristics. The extent to which this scale is able to sort cases into categories nearing the ideal is the extent to which the system has the necessary prerequisite for providing retributive justice.

Obtaining perfection is clearly impossible. But to what extent should variation in sentencing among similar cases be tolerated? Unfortunately, there is no standard overall measure that indicates at what level a system is considered proportionate, rather than arbitrary, in sentencing. Nevertheless, an overall pattern of sentencing does emerge from the data. It is clear from the graph below that the level of case aggravation is predictive of a death sentence. Further, particular types of capital murder can generally be identified that nearly either always result in death sentences or almost certainly result in an alternative sentence.

The results presented in Figure 4.1 show that death sentences are not imposed randomly. The probabilities of cases in the lowest and highest levels of case aggravation suggest that death sentences are quite predictable. The lowest three levels of aggravation result in death sentences in only 0.4 percent of cases (20/4,711). The highest three levels of aggravation resulted in death sentences in 85.3% of cases (29/34). Cases in the highest levels of aggravation are over two hundred times more likely to result in death sentences than those in the

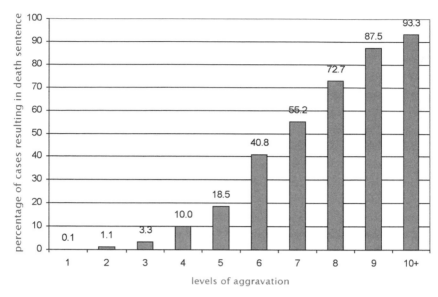

Figure 4.1. Percentage of cases resulting in death sentences, by aggravation scale

lowest levels. The percentage of cases receiving a death sentence consistently increased as the level of aggravation increased.

The underlying figures also include evidence that suggests the presence of arbitrariness in sentencing. Although the likelihood of a death sentence for the lowest three levels of aggravation was only 0.4 percent, there were still twenty cases in this range that resulted in death. Certainly, according to Justice Stewart's definition, these data support the idea that imposing the death penalty in these cases could be considered "freakish." In the next two levels of case aggravation (levels 4 and 5), the likelihood of receiving a death sentence increases, but only to 11.6 percent (111/956). Since the odds of receiving a death sentence are barely above one in ten, the sentence is far from consistently meted out in these cases. The midlevel cases (levels 6 and 7) hardly provide support for the consistency of the system: death sentences are handed down in 47.8 percent (66/138) of cases, close to the odds of a coin toss. Only in the highest ranges of aggravation do sentences appear proportionate: only five of the thirty-four defendants managed to avoid a death sentence.

This simple analysis of SHR data seems to provide support for both sides of the proportionality debate. First, sentencing appears to be fairly predictable, with certain case characteristics vastly increasing the odds that a case will result in a death sentence. And yet, most death sentences are issued in instances in which similarly situated defendants do not receive death sentences. One limitation to keep in mind, however, is that the SHR data suffer from a number of weaknesses and limitations that make a true assessment of proportionality impossible.[19]

To create a more sensitive scale that takes into account as many case characteristics as possible, the sample should be limited to arrests for murder that meet the statutory criteria making them eligible for the death penalty, and additional circumstances of the crime and the defendant should be coded. A more sophisticated methodology, pioneered by David Baldus and his colleagues, involves retrospectively following a group of murder cases through the criminal justice process and charting decisions made at each stage, from indictment through sentencing, to determine what factors influenced case outcomes.[20] Baldus and his colleagues sorted the cases into similar categories based either on the particular facts of the cases or the level of case aggravation. The likelihood of a death sentence was then calculated for each subset of murders. They used this methodology to study the levels of sentencing consistency in Georgia just before and just after the Supreme Court's decision in *Furman v. Georgia*. Those examining the level of consistency in death sentencing in various jurisdictions have most often relied on this methodology.[21]

For the current analysis, information was gathered from prison files on all inmates received in the Texas prison system for murders committed during 2000. The initial sample included 515 inmates convicted of murder or capital murder. Cases resulting in capital murder convictions were obviously eligible for capital punishment, but the files of those imprisoned for murder had to be manually searched to determine whether the murders contained elements that would have made them potentially eligible for capital-murder prosecutions. This exhaustive search resulted in a final pool of 248 inmates who had been involved in 193 separate incidents of murder during 2000, and all the murders either were, or could conceivably have been, prosecuted as capital murder.

The dispositions of these capital-murder cases are shown in Table 4.3. Of the 193 cases, 84 percent resulted in capital-murder indictments and 59 percent in capital-murder convictions. The remainder either pleaded guilty to, or were convicted of, the lesser offense of murder. Among the 114 cases resulting in capital-murder convictions, one-third (38/114) went forward to penalty trials in which the death penalty was sought. In the 38 penalty trials, three-quarters (29/38) returned a sentence of death. From the larger standpoint of the total number of death-eligible murder cases, the 29 cases resulting in death—the case of the Texas 7 described in Chapter 2 actually resulted in 5 death sentences at the time of data collection, for a total of 34 defendants sentenced to death for

Table 4.3 Disposition of capital murder cases in Texas (2000), by case characteristics

Type of Capital murder*	Death-eligible	Indicted for capital murder	Convicted of capital murder	Sent to penalty trial	Sentenced to death
		Number of Cases (% of death-eligible)			
Robbery	109	94	64	22	17
	(100)	(86.2)	(58.7)	(20.2)	(15.6)
Burglary	34	31	26	6	5
	(100)	(91.2)	(76.5)	(17.6)	(14.7)
Sexual assault	12	12	9	6	5
	(100)	(100.0)	(75.0)	(50.0)	(41.7)
Arson	9	7	7	2	2
	(100)	(77.8)	(77.8)	(22.2)	(22.2)
Multiple victims	39	34	28	12	9
	(100)	(87.2)	(71.8)	(30.8)	(23.1)
Child less than 6	28	24	15	5	3
	(100)	(85.7)	(53.6)	(17.9)	(10.7)
Remuneration	6	6	5	1	1
	(100)	(100.0)	(83.3)	(16.7)	(16.7)
Police killing	6	4	4	3	3
	(100)	(66.7)	(66.7)	(50.0)	(50.0)
Killing in prison	5	3	2	1	1
	(100)	(60.0)	(40.0)	(20.0)	(20.0)
Kidnapping	25	22	18	8	7
	(100)	(88.0)	(72.0)	(32.0)	(28.0)
Obstruction/ retaliation	5	3	3	1	1
	(100)	(60.0)	(60.0)	(20.0)	(20.0)
Total	193	162	114	38	29
	(100)	(83.9)	(59.1)	(19.7)	(15.0)

*These categories are not mutually exclusive.

murders committed in 2000—represent a small percentage of all those cases that theoretically could have garnered death sentences.

When specific types of murder are examined, some appear to result in death sentences more frequently than others. For instance, only 11 percent of murder cases involving children under six resulted in death sentences, but 50 percent of

Table 4.4 Case characteristics of capital murders in Texas and associated multipliers for the likelihood of receiving a death sentence, 2000

Predictor variable	Multiplier for likelihood of receiving a death sentence
Robbery	1.727
Burglary	2.047
Sexual assault	4.199
Arson	0.668
Multiple victims	6.016*
Child less than 6	3.799
Remuneration	13.554
Police killing	3.079
Killing in prison	80.771*
Kidnapping	11.000**
Obstruction/retaliation	4.448
Gunshot	16.746*
Stabbing	0.230
Bludgeoning	3.646
Mutilation	44.815*
Killing at place of business	2.821
Killing a stranger	4.123
Victim involved in criminal activity	0.178
Accomplice	0.190*
Triggerman	3.383
Prior homicide	5.520*
Prior sexual assault	71.193***
Fugitive	21.192

*p <.05; **p <.01; ***p < .001

those involving the murder of police officers resulted in death sentences. Even so, the imposition of a death sentence is far from certain for cases meeting any of the individual statutory criteria for capital murder. However, the statutory criteria are not mutually exclusive, so it is also necessary to consider their potential influence on death sentences in combination with one another. Further, as noted previously in the analysis of 1994–2000 arrests using the SHR data, additional factors are related to the imposition of death sentences, and must therefore be taken into consideration.

Table 4.4 presents the results of a logistic regression model used to predict death sentences among these capital-murder cases. In addition to the statutory

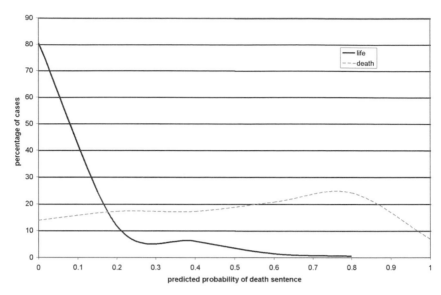

Figure 4.2. Predicted probability of death sentences for both life and death cases

criteria, a number of additional variables chosen from an inventory of over fifty potential predictor variables measuring the circumstances of the crime, the perpetrator, and the victims were found to influence case outcomes.[22] From this logistic regression model, the predicted probability of a death sentence was derived for each case.[23] The predicted probabilities for cases within each of the groups, those sentenced to death and those not sentenced to death, were then examined. The extent to which those cases *actually* sentenced to death have higher *predicted* probabilities of receiving death sentences than those actually receiving lesser sentences is an indication of how rationally the system distributes death sentences on the basis of the measured case characteristics.

The results, graphically presented in Figure 4.2, show that the factors included in the model were quite successful at separating cases actually resulting in death sentences from those receiving lesser sentences. Receiver-operating characteristic analysis was employed to calculate an omnibus measure of the predictability of death sentences. The resulting area under the curve of .911, which may be interpreted as the probability that a randomly chosen death-sentenced case would score higher on the logistic regression scale than a randomly chosen case resulting in a lesser sentence, confirmed that a high degree of predictability exists in the death sentencing process.[24] In other words, 91 percent of the time a randomly chosen death-sentenced case contains case characteristics that made it more likely to have resulted in a death sentence than another randomly selected case that received a lesser sentence. Nevertheless, there are a couple of highly aggravated cases that did not result in death sentences, and perhaps more troubling, a few death-sentenced cases that bore characteristics more similar to nondeath cases in their overall lower level of case seriousness.

Mentally Retarded

Beginning with its reaffirmation of capital punishment in 1976, the Supreme Court has insisted that individualized consideration is necessary in capital cases.[25] In particular, sentencers must be allowed to consider and give appropriate weight to any mitigating evidence present in a defendant's case.[26] Because of its reliance on special sentencing issues, the Texas death-penalty statute was bound to come under attack for lack of individualized consideration of mitigating circumstances. Although the Court had previously held that the second special issue, regarding future dangerousness, was broad enough to encompass a consideration of mitigating circumstances, it reconsidered this issue in *Penry v. Lynaugh* and reversed its findings.[27] Penry argued that instead of his mental disability working as a mitigating factor in his case, the jury was actually more inclined to view it as an aggravating factor that would support a finding of dangerousness. The Court agreed, and reversed Penry's sentence, remanding it for further proceedings. In response to the Court's decision in *Penry,* the Texas legislature amended its capital-sentencing scheme, adding a special-issue question that explicitly calls for the jury to consider any mitigating circumstances of the defendant.[28] The Court in *Penry* did not find that the execution of mentally retarded defendants was cruel and unusual, in violation of the Eighth Amendment, but only that the jury should consider a defendant's mental disability a mitigating circumstance.

John Paul Penry's case has been through three sentencing hearings, and each time the jury has found him deserving of a death sentence. Even when explicitly directed to consider Penry's subnormal intelligence, juries have not found this evidence to exculpate Penry from responsibility. Perhaps the reason can be found in the facts of the case, a very brutal murder, and Penry's level of deliberation in committing the killing:

> Penry, who was released from prison only three months prior to the killing after serving time for rape, forced his way into Carpenter's home and held an open pocket knife to her throat. While the two struggled, Carpenter, the sister of former Washington Redskins place-kicker Mark Mosely, managed to grab a pair of scissors and stab Penry. He then knocked the scissors from her hands

and dragged her into a bedroom where he raped her and then stabbed her in the chest with the pair of scissors. "I told her that I loved her and hated to kill her but I had to so she wouldn't squeal on me," Penry told police in a confession.[29]

Penry's saga, however, may not yet have come to an end. Though the Court had ruled in the first review of his case that the Constitution did not preclude the execution of the mentally retarded, in 2002 the Court overruled *Penry* in *Atkins v. Virginia*.[30] In *Atkins*, the Court relied on public-opinion data, the views of private religious organizations, and, most importantly, legislative changes in recent years to determine that "the evolving standards of decency that mark the progress of a maturing society" could no longer tolerate the execution of mentally retarded defendants.[31] The Court noted that since its decision in *Penry*, nineteen state legislatures had passed bills prohibiting the execution of mentally retarded defendants. The Court argued:

> Given the well-known fact that anticrime legislation is far more popular than legislation providing protections for persons guilty of violent crime, the large number of States prohibiting the execution of mentally retarded persons . . . provides powerful evidence that today our society views mentally retarded offenders as categorically less culpable than the average criminal.[32]

Chief Justice Rehnquist soundly criticized the majority's reliance upon the legislative changes of a minority of states, as well as the views of other countries, to effect this change in death-penalty jurisprudence.[33] He also criticized the majority's use of public-opinion poll data, which, he argued, were neither verified as reliable nor designed to gauge respondents' views regarding the appropriateness of capital punishment for mentally retarded defendants in all situations. Instead, the questions were phrased generically, asking only whether the respondent believed that a mentally retarded person should be executed, without providing any definition of a mentally retarded person or asking whether the respondent might agree or disagree that all mentally retarded persons by definition could never act with the level of culpability associated with the death penalty, regardless of the severity of their impairment or the individual circumstances of their crime. Rehnquist concurred with Justice Scalia's dissent in *Atkins*, concluding that "the Court's assessment of the current legislative judgment regarding the execution of defendants like petitioner more resembles a *post hoc* rationalization for the majority's subjectively preferred result rather than any objective effort to ascertain the content of an evolving standard of decency."[34]

In addition to describing the Court's sleight of hand in calculating the number of states that forbade the execution of the mentally retarded, Scalia criticized the Court for similarly fudging the number of jurisdictions actually executing mentally retarded offenders in recent years. The majority mentioned that only five jurisdictions had executed mentally retarded offenders during the years since *Penry,* but the same source showed that twelve states had executed thirty-five mentally retarded defendants during 1984–2000.[35] Given that mentally retarded offenders make up only 1–3 percent of the general population, and presumably the same percentage of those who commit murder, the "rarity" of executions involving the mentally retarded may be commensurate with their proportion of the population generally.

Although the Texas legislature was among those that passed a bill prohibiting the execution of mentally retarded defendants, Governor Rick Perry vetoed the bill on June 17, 2001, stating "We do not execute mentally retarded murderers today."[36] He believed that safeguards already in place protected mentally retarded defendants. The issue of mental retardation can be raised at several stages in the proceedings against a defendant charged with capital murder. First, if a defendant is found incompetent, meaning he does not have sufficient present ability to consult with his lawyer with a reasonable degree of rational understanding or a rational as well as factual understanding of the proceedings against him, he is not required to stand trial.[37] A defendant who is found competent to stand trial may still be relieved of criminal liability if "as a result of severe mental disease or defect [he] did not know that his conduct was wrong" at the time he committed the crime.[38] Also, during a murder trial the prosecution has the burden of proving that the defendant "intentionally or knowingly" committed the crime, otherwise he may be convicted of a lesser offense or acquitted.[39] Once a defendant is convicted of capital murder, jurors are specifically instructed during the sentencing phase to consider his personal moral culpability in deciding whether he is deserving of a sentence less than death.[40] Finally, *Ford v. Wainwright* and Texas law exclude from execution any offender unable to understand that he or she is to be executed, that the execution is imminent, and the reason he or she is being executed.[41]

Despite Perry's confidence that Texas has never executed a mentally retarded defendant, the Death Penalty Information Center (DPIC) asserts that Texas has executed at least six mentally retarded defendants.[42] The reason for this discrepancy lies in different interpretations of "mentally retarded." The Court in *Atkins* declared that the execution of a mentally retarded defendant was unconstitutional, but it did not specify how a state was to determine whether or not an individual was indeed mentally retarded. Some states that enacted statutes outlawing the execution of the mentally retarded drew a bright line, stating that an individual with an intelligence quotient (IQ) below 70 was to be considered mentally retarded. Apparently this is how the DPIC determined that Texas had executed six mentally retarded inmates, since Texas has executed six defendants whose IQs were near or below 70. According to the list, the following six executed defendants were mentally retarded: Johnny Ray Anderson, IQ 70; Johnny Frank Garrett, dual diagnosis of mental illness and retardation; Billy Wayne Wright, IQ 69; Mario Marquez, IQ 65; Terry Washington, IQ 58–69; Oliver Cruz, IQ 64–76.

Perry apparently does not adhere to this bright-line definition. Instead, he asserts that the current safeguards in the criminal-justice system were designed to identify those mentally disabled persons who are less culpable because they were unable to comprehend the nature of their acts or because they are unable to distinguish right from wrong. Therefore, unjust results may occur with a bright-line rule at an IQ of 70. For example, as David Rumley explains, the most widely used classification system classifies mental retardation as mild, moderate, severe, or profound, depending on the person's score on an intelligence test.[43] Mentally retarded persons who have been subjected to the death penalty are those considered mildly retarded, that is, scoring between 50 and 70 on an intelligence test. Rumley asserts that virtually all persons with mild retardation are now able to live successfully in the community, and most casual observers would be unable to detect that such a person is mentally retarded. He further asserts that virtually all mildly and moderately retarded persons have the ability to conform, without external direction or guidance, to the customs, habits, and standards of behavior in society. He asserts that there is a general societal misconception that all persons described as mentally retarded are unable to care for themselves and are "profoundly" retarded, meaning they have an IQ below 20. This is also the likely reason for the low level of support for the execution of retarded persons in public-opinion polls. In reality, 89 percent of all mentally retarded persons fall in the mildly retarded range. Therefore, the vast majority of persons who are considered "mentally retarded" are in reality perfectly capable of understanding the significance of their actions and carrying out daily activities. They may receive driver's licenses; they are not considered disabled for the purposes of receiving disability supplements; they may marry; they may have children, etc.

Although several states rely on this bright-line rule of exempting persons with IQs less than 70 from capital punishment, there are several reasons why such sole reliance on IQ scores is inappropriate. Most importantly, mildly retarded persons generally have a grasp of what is right and wrong, and they are able to make rational decisions and control their own behavior. There is no evidence that mildly retarded persons are responsible for committing more crimes than those with higher IQs. Additionally, intelligence tests are notoriously inaccurate.[44] Results vary, depending on the questions asked and the experience of the test-taker. Rapport with the examiner, incentives to excel on the exam, and test-taking skills all affect how well someone might do. Natural influences such as fatigue and illness affect scores. In fact, scores on successive IQ tests have been improved by as much as fifteen points by simply offering the participants a reward for doing well.[45] Of course, the opposite is also true: IQ scores can decline when the participant has a lack of motivation or desire to do well. Given that a defendant's reward for doing well on such a test is a sentence of death, the possibility of malingering is high. Scalia noted in his dissent in *Atkins* that

> one need only read the definitions of mental retardation . . . to realize that the symptoms of this condition can readily be feigned. And whereas the capital defendant who feigns insanity risks commitment to a mental institution until he can be cured . . . the capital defendant who feigns mental retardation risks nothing at all. The mere pendency of the present case has brought us petitions by death row inmates claiming for the first time, after multiple habeas petitions, that they are retarded.[46]

The American Association on Mental Retardation (AAMR), recognizing the fallibility of intelligence tests, has developed instead a three-part test to determine whether a person is mentally retarded.[47] First, the person must exhibit subaverage intellectual functioning, which is measured by an IQ score. Generally, this cutoff is 70 or below. Second, the person must display an inability to function properly in society, meaning an inability to meet normal standards of learning, personal independence, communication, and daily-living skills expected from his or her age group. Finally, the person must exhibit subaverage intellectual function and an inability to function in society during the "developmental period," generally thought to extend from birth until the age of majority.

According to this definition, therefore, a person who has an IQ as low as 55 and who displays no difficulty adapting to the norms of society should not be considered mentally retarded. This measure would meet the Court's concerns that a jury consider the influence of a defendant's mental disability on his or her moral culpability in the commission of a capital crime. In fact, most states, including those that have developed the bright-line exclusion for capital defendants with an IQ of 70 or below, have adopted this three-part test to determine whether a person is considered mentally retarded in all other circumstances. The practical result is a system in which the same person may be held morally culpable in every situation and for every crime except capital murder.

Perry's views on mental retardation are thus more consistent with the views of the AAMR than with the views of those who have adopted the simplistic bright line. In a recent case, the governor commuted a death-sentenced inmate when the state's own experts agreed that Robert Smith, an inmate with an IQ of 63, also met the AAMR requirements to be considered mentally retarded. This is an example where the last fail-safe available was used to prevent the execution of a mentally retarded offender. Of the commutation, Perry spokeswoman Kathy Walt stated:

> This is the first case I believe that has come to him where there is a finding post-conviction that the inmate is mentally retarded. . . . Obviously, the law is that people who are found to be mentally retarded cannot be executed, and the governor's going to uphold the law. He has no qualms whatever about upholding the law.[48]

Juveniles

Like the execution of mentally retarded inmates, the execution of juveniles has caused heated debate among those arguing for and against capital punishment. Public consensus is that juveniles are generally not deserving of a death sentence.[49] Juveniles are considered less mature and less responsible than adults, and therefore less deserving of a death sentence. Juveniles are also more apt to be influenced by peer pressure and to act without forethought. Therefore, they are less likely to be deterred by the thought that their punishment may be death. Finally, juveniles have a greater likelihood of being rehabilitated or reformed. Historically, the treatment of juveniles has reflected these notions that children are less culpable than adults. This can be seen in the development of juvenile courts and in other treatments that focus energy and resources mainly on the rehabilitation of juveniles.

However, in recent years there has been a countermovement to hold juveniles more accountable for their actions. Juvenile offenders who have demonstrated that they are sophisticated enough to understand the nature and extent of their actions, as well as the wrongfulness of their actions, have been deemed more deserving of harsh penalties than those juveniles who have demonstrated more naivete. Juveniles may be waived to adult courts for committing serious, violent, or predatory crimes, and they may be given "blended sentences," which are to be served in the juvenile system until they reach the age of majority and then finished out in the adult system. In Texas, for example, juvenile offenders as young as fourteen can be transferred to adult court, where, if charged with capital murder, they may be subject to a life sentence, meaning that they must serve a mandatory minimum of forty years before becoming eligible for parole. In fact, ten-year-olds who are charged with capital murder may receive a forty-year determinate sentence from a juvenile court.[50]

Yet, those arguing against the death penalty for juveniles hold it out as distinctly different from any other type of punishment. Even those supporting capital punishment agree that it is the ultimate sanction, to be reserved for those who most deserve it. The issue therefore becomes one of determining at what age a person becomes culpable in a capital-murder context. Several states have drawn a bright-line at eighteen, the age of majority in most U.S. jurisdictions. Those arguing against the execution of juveniles likewise define a juvenile as one less than eighteen years of age. Using loaded phrases such as "putting kids to death" and "killing kids," critics emphasize the lesser degree of responsibility and culpability associated with children.[51] They often cite the fact that those under eighteen are unable to enjoy certain rights and freedoms, such as the ability to enter into legally binding contracts, to vote, to marry, and to serve on juries. However, opponents of a juvenile death penalty seldom mention that minors younger than eighteen can consent to sex, can consent to an abortion without notifying their parents or a court, and can become emancipated and allowed to proceed as adults. Additionally, juveniles younger than eighteen are often given privileges and responsibilities usually reserved for adults, such as driving automobiles and obtaining employment. These facts indicate that society has agreed that persons younger than eighteen can demonstrate the maturity and responsibility of adults under many circumstances.

For years the Supreme Court refused to rule on the issue of executing juvenile offenders. Its first opportunity came in 1978 with *Bell v. Ohio*.[52] The defendant in *Bell* was sixteen when he committed capital murder. At the sentencing hearing, his attorney argued that his youth should be submitted as a mitigating factor, but Ohio law prohibited the use of any mitigating factors not explicitly listed in the statute, and youth was not listed. In *Lockett v. Ohio*, the companion case to *Bell*, the Court ruled that defendants must be permitted to introduce any available evidence that might mitigate against a death sentence, regardless of whether such mitigating factors were listed in the state's death-penalty statute.[53] *Bell* was remanded on that ground, so the constitutionality of executing juveniles would not be decided in that case.

The Court's second opportunity came in 1982, when it granted certiorari in a case in which a sixteen-year-old murdered a police officer.[54] Again, however, the Court avoided the issue of executing juveniles and instead relied on *Lockett* to reverse the case, since the trial judge had not allowed the introduction of the defendant's mitigating evidence. The Court finally addressed the issue of executing juvenile offenders during 1988 in *Thompson v. Oklahoma*.[55] Thompson was fifteen when he and three others murdered his former brother-in-law. The Court reversed Thompson's death sentence by a 5–3 vote, but failed to issue a majority opinion.[56] The case established, however, that capital punishment was cruel and unusual when applied to defendants who were younger than sixteen when they committed the offense. One year later, the Court made the affirmative declaration, in the 5–4 decision in *Stanford v. Kentucky*, that the Eighth Amendment does not prohibit the execution of a defendant who was sixteen or seventeen when he committed the offense.[57]

In 2002, the Court refused to revisit the constitutionality of juvenile executions in Stanford's case. In a strongly worded dissent from the Court's denial of certiorari, four justices argued that, in light of the Court's new analysis of "evolving standards" in *Atkins*, the Court should reconsider whether the execution of a defendant younger than eighteen was cruel and unusual punishment and in violation of the Eighth Amendment.[58] In January 2004, however, the Court granted certiorari in the case of *Roper v. Simmons*.[59] In *Roper*, the seventeen-year-old defendant was convicted of the premeditated murder of Shirley Crook and sentenced to death. The Missouri Supreme Court reversed his sentence in 2003, concluding that

> the Supreme Court of the United States would hold that the execution of persons for crimes committed when they were under 18 years of age violates the "evolving standards of decency that mark the progress of a maturing society," and is prohibited by the Eighth Amendment to the United States Constitution as applied to the states through the Fourteenth Amendment.[60]

The United States Supreme Court granted certiorari to answer two questions: 1. Once the Court holds that a particular punishment is not "cruel and unusual," and thus barred by the Eighth and Fourteenth Amendments, can a lower court reach a contrary decision based on its own analysis of evolving standards? and 2. Is the imposition of the death penalty on a person who commits murder at age seventeen "cruel and unusual," and thus barred by the Eighth and Fourteenth Amendments?[61]

Thus far, whenever the Supreme Court has placed limitations on the scope of capital punishment, its reasoning has relied on the concept of "evolving standards of decency that mark the progress of a maturing society," first enunciated in *Trop v. Dulles*.[62] The debate over the execution of juveniles, as with that over mentally retarded defendants, appears to be one of determining whether and under what circumstances such defendants deserve to be executed. Specifically, at what point can a person be said to have reached the level of maturity and sophistication that would render him or her completely responsible for committing capital murder? Several states, the international community, and opponents of juvenile executions have established a bright-line distinction, whereby a person younger than eighteen is considered a juvenile, and thus should not be subjected to the death penalty, regardless of his or her individual characteristics or the circumstances of the crime. What seems to be ignored in the debate over the classification of juveniles, however, is that chronological age is simply a proxy to help decision makers determine the underlying, and arguably more significant, issue of individual maturity and responsibility. In reversing Simmons's conviction, for example, the Missouri Supreme Court simply stated that

> less culpability should attach to a crime committed by a juvenile than to a comparable crime committed by an adult. The basis for this conclusion is too obvious to require extended explanation. . . . *Thompson* concluded, "The reasons why juveniles are not trusted with the privileges and responsibilities of an adult also explain why their irresponsible conduct is not as morally reprehensible as that of an adult." Although Mr. Simmons is 17 rather than 15, he is still an adolescent, and this Court finds the rationales set forth in *Thompson* and *Eddings* apply here.[63]

The injustice of this bright-line approach, however, is that a person who commits a capital murder on his eighteenth birthday will be considered culpable as an adult, whereas someone who commits the exact same crime the day before his eighteenth birthday is automatically considered less culpable, and thus less deserving of a death sentence than the offender whose birthday has already passed. In his article "On the Perils of Line-Drawing: Juveniles and the Death Penalty," Joseph Hoffman discusses how sentencing similarly situated defendants of slightly different chronological ages violates the concept of proportionality. He points out that the problem with using age as a bright line in juvenile death-penalty cases is that age is not the only reason why it is (at least arguably) unjust to impose the death penalty on many juveniles.[64] Instead, age is simply a proxy for a combination of factors related to an individual's deservedness, including maturity, judgment, responsibility, and the capacity to evaluate the possible consequences of one's conduct.

In *Roper v. Simmons,* for example, Christopher Simmons was just over four months away from his eighteenth birthday; that fact alone was reason enough for the Missouri Supreme Court to reverse his death sentence. Looking at overall indicators of personal culpability, however, Simmons had demonstrated that this robbery-murder was premeditated, and undertaken with full confidence that his status as a juvenile would allow him to "get away with it." Weeks before the murder of Shirley Crook, Simmons had discussed plans to commit a robbery and a murder, detailing specifically how the murder would take place. After finding someone to burglarize, he planned to tie the victim up and then push him or her off a bridge. Simmons believed that if he were caught, his status as a juvenile would allow him to escape the death penalty.

On September 9, 1993, Simmons planned to meet with two friends, ages sixteen and fifteen, to carry out the plan. After meeting with Simmons, the sixteen-year-old decided not to participate and left for home. Simmons and the fifteen-year-old went to the home of Shirley Crook. They reached through an open window and unlocked the back door to Ms. Crook's home. They turned on a hallway light, and Ms. Crook was awakened. When Simmons entered the bedroom, they recognized each other: Simmons had recently been in a car accident with her. They ordered Ms. Crook onto the bedroom floor, and then bound her hands behind her back with duct tape. They also taped her eyes and her mouth shut. They ordered her into the back of her minivan, which Simmons drove to a railroad trestle that spanned the Meramec River. Simmons discovered when he parked the minivan that Ms. Crook had managed to free her hands and had removed some of the duct tape from her face. Using her purse strap, the belt from her bathrobe, a towel from the back of the van, and some electrical wire found on the trestle, Simmons bound her hands and feet together, hog-tie fashion, and covered her face completely with duct tape. She was then pushed off the railroad trestle into the river below. The coroner determined the cause of her death to be drowning. She was alive and conscious during the entire ordeal.

Carrying out his plan to the letter, Simmons demonstrated premeditation and a full awareness of the possible ramifications of his actions. To allow Simmons to escape a punishment of death simply because he had not yet turned eighteen seems unjust. However, the use of chronological age as a bright-line barrier is well established in American jurisprudence and not likely to be abandoned. Given this fact, where should the line be drawn with regard to capital murderers? Hoffman argues that the lower the minimum age, the more likely that violations of proportionality will be avoided. If the minimum age were lower, jurors would be permitted to consider the defendant's age in their sentencing deliberations. The higher the age at which the bright-line is set, the more likely it is that those equally deserving of a death sentence may avoid the sanction simply because of their age.

Texas is an ideal state to demonstrate this concept because Texas has sentenced to death several defendants who were seventeen when they committed capital murder.[65] In fact, Amnesty International has determined that Texas was the most prolific executioner of children worldwide from 1994 through April 2003. In 2002, for example, Amnesty International asserts that Texas was responsible for the only three executions of children anywhere in the world. Part of the reason for this seemingly high number of juvenile executions is that Texas has executed the most offenders in the United States during the modern period, which makes it likely that it has also executed a disproportionate share of those who were age seventeen at the time of their offense. Texas also has a large pool of seventeen-year-old homicide offenders who committed capital murder. And Texas law has historically defined an adult as someone seventeen or older, so jurors are less likely to consider such a defendant a "child" for purposes of sentencing deliberations.

In fact, a breakdown of the precise ages of juveniles who have been sentenced to death in Texas illustrates that jurors are likely to consider age when deliberating the defendant's deservedness. Of the defendants sentenced to death for murders committed during 1974–2003 and who were seventeen at the time of their offense, most were on the high side of seventeen. Only 12 percent of those sentenced to death were not yet seventeen years and three months old, and none of those executed were younger than that. On the other hand, nearly 60 percent of those sentenced to death, and 70 percent of those executed, had reached seventeen and a half years of age. Two of these offenders committed their crimes just one day shy of their eighteenth birthday: Johnnie Bernal, who was born August 20, 1976, and committed capital murder on August 19, 1994; and Whitney Reeves, who was born August 21, 1981, and committed capital murder on August 20, 1999.

Several juvenile death-penalty cases that have been processed in Texas illustrate the danger that setting a high minimum age poses to achieving proportionality in capital sentencing. Consider the case of Charles Rumbaugh, the first juvenile executed in the United States during the modern era. On September 11, 1985, Rumbaugh became the tenth offender put to death in Texas during the modern era and the first juvenile executed in the United States in over twenty years. Although sources found on the Web contain many references to Rumbaugh, nearly all refer only to his unique status as the first juvenile executed in the modern era. Almost all are extremely sympathetic to his plight and opposed to executing juveniles. For example, several carry a quotation from the killer meant to illustrate his immaturity at the time of the offense. For these authors, the quotation demonstrates the purposelessness of his execution and, by extension, the execution of other juveniles: "I was 17 years old when

I committed the offense for which I was sentenced to die, and I didn't even start thinking and caring about my life until I was at least 20."[66] Although this quotation demonstrates at least a certain amount of reflection by Rumbaugh, and abolitionists cite it to support their argument that juveniles generally do not reflect upon their actions, his revelation is not one that is unique to juvenile offenders. Offenders generally neither repent nor experience any remorse for their behavior until they are caught, regardless of their age. Nor does it bolster the argument of those opposed to juvenile executions because of the age of the offender. If Rumbaugh had committed the murder a few months later, after his eighteenth birthday, he could have made the same statement, and it would have been just as valid.

Details regarding the circumstances of juvenile capital murders are generally difficult to find, despite their cases being quoted extensively by those who would see juvenile executions abolished. The only information available regarding Rumbaugh's case, for example, was that he had been sentenced to death for the murder of a fifty-eight-year-old person during the robbery of a jewelry store. Given this bare outline, it is difficult to see why Rumbaugh was sentenced to death for a somewhat ordinary capital murder, one in which defendants generally would have an equal chance of receiving life or a death sentence. In a situation such as this, his youth would seem to serve as a mitigating factor in favor of a life sentence.

However, further investigation revealed why Rumbaugh received a death sentence. First, Rumbaugh had a lengthy criminal record dating back to when he was just six. He committed his first armed robbery at twelve. Just under three months shy of his eighteenth birthday, he committed this capital murder. While being held on these charges, Rumbaugh and two other inmates escaped from the county jail by cutting through a ³/₈-inch steel plate and then lowering themselves with a rope fashioned from bedsheets knotted together. While on the run, the fugitives overpowered a state trooper who had pulled them over for a traffic violation, and took his gun. Fortunately for the trooper, another law enforcement official arrived in time to subdue the trio before another capital murder was committed. Later, at his sentencing hearing, Rumbaugh threatened the lives of his defense attorney, the prosecutor, the bailiff, and the judge before being disarmed of a seven-and-a-half-inch metal rod that he had sharpened to a point. Finally, in February 1983, long after making his statement regarding his repentance and his new view on life, Rumbaugh was critically wounded after lunging at a U.S. deputy during a court proceeding, again using a prison-made shank. Given these factors, it seems difficult to argue that Rumbaugh was less deserving of a death sentence than a similar defendant who happened to be three months his senior.

As Rumbaugh's case illustrates, some juvenile offenders may deserve a death sentence as much as offenders who are eighteen or older. One issue that arises in this debate is whether those younger than eighteen are less culpable overall—it is possible that Rumbaugh was a particularly extreme example of youthful criminality. Table 4.1 showed that defendants who were younger than eighteen at the time of their offense were actually more likely to receive a sentence of death than defendants who were eighteen at the time of their offense. These differences disappeared, however, when the types of offenses committed by those age seventeen (in Table 4.2) were controlled for. So why has Texas sentenced so many juveniles to death? A look at some of the case characteristics may provide clues to what influenced the juries' decisions in these capital cases and how bright-line age limits may exacerbate violations of proportionality.

One case from Laredo involved three juveniles who collectively decided to commit a sacrificial murder for Satan. Both Venegas and Hernandez were sixteen, and Martinez was seventeen. The trio decided to murder a local youth pastor, James Smiley, because they considered him a hypocrite. Upon arriving at the Smiley home, Venegas ordered Martinez to retrieve an axe from his car so that Venegas could murder Smiley and his overnight guests. Martinez brought the axe, and Venegas murdered Smiley and two guests. Hernandez, who was clearly the least culpable of the three, was sentenced to probation in exchange for his testimony against the other two. Although he did not commit the murders, the jury found Miguel Angel Martinez guilty under the law of parties and sentenced him to death for his role in the murders. He became the youngest person sentenced to death row. Venegas, who actually commanded and carried out the murders, escaped from custody and fled to Mexico. Upon his return and capture, he was certified to stand trial as an adult, and was eventually sentenced to forty-one years, but will be eligible for parole after serving one-fourth of his sentence. The death penalty was not an option in his case because of his age. Clearly, proportionality was violated here: a defendant who was more responsible for a crime than his accomplice was given leniency simply because he was a few months younger.[67]

In this case, the bright-line rule resulted in a death sentence for the less culpable of the two assailants simply because he had reached his seventeenth birthday. In many instances, including the cases of many of those currently sentenced to Texas's death row, the most culpable offender was seventeen at the time of the offense. It is likely that if the statutory minimum had been eighteen, then many of the accomplices would have been sent to death row to satisfy the public's demand for justice. Even if this could be prevented, proportionality would still be violated if seventeen-year-olds who are just as deserving of death as older offenders escape the penalty. Although the minimum statutory eligibility of seventeen also poses such a risk, as demonstrated in the above story, the higher the statutory minimum is set, the more often proportionality will be violated. In the interest of just deserts, it makes little sense to increase the statutory minimum age. If anything, comparative proportionality would be served by lowering the statutory age limit to sixteen.

One more example illustrates this point more directly. Jennifer Ertman and Elizabeth Peña were brutally murdered by the Black-White street gang in Houston. While walking home after visiting friends, the girls decided to cut through T. C. Jester Park, where they encountered six members of the gang. On the railroad tracks that marked their shortcut, the girls were kidnapped, repeatedly raped, brutally beaten, and strangled to death. Each of the six members of the gang was equally involved in the rapes and murders. Three of the gang members were eighteen or older, two were seventeen, and one was sixteen. The sixteen-year-old was not eligible for the death penalty, but all five of the others received death sentences. One of the seventeen-year-olds, Efrain Perez, admitted to raping and strangling sixteen-year-old Elizabeth Peña. The other seventeen-year-old, Raul Villarreal, bragged that he had stepped on the neck of fourteen-year-old Jennifer Ertman because "the bitch wouldn't die" after being strangled with a belt. These two defendants have been issued reprieves while awaiting the Supreme Court's decision in *Roper*. There will be no reprieves for the three others who happened to have crossed the bright line of eighteen.

Addendum

On March 1, 2005, the U.S. Supreme Court announced its decision in *Roper v. Simmons,* holding that imposing the death penalty on youths under the age of eighteen was cruel and unusual punishment and in violation of the Eighth and Fourteenth Amendments. In line with its earlier decision against executing the mentally retarded (*Atkins v. Virginia*), the Court found that a national consensus had developed against executing juveniles and, hence, that such executions violate evolving standards of decency. In this contentious 5–4 decision, the dissenters quibbled with the majority's definition of "national consensus" and argued that drawing a bright line at eighteen would exclude some of the worst murderers from death-penalty eligibility, thereby leading to violations of proportionality in sentencing. Texas, with twenty-four death-row inmates who were age seventeen at the time of their offense, is the state most affected by the decision. These murderers, including two members of Houston's Black-White street gang involved in the rape-murders described above, must be released from death row, and will likely have their sentences commuted to life imprisonment.

A week later, President Bush issued an executive order regarding fifty-one Mexican nationals now on death row in nine states: all of the inmates claim that their rights were violated when authorities failed to notify a Mexican consulate of their arrests, and the order requires states to conduct hearings to determine if this happened and, if it did, how their convictions will be affected. It is uncertain how states will comply with this order, but it could affect another fifteen inmates in Texas (there are sixteen Mexican nationals on Texas's death row, but one did not join the suit), including Jose Medellin, another member of the Black-White street gang. The remaining two gang members arrested for the rape-murders of Jennifer Ertman and Elizabeth Peña will have to seek other avenues of appeal.

These decisions were inevitable and bring the United States in line with international standards on the imposition of the death penalty. What remains to be seen is whether the decisions bring the United States closer to the end of its procedural tinkering with death-penalty statutes or whether they represent a continued chipping away at the sanction, a steady subtraction that will ultimately result in its abolition.

CHAPTER 5

Administration: Is the Death Penalty Carried Out Impartially, Reliably, and Efficiently?

[O]ne can object to the execution of innocent people based on their race or ethnicity without opposing capital punishment per se. Similarly . . . one can support constitutional principles of a fair trial and due process irrespective of one's views on the merits of the death penalty.

SCOTT ATLAS, HABEAS COUNSEL FOR RICARDO ALDAPE GUERRA, IN "HOW CAN WE BE SURE?" (2003)

Public opinion polls show that Texans, like Americans generally, are not philosophically opposed to capital punishment. When asked if they support the use of capital punishment, the majority of Texans invariably say yes. However, when asked specific questions about the application of the death penalty under particular circumstances, their level of support decreases. Most believe that capital punishment is an appropriate governmental response to particularly egregious murders, but their concerns about how the death penalty is implemented in particular cases gives rise to a certain amount of skepticism regarding its actual use. The greatest concern related to the implementation of capital punishment is whether the sanction is carried out impartially and reliably.

Whether the death penalty is parceled out to defendants impartially is a perennial question. The question implicates a host of factors potentially related to the disparate application of death sentences because of inappropriate considerations, such as the gender or economic status of the capital murderer. Gender and economic status tend to be of little consequence, since nearly all capital murders, as currently defined, are committed by males of lower socioeconomic status, which accounts for most of the perceived disparities in income and gender. Of greater concern is whether the death penalty is imposed against racial minorities, merely because of their minority status, more often than against whites. The historical pattern of executions has led to the inescapable conclusion that the death penalty has been unfairly applied to blacks in this country. Disparate application of the death penalty because of race influenced the Supreme Court's decision to declare, in *Furman v. Georgia* (1972), capital punishment, as then imposed, unconstitutional.[1] The question today is whether this concern has been adequately addressed by the new capital-punishment laws and bureaucratic procedures established during the modern era.

Another major concern in the implementation of capital punishment is whether it is applied reliably and so as to preclude the execution of innocent persons. The specter of executing innocent defendants has been the driving force behind the abolition of the death penalty in several U.S. jurisdictions and in other countries. Exonerations due to DNA testing, the release of death row inmates in Illinois by former governor Jim Ryan because of doubts concerning the guilt of some inmates, and even the influence of Hollywood after the release of *The Life of David Gale* have recently caused many Americans to question whether all those awaiting execution are guilty of the crimes for which they were sentenced to death. Most Americans now believe that the death-penalty system has or will execute an innocent person. Such speculation involves the actual odds of executing an innocent person and the evidence upon which such estimates are based.

Finally, a pragmatic issue often arises in the implementation of the death penalty: is it more or less expensive than a life sentence? At the crudest level, common sense suggests that executions should be far cheaper than warehousing a prisoner for life. Historical practices certainly bear out the proposition that executions can be conducted with fiscal efficiency. Neither the rope used to hang offenders nor the electricity used in electrocution was costly. In the modern era, the drugs for lethal injection are similarly inexpensive. However, the modern era has brought increased protections through extensive legal procedures; these cost money in themselves, increase waits on death row, and sometimes result in overturned cases. The cost of this "super due process" in death-penalty cases has been found to exceed the projected cost of incarcerating an offender for life. The question then becomes whether it is possible to carry out a death sentence at a cost lower than or commensurate with the cost of life imprisonment, while still providing the constitutional safeguards that must be afforded capital defendants.

Racial Bias

Each of the three cases joined in *Furman v. Georgia* (1972) involved black defendants and white victims. Furman had murdered his victim; the other two appellants had raped, but not murdered, their victims. One of these rape cases involved an appellant, Elmer Branch, from Texas.[2] Branch had "entered the rural home of a 65-year-old widow, a white, while she slept and raped her, holding his arm against her throat. Thereupon he demanded money and for 30 minutes or more the widow searched for money, finding little. As he left, [Branch] said if the widow told anyone what happened, he would return and kill her."[3] Although unsure whether it was in fact the race of the offender that led to the imposition of the death penalty in the case of Branch or the other appellants, Justice Douglas cited statistical evidence showing such patterns to be widespread. He quoted a study by Rupert Koeninger concerning disparate treatment of white and black defendants accused of capital crimes in Texas during the electrocution era, 1924–1968:

> Seventy-five of the 460 cases involved codefendants, who, under Texas law, were given separate trials. In several instances where a white and Negro were co-defendants, the white was sentenced to life imprisonment or a term of years, and the Negro was given the death penalty.
>
> Another ethnic disparity is found in the type of sentence imposed for rape. The Negro convicted of rape is far more likely to get the death penalty than a term sentence, whereas whites and Latins are far more likely to get a term sentence than the death penalty.[4]

There can be little doubt that executions for rape in Texas and throughout the South constituted a perpetuation of historical oppression, carried on previously through lynching, that acted as a mechanism to keep blacks "in their place." Evidence of discrimination in the sentencing of black rapists throughout the South was overwhelming.[5] The National Prisoner Statistics Bulletin, published by the U.S. Department of Justice, showed that from 1930, when statistics were first kept, through the last pre-*Furman* execution in 1967, "blacks . . . made up 89 percent of those put to death for rape. . . ." With the exception of seven executions for rape in Missouri, all executions of blacks for rape took place in the South.[6]

This peculiar form of chivalry was carried out in Texas much as it had been in more traditional southern states, particularly in East Texas, the area that had had the highest proportion of slaves. Death sentences imposed for rape in Texas during 1924–1971 involved black offenders in 76 percent of the cases and white victims in 95 percent of the cases overall.[7] Death sentences for rape, however, were becoming increasingly uncommon by the time of the *Furman* ruling. Georgia, one of the few states to reenact the death penalty for rape after *Furman,* quickly found that the Supreme Court considered the death penalty to constitute cruel and unusual punishment for the rape of an adult woman.[8] Discrimination in the imposition of the death penalty for rape is therefore no longer an issue, except when a black defendant is accused of raping and then murdering a white victim.

The pattern for murder during this period, although not nearly so stark, paralleled that of rape. The racial combination of black offender and white victim was by far the most likely case to result in a sentence of death during this era, even controlling for the fact that African Americans had a much higher rate of involvement in murder than other races.[9] In Texas during the era of electrocution, just over 50 percent of those sentenced to death for murder were black, while 75 percent of the victims overall were white.[10] However, the proportion of blacks sentenced to death for murder, relative to whites, consistently decreased from nearly 80 percent in the 1920s to less than 50 percent by the 1960s.[11] A shift, then, had also occurred in the sentencing of murderers, at least in Texas, even by the time of *Furman*.

In *Furman*, the justices devoted their attention to the lack of standards in sentencing, and so were most concerned with discrimination by jurors in imposing death sentences on black defendants during trial. Most death-penalty studies before this period similarly focused on race-based decisions made at trial or in postconviction proceedings.[12] Studies completed in the wake of *Furman*, however, have found little evidence of any direct discrimination against black defendants by jurors deciding on a sentence of life or death. Rather, researchers have noticed a more subtle pattern of discrimination that occurs during the pretrial stages of case processing: certain types of cases are set on a death-penalty track during the charging process more often than other types of cases. Race has been implicated in many of these studies, but now typically in the form of victim-based discrimination, as prosecutors pursue cases involving white victims more vigorously than those involving black victims.[13] These studies have consistently found that cases involving white victims are more likely to be charged as capital murder and to proceed to capital trials with death-qualified juries. Many have found that these pretrial processes are also influenced by the conjunction of the race of the victim and the race of the offender: black defendant–white victim is the racial combination most likely to proceed to a death-penalty trial. However, researchers' failure to adequately parcel out the effects of the defendant's and victim's race while observing their effects in combination has led those reviewing the studies to remain skeptical of these findings.[14]

Post-*Furman* studies rarely find evidence of any racial effects in jurors' decision making during the guilt and penalty stages of case processing. Certainly there is little evidence of any intentional discrimination on the part of jurors, or even prosecutors, in making their decisions.[15] Some have suggested that cases involving the murder of whites, particularly if committed by blacks, elicit the most fear from predominantly white jurors, whereas jurors are more likely to view the types of murders committed against blacks, usually by black defendants, as less serious. The pattern of "racial disparity" found in pretrial processing may then result from a process of "case typification": prosecutors, though not consciously discriminatory, decide to pursue cases with characteristics that they believe conform with jurors' views of the seriousness of a case.[16]

The validity of the findings in these studies depends on the ability of researchers to control for other possible explanations of the racial differences found. For example, Jesse Jackson noted that just over 40 percent of death sentences and 35 percent of executions in the United States during 1977–2001 involved blacks, who comprised only 12 percent of the population.[17] He argued that this overrepresentation was evidence of discrimination. What such figures fail to reflect is that blacks are disproportionately involved in murders: over 50% percent of homicide offenders arrested across the United States during 1976–2000 were black.[18] Studies that use the proportion of blacks involved in murder as the baseline often conclude that there is no discrimination against black defendants; whites, in fact, appear overrepresented among death-row inmates relative to their presence among murder arrests.[19]

These simple comparisons cannot be relied on when determining whether capital punishment is administered in a racially biased manner. To gauge whether the system is discriminatory—and if so, by how much—one must fully control for legally relevant factors that could have influenced the imposition of the sanction. Only then can one presume that some of the residual disparity could be due to inappropriate racial considerations.

To determine whether any racial disparities remain unexplained after controlling for case characteristics that could legitimately be expected to influence pretrial and death-sentencing decisions, researchers generally rely upon the two approaches described in the previous chapter to control for the level of case seriousness, those pioneered by Gross and Mauro and by Baldus and his colleagues.[20] The first approach compares death-sentenced cases to statewide homicides arrests, controlling for all variables available in the Supplemental Homicide Reports.[21] The first study applying this approach to Texas found that among arrests for felony murder during the 1970s, black offenders with white victims were 9.5 times more likely to receive the death penalty than blacks who killed black victims, and 5 times more to receive the death penalty than whites who killed white victims.[22] Relying on this methodology to analyze specific forms of felony homicide, Ekland-Olson found that rape-murders involving black offenders and white victims, at a ratio of 4.82:1, were the most overrepresented types of felony murder cases on death row, relative to their presence among arrests during the early 1980s.[23] In a reanalysis and extension of Ekland-Olson's work, a study used logistic regression to simultaneously control for all of the factors present in the SHR data in order to determine which were most influential in prosecutorial charging practices for homicides involving felonies. This study found that though the race of the victim appeared to influence the charging decision, the race of the offender in combination with that of the victim had no effect.[24]

The second approach developed by Baldus and his colleagues involves retrospectively following up a sample of cases from individual files, which allows for the collection of a larger amount of data both on the legitimate characteristics of particular cases and on how they were processed at each stage of criminal-justice processing.[25] There has never been a true Baldus-style study completed in Texas, but one study emulated Baldus's methodology by examining the extent to which legitimate case characteristics and race influenced jury decisions in death penalty trials among capital-murder convictions during 1974–1988. Included in the study were additional variables not available in the SHR data—most significantly, the defendant's prior criminal record. In this study, none of the racial combinations were found to significantly influence the likelihood of a capital defendant being sentenced to death. Because this study did not take into account the cumulative race effects that may have resulted from earlier prosecutorial decisions, however, the findings regarding the lack of race effects on sentencing must be received cautiously.[26]

The study undertaken herein draws on the strengths of both types of analysis to determine whether the race of offenders or victims, either separately or in combination, increased the likelihood of a death sentence in Texas during recent years. First, an analysis in the style of Gross and Mauro's was used to compare those sentenced to death with those arrested for homicide during 1994–2000. This method has the advantage of facilitating a comparison among the broadest possible pool of cases and generating a global measure of disparity that includes the effects of prosecutors' and juries' decisions during pretrial and sentencing stages. The method is limited by the number of control variables included in the SHR data, and by its inability to pinpoint the stage of case processing at which any discovered disparity entered into the system. Second, an in-depth Baldus-style analysis was used to examine the characteristics of the murders in 2000 that resulted in death sentences. Using this approach, and taking into account additional case characteristics, it is possible to determine at which stage disparities enter the system and to get a better view of whether race is related to case-processing decisions. The main weakness of this approach stems from the smaller pool of available cases, which impinges on the ability to generalize the findings. However, these two approaches complement each another, and to the degree that they concur, the ability to draw conclusions from the analyses is improved.

Homicide Arrests Resulting in Death Sentences (1994–2000)

Simply comparing the percentage of black offenders sentenced to death to the percentage of blacks in the general population would find an overrepresentation of blacks sentenced to death; blacks made up 37.7 percent (86/228) of Texans given death sentences for murders occurring during 1994–2000, but only 11.5 percent of Texas residents.[27] When the comparison group is changed from the percentage of blacks in the general population to the percentage of blacks potentially at risk of receiving the death penalty, the racial disparity disappears: blacks constituted 36.7 percent (2,176/5,934) of those arrested for homicide, a figure very close to the percentage of blacks among those sentenced to death, 37.7 percent (86/228). The first set of figures in Table 5.1 shows the percentage of homicide cases that result in death sentences, broken out by the race of the offender. White and black offenders tend to receive the death sentence at similar rates, at around 4 percent; Hispanics and Asians receive the death penalty slightly less often.

Studies completed during the modern era, however, have shown that the race of the victim is more likely to influence death sentencing than the race of the offender. The second set of figures in Table 5.1 shows that cases involving black and Hispanic victims are the least likely to result in death sentences. Those with black victims result in death sentences about a third as often as cases involving white victims. Those involving Hispanic victims result in death sentences about half as often as those involving white victims. The cases most likely to result in death sentences are those with Asian victims, which are more than twice as likely to result in death as cases involving white victims.

The finding that cases with Asian offenders are least likely to result in the death penalty, but that those with Asian victims are most likely to result in the death penalty, suggests the importance of controlling for offender-victim racial combinations, for it is obvious that interracial killings of Asians are most likely to result in the death penalty. The final set of figures in Table 5.1 shows the validity of this supposition. Cases involving the racial combinations of either blacks or Hispanics who kill Asians are most likely to result in the death penalty; over a quarter of all such murders result in death sentences. The category next most likely to receive death is black-kill-white, followed by Hispanic-kill-white. For the killing of whites, blacks are three times more likely than

Table 5.1 Racial characteristics of murder arrests in Texas and the likelihood of receiving a death sentence, 1994–2000

	Total arrests	Cases resulting in a death sentence	
		Number	Percentage
Offender's race			
White	1,680	69	4.1
Black	2,176	86	4.0
Hispanic	2,014	71	3.5
Asian	64	2	3.1
Victim's race			
White	1,949	126	6.5
Black	1,825	38	2.1
Hispanic	2,013	66	3.3
Asian	83	12	14.5
Race of offender/victim			
White/White	1,395	60	4.3
White/Black	107	3	2.8
White/Hispanic	183	11	6.0
White/Asian	7	0	0.0
Black/White	323	42	13.0
Black/Black	1,640	33	2.0
Black/Hispanic	202	8	4.0
Black/Asian	23	6	26.1
Hispanic/White	268	26	9.7
Hispanic/Black	91	2	2.2
Hispanic/Hispanic	1,651	46	2.8
Hispanic/Asian	13	4	30.8
Asian/White	9	0	0.0
Asian/Black	3	0	0.0
Asian/Hispanic	13	1	7.7
Asian/Asian	42	2	4.9

whites to get death, and Hispanics get death twice as often as whites. Among black offenders, those who kill whites get death six and a half times more often than those who kill blacks. Among Hispanic offenders, those who kill whites get death three and a half times more often than those who kill Hispanics.

These findings parallel those of other studies that have used this methodology, with the exception of the new findings related to interracial killings of Asians. Interesting too is the finding that among those who kill blacks, whites are most likely to receive death.[28] However, these findings represent only the raw totals of racial disparity between homicide arrestees and those sentenced to death, unadjusted for case characteristics that could legitimately influence the severity of punishment. Just as it would be a misrepresentation to compare the percentage of blacks on death row to the proportion of blacks in the general population, this simple comparison also misrepresents the actual level of racial disparity.

As found in Chapter 4, a host of relevant case characteristics available in the SHR data were useful for predicting death sentences among homicide arrests. The likelihood that a death sentence would be imposed varied drastically with the presence or absence of these characteristics in a given case, and these factors could also account for much of the unadjusted racial disparity found in Table 5.1. For example, it is possible that black-kill-white homicide cases may regularly involve robbery, whereas black-kill-black cases may not regularly involve this aggravating feature and therefore may be less likely to result in a death sentence. Because the racial disparities that took only race into account may actually result from such aggravating case characteristics, it is necessary to control for the effects of these potentially influential factors to more accurately gauge the effect of race on death sentences. To control for specific case characteristics that may legitimately influence the imposition of the death penalty, the logistic regression model from Chapter 4 was once again utilized (see Table 4.2 and note 17 to Chapter 4).

Table 5.2 presents the effects of race on death sentences for three logistic regression models that include the race of offender, the race of the victim, and offender-victim racial combinations, controlling for legitimate case characteristics.[29] The figures presented in Table 5.2 may be interpreted as the increase in the likelihood of a death sentence for a racial category, compared to an omitted reference category.[30]

The first model includes the effects of the race of an offender on the likelihood of a death sentence. Since the main concern is with minority offenders, the results are reported for blacks and Hispanics; cases with Asian and white offenders serve as the reference category. The results show that cases involving black offenders are significantly less likely than those of whites and Asians (the reference category) to result in death sentences, holding the other case characteristics constant. The odds multiplier for black offenders is .528, meaning that cases involving blacks are about half as likely as cases involving whites and Asians to result in death. If the Hispanic coefficient had been statistically significant, the odds multiplier would indicate that Hispanics are about three-quarters as likely as whites and Asians to receive a death sentence. These preliminary findings show no support for the argument of discrimination against

Table 5.2 Impact of race on death sentences, controlling for legitimate case characteristics of arrests, 1994–2000

Model	Times as likely to result in a death sentence	Reference category
I. Offender's race		
Black	.528**	White and Asian
Hispanic	.719	offenders
II. Victim's race		
White	1.984***	Black and Hispanic
Asian	3.771***	victims
III. Race of offender/victim		
White/White	.966	Asian offenders/
White/Hispanic	1.010	all victims; White
Black/White	1.117	offenders/Black
Black/Black	.426**	and Asian victims;
Black/Asian	1.751	Hispanic/Black;
Hispanic/White	1.257	Black/Hispanic
Hispanic/Hispanic	.740	
Hispanic/Asian	4.722*	

*$p < .05$; **$p < .01$; ***$p < .001$

minority offenders. The apparent leniency extended to minority offenders, however, could result from the fact that most homicides are intraracial, and those with minority victims are less likely to result in death sentences.

The second model confirms the importance of the race of the victim in death sentencing. Herein, the racial categories of most import, Asian and white, are reported; Hispanic and black victims serve as the reference category. Odds multipliers show that homicides involving white victims are nearly twice as likely to result in death sentences as those with black or Hispanic victims, other case characteristics held constant. Homicides involving Asian victims are nearly twice as likely as those involving white victims to result in death, which is nearly four times greater than those involving blacks and Hispanics, all other factors held constant. The results concerning white victims are consistent with previous studies in Texas, while the death-sentencing rates for crimes involving Asian victims represent a new finding in Texas.[31] But again, as noted in Table 5.1, the race of the offender appears to work in conjunction with the race of the victim to influence death-penalty sentencing outcomes.

The final and most telling model includes the offender-victim racial combinations.[32] The results show that whites who kill either whites or Hispanics are no more or less likely to receive the death penalty than any other racial combination, all other factors held constant. In the category of most concern—black and Hispanic offenders who kill whites—the odds are also not significantly different from 1.0, suggesting that these minorities are no more likely to receive the death penalty for killing whites than deaths associated with other racial combinations. The largest racial difference found in the model is for Hispanics who kill Asians: they are 4.7 times more likely to receive a death sentence than the other cases. If it were statistically significant, the odds multiplier for black-kill-Asian would be the second largest positive coefficient. The relationship that attained the highest level of statistical significance was that of black-kill-black; it was the combination least likely to receive a death sentence. All other factors held constant, black offenders who kill black victims were less than half as likely to receive the death penalty as similarly situated cases involving other racial combinations. Although not statistically significant, the odds multiplier for intraracial killings involving Hispanics follows a similar pattern.

What do these findings suggest about the imposition of the death penalty in Texas currently? Are some groups of offenders treated with undue harshness? Do some racial groups receive more protection from the justice system, while others are discounted? The answer to the question of disparate, undue harshness appears to be a clear no. Only in situations of Hispanics killing Asians does it appear that a group of minorities receives death sentences significantly more often than would be expected given other legitimate case characteristics. For two reasons, however, this relationship should be interpreted with a great deal of caution. First, this is a very small group of cases: thirteen homicides, which resulted in four death sentences. Although the evidence of discrimination against other minorities in killing Asians becomes stronger if cases involving black and Hispanic offenders are combined, a question arises: under what theory would one expect these groups to be treated more harshly for killing members of another minority group? The usual explanation for the harsher sentencing of minorities who kill whites is that whites, who are members of the dominant majority, are able to mobilize the resources of the criminal-justice system in their favor and to encourage prosecutorial charging decisions that protect them from violence perpetrated by minorities. This will not serve as an explanation for the harsher treatment of minorities who kill Asians, members of another minority group.

A second reason for caution is that several variables, some of which appear to affect the seriousness of a case, are not available in the SHR. To the extent that these unavailable variables influence the processing of those cases involving the killing of Asians by other minorities, their effects remain unmeasured, and may be the true explanation for the disparate sentencing. Specifically, many of the death sentences in this category resulted from crime sprees in which offenders systematically robbed Asian businesses. Such crimes are much more likely to result in the death penalty, but its quantification is unavailable as a variable in the SHR.

More support exists for the supposition that some groups receive less protection from the criminal-justice system because of their relative inability to mobilize the capital-punishment process on their own behalf. For intraracial cases involving minorities, particularly blacks, it appears that the death penalty is much less likely to be imposed than in other cases with similar case characteristics. Although this is a much larger pool of cases, and therefore does not suffer from the same potential defect as the findings related to the killing of Asians described above, these findings related to intraracial killings among minorities do not escape the criticism that important case considerations may not have been taken into account. For example, the relationship between the offender and the victim was not included here because it lacked significance in the overall model and because it is notoriously inaccurate in the SHR data.[33]

Previous studies, however, have shown that intraracial cases involving blacks are likely to involve acquaintances. Previous research has also shown that these crimes are much more likely to involve some form of provocation on the part of the victim, something else not included in the SHR data.[34] Additionally, intraracial black robbery-murders may involve drug dealers, and homicides involving multiple victims may be more likely to involve members of street gangs. In either situation, the victims may be seen as unworthy of the death penalty for reasons other than their race. Other problems arise in prosecuting these cases, such as the reluctance of witnesses to testify and the impeachability of such witnesses when they do agree to cooperate. That interracial cases involving minority victims result in the death penalty as often as cases with white victims suggests that minorities' ability to mobilize the death penalty is probably more contingent on the fact patterns in the case than on the victims' status as minorities.

An additional hypothesis suggests that the effects of race may not be constant across levels of case seriousness. In *The American Jury*, Kalven and Zeisel first described the relationship between the seriousness of the case and the likelihood that jurors would consider inappropriate or extralegal factors.[35] They found that when the evidence was strong and the facts of the case supported a severe sentence, jurors tended to base their decisions solely on the strength of the evidence. However, in less clear-cut cases, jurors felt "liberated" from the facts of the case and looked to extralegal factors to help them decide, suggesting that jurors may have based their decisions on their personal biases. This

Table 5.3 Murder arrests resulting in death sentences, by offender/victim racial combinations and level of case aggravation, 1994–2000

Level of case aggravation	Death sentences, % (no. death sentences/no. cases)			Ratio of death sentences	
	WkW	BkW	BkB	BkW:WkW	BkW:BkB
1–3	0.5	1.4	0.1		
	(6/1,172)	(2/138)	(1/1,374)		
4–5	15.9	13.0	5.4	0.8:1	2.3:1
	(29/182)	(20/154)	(12/224)		
6–7	51.7	60.9	40.5	1.2:1	1.5:1
	(15/29)	(14/23)	(15/37)		
8+	83.3	75.0	100.0		
	(10/12)	(6/8)	(5/5)		

Note: WkW: white kills white; BkW: black kills white; BkB: black kills black.

"liberation hypothesis" (as it has come to be called), when applied to homicide cases, predicts that in the most serious and brutal homicide cases, juries sentence on the basis of legally relevant factors, but in less aggravated cases, juries are liberated by the lack of weighty evidence to consider extralegal factors (e.g., race of the offender or victim). By extension, the same can be said of prosecutors making pretrial decisions.

That studies have found support for the liberation hypothesis in death sentencing suggests the importance of considering the interaction of race and case seriousness on death-penalty decisions.[36] To test for this possibility, an additional evaluation was conducted by, first, sorting the cases into the levels of case seriousness presented in Figure 4.1. The probability of a death sentence was then calculated for each subcategory of racial combination of interest, at each level of case aggravation. Since the greatest concern, historically and legally, has been with discrimination against black offenders, these figures are presented in Table 5.3. The racial combination of white-kill-white serves as the reference category.

These new results continue to support the overall effects of race found in the previous analyses, but offer only limited support for the liberation hypothesis. First, for killers of whites, the race of the offender does not appear to make a difference, regardless of the level of case aggravation. Although the categories at the extremes are too small for ratios to be legitimately calculated, it appears that at the highest levels of aggravation, white victim cases are likely to result in death sentences regardless of the race of the offender. Although the proportion of black-kill-white at the lowest levels of aggravation is higher than that for white-kill-white, these cases should not be construed as providing support for the liberation hypothesis, because both of these cases involved the murder of white Houston police officers by black offenders.[37] Differences among cases in the midrange level—those in which other researchers have typically found evidence of racial disparities to be the strongest—tend to cancel one another out. Blacks are slightly less likely than whites to receive the death penalty for killing whites in the low-middle range of case aggravation, and slightly more likely in the high-middle range.

The evidence provides some support for the liberation hypothesis among black-offender cases, depending on the race of the victim. While the rate of death sentencing is 100 percent for blacks who kill blacks at the highest levels of case aggravation, the level of disparity between black-kill-white versus black-kill-black increases as one moves down the level of case severity. In the high-middle range, blacks who kill whites are 1.5 times more likely to receive a death sentence than blacks who kill blacks; in the low-middle range, the same disparity ratio increases to 2.3 times. These findings support the results from the logistic regression models, that the justice system discounts black-on-black homicides, but suggest that this discounting occurs among the less serious cases. However, without a more intensive case analysis, it is not possible to determine whether this observed discounting of black-on-black killings results solely from the racial combination of the killing or from some other circumstance.

Intensive Examination of Murders in 2000

The disposition of capital murder cases, by race, is presented for each stage of processing in Table 5.4. Although the overall percentage of cases eventually resulting in death is much higher for capital-murder cases than for arrests, in this unadjusted comparison of racial categories, a pattern similar to the one found in the earlier analysis was detected, although in an attenuated form. The rate of death sentencing tends to be similar across offender race, although black offenders appear to receive death sentences slightly more often than those of other races. The largest disparity occurs when the race of the victim is taken into consideration. Cases involving black victims are about half as likely to result in death sentences, compared to the other cases; cases involving Asian victims are about three times more likely than the other cases to result in death sentences.

Table 5.4 Disposition of capital murder cases in Texas (2000), by racial characteristics of offenders and victims

		Number of cases (% of death-eligible)			
	Death-eligible	Indicted for capital murder	Convicted of capital murder	Sent to penalty trial	Sentenced to death
Offender's race					
White	62	51	35	11	8
	(100)	(82.3)	(56.5)	(17.7)	(12.9)
Black	86	77	59	19	16
	(100)	(89.5)	(68.6)	(22.1)	(18.6)
Hispanic	58	46	31	11	8
	(100)	(79.3)	(53.4)	(19.0)	(13.8)
Asian	1	1	1	0	0
	(100)	(100)	(100)	(0)	(0)
Victim's race					
White	80	67	50	18	15
	(100)	(83.8)	(62.5)	(22.5)	(18.8)
Black	48	41	31	7	4
	(100)	(85.4)	(64.6)	(14.6)	(8.3)
Hispanic	63	51	31	13	10
	(100)	(81.0)	(49.2)	(20.6)	(15.9)
Asian	9	9	8	4	4
	(100)	(100)	(88.9)	(44.4)	(44.4)
Race of offender/victim					
White/White	45	36	25	7	5
	(100)	(80.0)	(55.6)	(15.6)	(11.1)
White/Black	1	1	1	0	0
	(100)	(100)	(100)	(0)	(0)

(continues)

Since only one killing of an Asian was intraracial, it necessarily follows that the interracial killings of Asians, all committed by blacks and Hispanics, have the highest likelihood of garnering death sentences. Interracial killings involving white victims, also all committed by blacks and Hispanics, also had a higher likelihood of resulting in death sentences. Hispanics who killed whites were twice as likely to receive death sentences as whites who killed whites; for blacks who killed whites, the odds were nearly three times as high as for intra-

Table 5.4 (*continued*)

	Death-eligible	Number of cases (% of death-eligible)			
		Indicted for capital murder	Convicted of capital murder	Sent to penalty trial	Sentenced to death
White/Hispanic	16	14	9	4	3
	(100)	(87.5)	(56.3)	(25.0)	(18.8)
Black/White	26	23	21	9	8
	(100)	(88.5)	(80.8)	(34.6)	(30.8)
Black/Black	45	38	28	6	4
	(100)	(84.4)	(62.2)	(13.3)	(8.9)
Black/Hispanic	13	13	8	2	2
	(100)	(100)	(61.5)	(15.4)	(15.4)
Black/Asian	6	6	5	3	3
	(100)	(100)	(83.3)	(50.0)	(50.0)
Hispanic/White	18	16	12	4	4
	(100)	(88.9)	(66.7)	(22.2)	(22.2)
Hispanic/Black	3	3	3	1	0
	(100)	(100)	(100)	(33.3)	(0)
Hispanic/Hispanic	38	28	17	8	6
	(100)	(73.7)	(44.7)	(21.1)	(15.8)
Hispanic/Asian	2	2	2	1	1
	(100)	(100)	(100)	(50.0)	(50.0)
Asian/Asian	1	1	1	0	0
	(100)	(100)	(100)	(0)	(0)

Note: Some cases involve multiple offenders or multiple victims of different races. In these instances, the figures presented in the third panel (race of offender/victim) may not sum to those presented in the first or second panels (offender's race or victim's race).

racial white killings. In comparison to their own intraracial killings, blacks who killed whites were also over three times as likely to receive a death sentence, while the same disparity for Hispanics was about 1.5:1.

Once again, however, these raw disparities are unadjusted for any other characteristics that could legitimately influence the outcome. To test for the influence of race independently of other case characteristics, it is necessary to once again control for these other legitimate factors that could be paired with race and thus account for the previous unadjusted relationship between race and case outcome. Two different techniques were used to test for independent race effects in this manner. The first began with the logistic regression model used to predict death sentences in Table 4.4.[38] Using the method of forward conditional selection, racial characteristics were allowed to compete with all of the legitimate predictors of sentence in predicting case outcome. However, none of the racial variables found a place in the model with the remaining nine legitimate predictors. When forced into the model, none of the racial characteristics came close to attaining statistical significance.

The next test involved using ordinary least-squares multiple regression with each stage of processing, from indictment through death sentence, coded 1–4 in the dependent variable, with 0 assigned to those cases not indicted for capital murder. Such an analysis considers not just the final outcome, but all the steps along the way, and as such is sensitive to any differences occurring throughout the process. A stepwise procedure was used to select variables from among the same inventory of variables found to be successful predictors in the logistic regression analyses. Racial characteristics were allowed to compete simultaneously with these legitimate predictors. Once again, this test failed to support any inference of racial bias; the only racial characteristic to enter the model was intraracial cases involving Hispanics, which were treated more leniently in comparison to other similar cases.

Potential Innocence

One of the greatest fears among opponents and proponents of the death penalty alike is that an innocent person may be executed. The use of DNA testing in recent exonerations of noncapital inmates, combined with reversals in capital cases, has painted a picture in the minds of many citizens that an innocent person will inevitably be sentenced to death and executed. The impaneling of a commission to study the administration of the death penalty in Illinois and the subsequent commutation of all death-sentenced inmates to life by Governor Ryan was in large part due to his fear of executing an innocent person.[39] Hollywood has also weighed in with the movie, *The Life of David Gale*, which portrays Texas's execution of an innocent man.

The possibility of a miscarriage of justice is one of the most persuasive arguments against the death penalty, since the punishment is irreversible. As with other crime-related policies, the public tends to be influenced by one particularly egregious case example rather than by statistical evidence concerning this issue. For example, research on the selective incapacitation of violent offenders and career criminals had been ongoing for years, but it took the abduction, rape, and murder of Polly Klaas by a recently paroled rapist to spark development of "three strikes" policies.[40] Similarly, although researchers had known for years that sexual offenders often do not respond well to treatment and have extremely high rates of recidivism, it took a similar crime to spark sexual-offender registration programs, called Megan's Laws, named for the victim in this crime. One particularly gory, high-profile crime has the power to change criminal laws throughout the United States.

The same is true for capital punishment. Many instances exist where the implementation of capital punishment, or its re-implementation after a period of abolition, has come on the heels of a widely publicized, horrendous murder. Similarly, abolition has resulted from one atrociously botched execution or a question of the guilt of a particular party. The abolition of capital punishment in England in 1962 is credited to the execution of James Hanratty, who was widely believed to be innocent. Ironically, a recent DNA test carried out at the behest of his family proved that he was in fact guilty of the crime.[41]

It should not come as a surprise that the specter of executing an innocent person is the engine that currently drives the abolitionist's car. This is, by far, the most persuasive argument in their favor. To say that capital punishment is cruel and unusual when inflicted on a defendant convicted of a horrible murder does not invoke much sympathy. When the offender is less culpable because of youth or mental retardation (or from playing a secondary role in the crime), this causes more concern among the public than the usual death-penalty case, but does not even compare with the level of angst caused in people's hearts and minds when they imagine the execution of an innocent person.

This also happens to be an issue that empirical methods are ill equipped to address. Most of the empirical studies in this area are only tangentially related to the question of innocence. For example, the most ambitious study of its type, by James Liebman and his colleagues, studied reversals in capital cases across the United States.[42] In *A Broken System*, they describe the high rate of reversal throughout the United States — 68% percent of cases were overturned during 1973–1995 — along with the reasons for these "errors." Their description of the errors in these cases informs readers of the types of procedural mistakes that could conceivably cause an innocent person to be wrongly subjected to the death penalty, but the "error rate" bears no relationship whatsoever to the probability that someone sentenced to death was innocent of the crime for which he was convicted. In other words, although a technical or procedural error may cause a case to be overturned, this does not necessarily mean that the individual did not commit the crime. More limited studies have attempted to find correlates among those cases deemed to be wrongful convictions in an attempt to identify the reasons for these wrongful convictions.[43] These studies suffer from a number of limitations, however, the most important of which is the identification of cases as "wrongful convictions."

In attempting to identify "wrongful convictions," criminologists have had to rely on a case-by-case approach in which they subjectively identify which convictions they believe were convictions of innocent persons. The methods and evidence relied on to identify potentially innocent individuals, as well as to estimate the likelihood of such errors occurring, are best illustrated by the most comprehensive analysis of the issue, *Miscarriages of Justice*, by Hugo Bedau and Michael Radelet.[44] In this study, which serves as the basis for the Death Penalty Information Center's (DPIC) "Cases of Innocence, 1973–Present" (which in turn serves as the basis for most of the subsequent studies on the issue), the authors catalogued the cases of 350 persons who they believed had been wrongly convicted of capital or potentially capital murder from 1900 through 1987 (when the article was published). In a later book, the authors extended the time period under review through 1991, adding an additional 66 cases, for a total of 416 wrongful convictions.[45] They also described their reasons for believing that these wrongful convictions had likely occurred: mistaken eyewitness identification, prejudice, corrupt police and prosecutorial practices, and the rush to judgment, so common in capital cases, meant to quell a community's outrage. From their case scenarios, they provide a compelling argument that innocent persons were regularly convicted of capital crimes throughout the twentieth century.

The immediate effect of their landmark study was so stirring that the federal government felt it necessary to respond. In their published response, Assistant Attorney General Stephen J. Markman and Special Assistant U.S. Attorney Paul G. Cassell pointed out several flaws with the Bedau/Radelet study, flaws that illustrate the more general problems of carrying out this type of study.[46] First, they take issue with the pool of cases included as "miscarriages of justice." Of the 350 "potentially capital crimes" in the original study, Markman and Cassell pointed out that only 139 actually resulted in death sentences, of which only 23 were carried out. The others were often convicted of lesser offenses or given a term of years. Assuming that the 23 executed individuals were actually innocent, they calculate the likelihood of executing an innocent person to be less than one-third of 1 percent (23 of approximately 7,000 executions carried out during that period).

Markman and Cassell also argued that the evidence Bedau and Radelet relied upon to conclude that these 23 executed individuals were "actually innocent" is weak and subjective. Bedau and Radelet even admitted that "no state or federal officials have ever acknowledged that a wrongful execution has taken place in this century."[47] The evidence that they relied upon to "prove" innocence consisted of "another person's confession (6 cases), the implication of another person (3 cases), a state official's opinion (6 cases), and 'subsequent scholarly judgment' that the defendant was innocent (8 cases)."[48] Of course Bedau and Radelet realized that their standards of proof would be challenged, but they argued that such a study, in order to proceed, must rely on some standards other than an official admitting to a wrongful execution, since none had ever been forthcoming. Markman and Cassell proceeded to question, on a case-by-case basis, each of the instances in which Bedau and Radelet claimed that an innocent person had been executed. Relying entirely on official accounts, their descriptions differ greatly from the scenarios presented by Bedau and Radelet. In rebuttal, Bedau and Radelet charged that Markman and Cassell's descriptions were biased and designed solely to confirm the decedents' guilt.[49]

Nonetheless, Bedau and Radelet's compilation served as the beginning point for cataloguing wrongful convictions in post-*Furman* death sentences. The list of potential innocents has since been maintained on the DPIC website, and is regularly updated with additional names. By March 1, 2004, the list contained the names, along with a brief case synopsis, of 113 persons sentenced to death, but now considered innocent, since 1973. Despite questions about the definition of "wrongful conviction," this list is considered the authoritative source for those working in this area, and it has spawned many analyses wherein the authors simply assume the validity of the list, often with an eye toward determining which types of errors in case processing are most likely to result in a miscarriage. The DPIC restricts the list to those meeting the following criteria:

> They had been convicted and sentenced to death, and subsequently either a) their conviction was overturned and they were acquitted at a re-trial, or all charges were dropped; or b) they were given an absolute pardon by the governor based on new evidence of innocence.[50]

They note that they have strayed from this definition five times by including cases in which the defendants were released but charges were not dropped, or the defendants pleaded to, or were convicted of, a lesser charge. This addendum in itself illustrates the blurred lines used to make determinations of innocence. Many would take issue with the list as being either too inclusive or not inclusive enough. According to the DPIC, the strength of evidence suggesting innocence varies considerably among these cases, from the five mentioned above that resulted in reductions to lesser charges, to thirteen cases in which "DNA played a substantial factor in establishing the innocence of the inmate."[51]

In those cases involving DNA evidence, the likelihood of "innocence" may seem certain, but it must be remembered that other explanations may exist that do not completely exonerate an accused. For example, it may simply suggest the presence of a coconspirator. Further, in many of these cases the piece of evidence, such as a hair, that either was excluded by DNA or for which the test was determined to be inconclusive is typically only part of a series of evidence linking the defendant to the crime. After undertaking a comprehensive study of the implementation of capital punishment in Indiana for the governor, the Indiana Criminal Law Study Commission clearly stated some reasons for caution when encountering claims of wrongful convictions:

> Although some well-meaning journalists and capital punishment opponents have characterized these reversals as the formerly convicted now having been proven "innocent," this misstates the situation. It is difficult to say exactly how many reversals involved defendants who were actually guilty. What can be said with certainty is that reviewing courts, utilizing more sophisticated and evolving standards of both science and jurisprudence, have reversed capital cases where the reviewing court's full confidence in the conviction has been undermined to some extent or the proceedings were found to be unfair in some way. For example, post-trial DNA testing showing that semen evidence belonged to the rape-murder victim's husband, not the defendant, does not prove that the defendant did *not* rape and murder the victim. Few convictions are the result of a single piece of evidence. However, if a reviewing court finds that the semen played a strong part in proof of guilt, the remaining evidence, depending on its strength, may or may not be sufficient to maintain the court's full confidence under the law in the defendant's conviction. The societal benefit of the reasonable doubt standard in criminal law is protection of an innocent defendant; the cost of protecting the innocent is that sometimes the guilty will escape justice.[52]

While DNA can exonerate persons years after the fact, DNA can also have the opposite effect, of confirming guilt. In both types of cases, along with other reforms to the system, DNA analysis has the potential to make the system much more accurate when dealing with certain types of key physical evidence. The case of Robert Kleasen provides an example of how DNA analysis finally resolved doubts in a case nearly three decades after its occurrence.

THE TEXAS BAND SAW MASSACRE[53]

A 1974 movie filmed near Austin began with the introduction:

*The film which you are about to see is an account of the tragedy
which befell a group of five youths, in particular Sally Hardesty and her
invalid brother, Franklin. It is all the more tragic in that they were young.
But, had they lived very, very long lives, they could not have expected nor
would they have wished to see as much of the mad and macabre as they
were to see that day. For an idyllic summer afternoon drive became a
nightmare.*

*The events of that day were to lead to the discovery of one of the most
bizarre crimes in the annals of American history, the Texas Chain Saw
Massacre.*

Although the tag on the film stated that the story was true, the
events portrayed in the legendary horror classic did not really occur.
Filmmaker Tobe Hooper was influenced by crimes of Ed Gein, a Wisconsin serial killer who saved the flesh and body parts of his victims
in his home, crimes that also inspired the films *Psycho* and *The Silence
of the Lambs*. However, in 2001 the details of a real crime surfaced
twenty-five years after the fact, leading many to surmise that this
incident had inspired the movie. It was simply a historical irony, however, that the same year the movie *The Texas Chain Saw Massacre* told
the tale of a cannibal family that hacked up unsuspecting passersby
for barbeque, Robert Elmer Kleasen was charged in a true-life crime
that nearly paralleled the macabre killing portrayed in the movie.

On October 28, 1974, two young Mormon missionaries, Mark
Fischer and Gary Darley, went to a scheduled appointment to min-
ister to Kleasen. They never returned. On November 5, authorities,
armed with a federal search warrant requested by an agent with the
Bureau of Alcohol, Tobacco and Firearms, found substantial evidence
linking Kleasen to the murder of these two men, along with evidence
of federal firearms violations. Personal effects belonging to the
victims, including a key ring containing keys to the decedents' car
and apartment, a watch, and Mormon bibles were found in Kleasen's
trailer. During additional searches of the property, a bullet-riddled
prayer book and nametag belonging to one of the young Mormons
was found. Wheels, tires, and the license plates from their stripped
and abandoned car were found in a structure adjacent to the
defendant's trailer. But the most telling piece of evidence was a grisly
discovery found in a taxidermy shop behind Kleasen's trailer. Blood,

(continues)

THE TEXAS BAND SAW MASSACRE (*continued*)

hair, and tissue that matched the victims' was found on a band saw. Clothing belonging to Kleasen was found in a trash receptacle near his trailer and was stained with human blood. Hairs found on this clothing also matched those of the victims. The bodies were never found, but it was clear from the evidence that Robert Elmer Kleasen, an avid poacher, had cut up the corpses and disposed of them in the same manner detailed in a manuscript he kept on how to dispose of the carcasses of illegally killed deer.

A jury convicted Robert Elmer Kleasen of capital murder, deliberating only two hours before sentencing him to death for the crime. He became the third inhabitant of Texas's newly reconstituted death row. The Court of Criminal Appeals overturned his sentence in 1978, however, because the federal search warrant lacked probable cause. After his release from Texas death row, Robert Kleasen served time in a federal prison in New York for the weapons violations. While in federal prison, he became a pen pal to an English woman, convincing her that he had a prison address because he was a college professor who taught inmates.

Upon his release, and after completing parole, he moved to England, where the self-proclaimed "Dr." Robert Elmer Kleasen married his pen pal, Marie Longley. In England, Kleasen created a fictitious past that included a stint as a fighter pilot in Korea, where he had shot down thirty-four Chinese MIG fighters, a feat for which he had received the Congressional Medal of Honor from President Eisenhower. He also regaled locals with stories of how he had served his country as a CIA agent and as a government assassin. With this cover story he was able to convince Humberside police that he was worthy of a firearms permit. He became a regular at local gun clubs, and amassed an arsenal of over forty weapons. The esteemed American, known to locals as "Odd Bob" for his eccentricities and quick temper, was even called on to advise the Humberside police department on the use of these weapons.

This life came to a close when his wife, fearing that he would carry out threats he had made against her, turned him in to the police in 1999. They found many illegal weapons among his cache. An Interpol background check revealed his less-than-illustrious prior record in the United States. He was sentenced to three years in prison for

(continues)

THE TEXAS BAND SAW MASSACRE (*continued*)

illegal possession of firearms. His case led to a tightening of firearms restrictions in England to prevent individuals from amassing weapons. In particular, foreigners would have to undergo an Interpol criminal-history check before being issued a permit to possess firearms.

The case was big news in England and the United States, particularly in the Austin area, where prosecutors, encouraged by the publicity, decided to reopen the case. A DNA test of the decades-old blood on Kleasen's pants was a perfect match with the DNA of one of the victims. A grand jury indictment was issued in August 2001, and Austin prosecutors agreed not to seek the death penalty against Kleasen if England would extradite him to the United States. While awaiting extradition, Kleasen succumbed to heart failure in April 2003 at the age of seventy.

The distinction between legal and factual guilt is also blurred by prosecutors' reluctance, or failure, to retry overturned cases. Some view this as "exonerating" the defendant, but the reluctance or failure may not be related at all to the factual innocence of the defendant. In nearly all these cases, prosecutors remained convinced of the defendant's guilt, but perhaps could not retry the case, for various reasons. Remember that "proof beyond a reasonable doubt" has never meant that a person found "not guilty" was factually innocent, but merely that this high standard was not met. The more time that passes between the offense and the new trial, the more difficult it is to meet this standard. For example, key witnesses may no longer be available, either because of an unwillingness to get reinvolved, or because their memory has weakened, or because of death. Evidence may have been lost or destroyed. Courts may declare that evidence clearly establishing the individual's guilt must be excluded because of procedural violations committed when gathering the evidence. Therefore, when the DPIC or other authors describe a person as "exonerated" because a prosecutor did not retry the person, or when a jury acquits a defendant, it is somewhat misleading. What they are referring to is the person's legal, not actual, innocence.

With this in mind, the seven cases in the DPIC list that are from Texas have been extracted for perusal. The following vignettes have been copied verbatim from the DPIC's Web site.[54]

TEXAS CASES FROM THE DPIC "CASES OF INNOCENCE: 1973–PRESENT"

Vernon McManus. Texas conviction 1977. Released 1987.
After a new trial was ordered, the prosecution dropped the charges when a key prosecution witness refused to testify.

Randall Dale Adams. Texas conviction 1977. Released 1989.
Adams was convicted of killing a Dallas police officer and sentenced to death. After the murder David Harris was arrested for the murder when it was learned that he was bragging about it. Harris, however, claimed that Adams was the killer. Adams trial lawyer was a real estate attorney and the key government witnesses against Adams were Harris and other witnesses who were never subject to cross examination because they disappeared the next day. On appeal, Adams was ordered to be released pending a new trial by the Texas Court of Appeals. The prosecutors did not seek a new trial due to substantial evidence of Adam's [sic] innocence. Adams case is the subject of the movie, *The Thin Blue Line*.

Clarence Brandley. Texas conviction 1980. Charges dropped 1990.
Brandley was awarded a new trial when evidence showed prosecutorial suppression of exculpatory evidence and perjury by prosecution witnesses. An investigation by the Department of Justice and the FBI uncovered more misconduct, and in 1989 a new trial was granted. Prior to the new trial, all of the charges against Brandley were dropped. Brandley is the subject of the book *White Lies* by Nick Davies.

John C. Skelton. Texas conviction 1982. Released 1990.
Despite several witnesses who testified that he was 800 miles from the scene of the murder, Skelton was convicted and sentenced to death for killing a man by exploding dynamite in his pickup truck. The evidence against him was purely circumstantial and the Texas Court of Criminal Appeals found that it was insufficient to support a guilty verdict. The Court reversed the conviction and entered a directed verdict of acquittal.

Federico M. Macias. Texas conviction 1984. Released 1993.
Macias was convicted and sentenced to death for the murder of a man during a burglary. Macias was implicated by a co-worker, who in exchange for his testimony was not prosecuted for the murders,

(continues)

TEXAS CASES FROM THE DPIC "CASES OF INNOCENCE: 1973–PRESENT" (*continued*)

and from jail-house informants. Post-conviction investigation by pro bono attorneys discovered substantial evidence of inadequate counsel. A federal district court ordered a new hearing finding that "[t]he errors that occurred in this case are inherent in a system which pays attorneys such a meager amount." Macias's conviction was overturned and a grand jury refused to re-indict because of lack of evidence.

Muneer Deeb. Texas conviction 1985. Released 1993.

Deeb was originally sentenced to death for allegedly contracting with three hit men to kill his ex-girlfriend. The hit men were also convicted and one was sentenced to death. Deeb consistently claimed no involvement in the crime. Deeb's conviction was overturned by the Texas Court of Criminal Appeals in 1991 because improper evidence had been admitted at his first trial. With an experienced defense attorney, Deeb was retried and acquitted in 1993.

Ricardo Aldape Guerra. Texas conviction 1982. Released 1997

Guerra was sentenced to death for the murder of a police officer in Houston. Federal District Judge Kenneth Hoyt ruled on Nov. 15, 1994 that Guerra should either be retried in 30 days or released, stating that the actions of the police and prosecutors in this case were "outrageous," "intentional" and "done in bad faith." He further said that their misconduct "was designed and calculated to obtain . . . another 'notch in their guns.'" Judge Hoyt's ruling was unanimously upheld by the U.S. Court of Appeals. Although Guerra was granted a new trial, Houston District Attorney Johnny Holmes dropped charges on April 16, 1997 instead. Guerra returned to his native Mexico.

The brief vignettes on the DPIC Web site naturally portray exculpatory information in a light most favorable to the defendant. Limiting one's analysis to these brief descriptions, however, results in an incomplete picture of the actual events. When all of the available information is taken into account, it is clear that most defendants had their death sentences reversed because of procedural rules, related, for example, to the admissibility of evidence at trial, and not because their actual innocence was demonstrated. This is not to imply that the reversals were unwarranted. In fact, many of the errors were quite egregious and involved the coercion of witnesses or a failure to provide potentially exculpatory evidence to the defense, behavior that is completely unacceptable in capital cases.

The problem that arises in describing these persons as "exonerated" is that that word implies factual innocence, admitted or proven. A factually innocent person evokes much greater sympathy and outrage than someone who may be guilty, but just got off on a technicality. A description implying that an individual is truly innocent, or exonerated, appeals to the emotions of most people and attempts to persuade them that because of cases such as the ones described, the death penalty violates the sense of justice and fair play and should thus be abolished. In reality, however, even the court opinions that overrule these cases often recognize that there is convincing evidence of the defendant's guilt. The courts, while acknowledging that the defendant may be culpable, simply demand that the requirements of the Constitution be observed.

To illustrate the importance of having complete information, the stories behind the DPIC's seven "exonerated" individuals are outlined in greater detail below.

Vernon McManus

The brief description provided by the DPIC for this case simply states that upon retrial, prosecutors dropped the charges when a key witness refused to testify. It is difficult to tell from this one-line description what made this case a miscarriage of justice. McManus, a former All American college football star and coach at Lamar University, had branched into the plywood brokerage business. An attractive young secretary named Paula Cantrell Derese came to work for him. Paula, an only child, complained excessively about her parents' interference in her personal life, particularly with the relationships between herself, her son, and her ex-husband. The prosecution alleged that McManus hatched a plot to kill Paula's affluent parents for a share of their estate. After being warned to leave her parents' house on July 24, 1976, Paula returned the next morning to find her parents strangled and their throats slit.

The evidence against McManus seemed solid. He was shown to have made $12,000 in payments to procure a hit man; he made statements to several persons that he would "come into" money in August; a car that he rented from the airport matched eyewitness descriptions of a car seen at the house on the day of the murders; he was identified as the driver of the car by one of the witnesses; he altered his physical appearance on the day of the murders; and he faked his own abduction and fled to Florida after the murders. Additionally, at the punishment phase of the trial, a former girlfriend of his testified that he had attempted to extort money from her months before the killing. He also told her of his plan to kill her husband, an attempt that was foiled by the presence of a police officer in the vicinity. The targeted husband corroborated this allegation, saying that he had been confronted by the defendant, who was wearing a disguise.

Why, then, was this case overturned? Initially the case was overturned and remanded for a new trial by a U.S. District Court judge because a juror had been improperly excluded, in violation of the Supreme Court's ruling in *Adams v. Texas*. The state was set to retry the case, but waited for a ruling from the trial court judge on whether the previous testimony of Paula Derese would be allowed into evidence. Paula Derese, the star witness for the prosecution, refused to testify at the retrial because the prosecutor had reneged on his plea-bargain arrangement with her in the first trial. In exchange for her testimony, Paula was supposed to receive a lighter sentence for her involvement in the murders. Instead, she was sentenced to two life terms. She was paroled, however, in the same year that Vernon McManus was released, ten years after her parents were murdered. Without Paula's cooperation, the only way to get her testimony presented to the new jury would be to have her previous testimony admitted into evidence.

A week before the trial was to commence, the judge ruled that Paula's testimony would not be allowed because of possible improprieties by defense counsel during the first trial. The judge held that McManus may have suffered prejudice or inadequate counsel as a result of his lawyer's involvement with his, McManus's, wife. The defense attorney later married McManus's wife, but claimed that they got together only after McManus had been convicted. Without the testimony of its key witness, the prosecution felt unable to proceed with the case. Although the prosecutors decided not to retry McManus, there is currently no bar to prosecuting him should additional evidence become available in the future.[55]

Randall Dale Adams

The basic facts of this murder are undisputed.[56] At about 12:30 a.m. on the morning of November 28, 1976, Dallas police officer Robert Wood and his partner, Teresa Turko, pulled a car over in a routine traffic stop. When Officer Wood neared the driver's window, he was shot and killed by the driver. There were two suspects in this murder: David Harris and Randall Dale Adams. David Harris had stolen the car and the gun used in the murder from a residence in Vidor and then fled to Dallas. The day before, Harris had given

Adams a ride; Adams had been hitchhiking because his car ran out of gas. They spent the day together drinking, smoking marijuana, and attending a drive-in movie.

At this point, the evidence and the testimony of the events diverge. The state's chief witness at trial was David Harris, who stated that he and Adams left the movie around midnight to return to Adams's motel. On the way, they were pulled over by the police. Harris, who was in the passenger side, slumped down because he feared being identified. According to Harris, when the officer approached, Adams, who was driving, pulled the stolen .22-caliber pistol from under the front seat and shot the officer several times. In addition to Harris's testimony, the state relied on the testimony of the slain officer's partner, Teresa Turko, and three eyewitnesses to show that Adams was the triggerman. In Adams's version of the events, he and Harris returned to the motel from the drive-in around 9:30 p.m., and he was asleep by 10:00. He maintains that Harris was alone at the time of the offense and was simply trying to shift the blame to him.

Based on the evidence presented at trial, Adams was found guilty of the murder of Officer Wood. His conviction was affirmed on direct appeal, but was reversed by the U.S. Supreme Court in 1980 because the procedure then used to select juries in Texas was found to violate the Court's holding in *Witherspoon v. Illinois*.[57] While the case was on remand, Governor Clements, at the behest of prosecutors, commuted Adams's sentence to life imprisonment, and the Texas Court of Criminal Appeals affirmed the life sentence in 1981.[58]

At a habeas hearing in 1988, District Judge Larry Baraka ordered a retrial based on the facts before him. Specifically, the government's chief witness, Harris, had recanted his testimony and admitted that he alone had gunned down Wood. Further, the judge noted extensive prosecutorial misconduct in the case. The prosecution had suppressed contradictory and exculpatory statements made by the state's other eyewitnesses, knowingly used perjured testimony, and failed to acknowledge deals made by prosecutors with Harris and other witnesses in exchange for their testimony, thus denying Adams the right to a fair trial. The misrepresentations made by the state and other "holes" in the state's argument are detailed in the documentary film *The Thin Blue Line*. As for the likelihood of Adams's innocence, Judge Baraka concluded:

> Although the court cannot determine the applicant is 'innocent' of the Wood murder ["Since innocence is not a basis in Texas for a new trial . . ."], on the basis of the evidence presented at the habeas corpus hearing, applying the law which places the burden of proof on the State beyond a reasonable doubt, the court would have found applicant not guilty at a bench trial.[59]

Adams was released from prison in 1991. Adams may not be considered *legally* guilty of the crime, but what of his *actual* guilt or innocence? It may never be possible to definitively conclude whether the event occurred as David Harris originally described it or as he described it later at the habeas hearing—a description consistent with Adams's initial account—but the weight of the evidence appears to implicate Harris. Adams, twenty-five at the time of the murder, had nothing in his background that would have predicted this sort of crime. He had no previous record at all. Harris, who already had an extensive criminal record at sixteen, was on a crime spree. He had stolen the automobile, and was in possession of a stolen pistol. For the two burglaries and aggravated robbery in Vidor, he was facing charges that would have resulted in revocation of his probation and confinement in prison if he were taken into custody. Harris was only sixteen at the time and thus not eligible for the death penalty; this type of case, the murder of a police officer, always generates tremendous pressure for a death sentence. Further, after his pending charges were dropped in exchange for his testimony, Harris continued in his criminal career. After enlisting in the army, he was charged with assault (dismissed), several burglaries, and theft, for which he was court-martialed and sentenced to Leavenworth Federal Penitentiary. Months after being released from Leavenworth, he was convicted of kidnapping, armed robbery, burglary, attempted burglary, and attempted robbery, for which he was sentenced to six and a half years in the California prison system. Shortly after being paroled, he returned to Vidor, and after burglarizing a Beaumont apartment and kidnapping the female inhabitant, he killed a man who was attempting to rescue her. Sentenced to death for this crime, he is currently on Texas death row.

Among these seven cases from the DPIC list, this one has the most compelling evidence of actual innocence. Ultimately, however, it is simply impossible to determine whether Adams was present at the killing, and if he was, the extent of his participation. Much of this uncertainty stems from inconsistent statements Adams made. In his initial statement to police, Adams admitted that he drove the car to the hotel from the movie down the same stretch of road where the policeman was shot, but that he blacked out after turning on the road and could remember nothing further until he reached the motel. If Harris was slumped down in the passenger seat, as he originally testified, he could have come up across Adams's chest with the gun to shoot the police officer. If this occurred, Adams would understandably never have admitted to being there; his presence would have implicated him directly in the shooting. This would explain why he remained silent even if Harris was the triggerman. Harris, who was convicted of another capital murder, however, had nothing to lose, and may have recanted to repay Adams for not implicating him in the original crime, or even as a means of injecting doubt into the system of capital punishment in which he also found himself.

Clarence Brandley

This case is probably the most controversial of the seven since it involves a black defendant sentenced to death for the rape and strangulation-murder of a sixteen-year-old white girl in Conroe, Texas.[60] The victim, Cheryl Ferguson, a native of Bellville, was participating in a volleyball match at Conroe High School on Saturday, August 23, 1980. Shortly after arriving at the school, Ferguson left her friends and headed out of the gymnasium to use a restroom. After the match, a brief search for Ferguson ended when her nude body was found in a loft area above the stage in the school auditorium. Clarence Brandley and Henry "Icky" Peace, two school custodians, found her body. She had been raped and strangled to death. The investigation that ensued pointed to Brandley as the prime suspect, and he was charged with capital murder. During the first trial, the jury could not decide on guilt, the 11–1 deadlock in favor of guilt resulting in a mistrial. During the next trial, Brandley was found guilty and sentenced to death.

Defense attorneys investigating the case on habeas corpus review made a number of allegations concerning improprieties in the investigation and prosecution of the case. Many of these allegations were tied to the race of the defendant and the victim. The Montgomery County courthouse had historically been the site of several regrettable incidents, some quite horrific, relating to race and capital punishment. A black man accused of raping a white woman had been staked to a pole and burned on the courthouse lawn in 1922. In the 1937 trial of a black defendant accused of raping a white woman, the husband of the alleged victim murdered the defendant in the courtroom, a crime for which he was acquitted. In some ways, the investigation and trial of Brandley had the same markings of racism. After determining that the search for suspects had been narrowed to the two custodians who found the victim's body, an officer investigating the murders was alleged to have stated quite candidly to his prime suspects that since the white janitor, who was less than five feet tall and weighed less than 150 pounds, obviously lacked the physical strength to have perpetrated the crime, "the nigger is elected."

Defense attorneys capitalized on this remark and attempted to show that the entire process, from investigation through prosecution, was tainted by the race of the defendant and the victim. Brandley, they alleged, became the sole focus of the investigation from the very beginning, before facts had even been gathered to exclude others. This "blind focus" led police to ignore all evidence to the contrary, and resulted in their failure to follow up on other leads. Prosecutors were charged with failing to provide exculpatory evidence to the defense, using peremptory strikes to seat an all-white jury, and using perjured testimony to secure a conviction. The testimony of the other custodians, three white and one Hispanic, was called into serious question. Two recanted their trial testimony in taped interviews with the defense investigator, only to subsequently recant these recantations in the habeas proceedings. Witnesses at the habeas corpus proceedings testified about the racially charged atmosphere before and during the trial. Civil-rights leaders marched in protest and raised money for Brandley's defense. The FBI was called in to investigate civil-rights abuses that may have occurred during the trial, and the Texas attorney general's office compiled the results of its own independent investigation in a 203-page report.

Special Judge Perry D. Pickett, after an extensive hearing in the habeas proceedings, concluded that the "state's investigative procedures denied defendant due process of law and a fundamentally fair trial." With strong words, Judge Pickett condemned the process used to convict Clarence Brandley:

> The litany of events graphically described by the witnesses, some of it chilling and shocking, leads me to the conclusion the pervasive shadow of darkness has obscured the light of fundamental decency and human rights. I can only sadly state justice has been on trial here, but of more significance, injustice has been on trial.[61]

Based on Judge Pickett's findings, the Texas Court of Criminal Appeals set aside Brandley's conviction, and he was freed in 1990 after serving more than ten years in prison. According to many, a great injustice has been to some extent resolved, although Brandley was unable to recover any monetary compensation from a lawsuit against county officials. The recantations by state witnesses, the conclusions of Judge Pickett, and the publication of *White Lies* by Nick Davies all seem to substantiate what supporters have suggested, that Brandley was wrongfully convicted.

However, there is another side to the story, one that is much less exciting and seldom, if ever, referred to in discussions of the case. Most of those involved in the case, including the members of the Court of Criminal Appeals, remain convinced of Brandley's guilt. The court's 6–3 decision in favor of reversing Brandley's conviction may be somewhat misleading. Two of the six members concurring in the majority opinion stated that they did so only as a matter of law, which required them to defer to the findings of the hearing-court judge as long as they were supported by the record, even if the appellate judges disagreed with his findings. As Justice Duncan, joined by Justice Miller, stated, "I have read every page of the writ hearing and although I may not have made the same findings of fact or conclusion of law as Judge Pickett, I do find that they are supported by the record."[62] Even the remaining four members of the majority fell far short of accepting the defense's theory that someone else committed the crime. They merely agreed that the "state's investigative procedure produced a trial lacking the rudiments of fairness," and they therefore agreed with Judge Pickett that the defendant's conviction be set aside. However, they also noted that "the error attendant in this case would not prevent the readmission of evidence upon retrial, assuming, of course, that the procedural prerequisites to its admission are met."[63] The assumption of the majority, then, was that the case against Clarence Brandley would be retried.

The "exoneration" in this case came when Montgomery County District Attorney Peter Speers agreed to dismiss charges against Brandley because "existing circumstances do not permit the state to retry the case," circumstances including lost evidence and the recantation of testimony by two key witnesses. However, the charges were dismissed by visiting judge Curt Strieb without prejudice, meaning the state could refile the charges if new evidence comes to light in the case. But does the state's decision not to proceed with the case mean that Brandley is factually innocent?

Although the question in the habeas hearing and the Court of Criminal Appeals review was simply whether the defendant deserved a new trial, the opinions also provide information about the strength of any exculpatory evidence regarding Brandley's possible innocence. The dissenting opinion, penned by Presiding Justice McCormick, offers the most insight into whether Brandley was in fact guilty of the crime. After an extensive review, not just of the habeas proceedings but also of the grand jury proceedings, the trial transcripts, and other evidence and reports related to the case, McCormick concluded:

> Although the findings in the habeas court, if taken as factual, may raise the specter that another or others may have been involved *with* applicant in the commission of this murder, there is absolutely no evidence which remotely tends to exculpate applicant or to show that he is not guilty.[64] (emphasis added)

In the original arrest warrant, the following facts were set forth:

1. Brandley was arrested by CPD officers for committing an attempted rape and abduction on 3/7/79 according to CPD offense reports.

2. Said Brandley is presently on felony probation for possession of a prohibited weapon.

3. Said Brandley, according to four other custodians, was the only school employee in or around the main building who had keys to the auditorium, storerooms and other doors in the building at the time of the offense.

4. According to the other custodians, Brandley's whereabouts are unaccounted for during a 45-minute period at about the same time as that of the victim's disappearance.

5. A pubic hair found on the victim's body has been determined by the Department of Public Safety Lab in Austin, Texas, to be that of a black male, and appears identical to pubic hairs removed from Brandley's person.

6. Said Brandley is the only custodian or employee who was on duty at the location who is a black male.

7. A Houston Police Department Polygraph Supervisor advised Captain Monty Koerner that said Brandley had failed a polygraph test administered to him on August 25, 1980, in connection with the offense.

Evidence later produced at trial demonstrated that the mark on the victim's neck was consistent with the belt the defendant was wearing at the time of the offense. Another custodian who had previously worked for the school testified that after a group of female students walked by, Brandley made the remark that "if he got one of them alone, ain't no telling what he might do." The victim's clothes had been cut off and discarded in a yellow bag that included a mop string similar to those from the janitors' closet. Testimony at trial also showed that Brandley worked part time for a funeral home; standard procedure there was to remove the clothes of the victim by cutting them off and then disposing of them in a bag, as had been done in this case. Two women testified during the punishment phase of the trial that Brandley had sexually assaulted them. (He has since been convicted of assault for hitting a live-in girlfriend on the shin, pointing an unloaded gun at her, and pulling the trigger when she refused to make him a meal after he returned to his apartment at 3:30 a.m. on a summer day in 1997.)

Judge McCormick points out that none of these facts are in dispute. Rather, the evidence relied on by supporters to convince others of Brandley's innocence stems mainly from the recantations of the original statements that the other custodians made to the police. One of the custodians, John Sessions, implicated another custodian, Gary Acreman, in the crime nine years after the fact. During the course of the habeas investigation, a woman came forward from the town of Cut'n Shoot (six miles east of Conroe) to testify that on the day in question, her estranged common-law husband, James Robinson, a custodian who had quit three weeks before the crime occurred, returned home on the day of the crime with bloodied tennis shoes and announced that he had taken part in the killing and was leaving for North Carolina. In a taped interview conducted by defense investigator Richard Reyna, Reyna told Acreman that he was now being implicated in the murder along with Robinson. At that point, Acreman, who was not under oath, placed Robinson at the scene but denied his own involvement in the offense. He later recanted this recantation under oath during the habeas proceeding.

The testimony of Brandley at the grand jury indictment also directly contradicts the theory that another custodian was the sole perpetrator. Brandley testified that only he was near the restroom at the time the girl was abducted. He provided alibis for the other janitors, whom he claimed he had sent to another building. When asked who else he saw in and around the building at that time, he never mentioned James Robinson.

Aside from Brandley's own statement regarding Robinson's whereabouts, an investigation of Robinson found that he was in North Carolina during the week before the crime. He had failed to pick up his last paycheck from Conroe High School, dated August 17. Further, he passed three polygraph tests supporting his alibi. Of course, some witnesses have placed him in and around Conroe during the week of the murder, and there is still the statement from his ex-wife.

Some evidence was found that suggested the possible involvement of a white person. A couple of hairs from a white person were found on or near the victim, along with the pubic hairs from a black man, suggesting that a white person may have been involved in the crime. However, unlike the numerous pubic hairs from a black man, which closely matched those of Brandley, the white person's hairs had not been forcibly removed. It is also unclear whether these were pubic hairs. These hair samples were tested against Henry "Icky" Peace's hair by Brandley's expert and found not to match. Because they have since been lost, there is no longer an opportunity to compare them to Robinson's and Acreman's hair.

A final piece of evidence supporting the idea that another person may have been involved in the crime includes a report by a volleyball player who called in after seeing a *60 Minutes* news segment on the Brandley case in 1989. She stated that she had seen two men running from the gymnasium about the time that Ferguson was murdered. It is not known whether she reported this to police at the time, but even if she had, none of the other players verified her report, and therefore no follow-up would have been made. There was little basis for her testimony, and she described the men only after seeing the news program.

The defense used the loss of the hair sample to call into question the reliability of police procedures. Brandley's habeas attorney also railed against the prosecution because the vaginal swab, which could have been used to vindicate Brandley in the era of more advanced DNA testing, had been discarded. The state, however, showed that despite the defense's attempt to show otherwise, the Harris County medical examiner who analyzed the swab and then discarded it after one month was following acceptable standard procedures at the time.

In sum, it appears that some irregularities may have occurred during the investigation of the murder of Cheryl Ferguson. The evidence, nonetheless, also shows a strong probability that Clarence Brandley was involved in her rape and strangulation. The evidence concerning the presence of coperpetrators is less certain. The defense theory first focused on Icky Peace as the actual murderer (he has since been charged with aggravated sexual assault for molesting the children of a nearby family, two boys and two girls aged seven to ten). But when the physical evidence and testimony failed to support this possibility, the defense's theory turned to another custodian, Gary Acreman, and a previously employed custodian, who had moved to another state, James Robinson. The testimony of the other custodians is certainly questionable. Brandley himself, however, provided alibis for the other custodians in his statements to the police and in his grand jury testimony. The facts that an investigating peace officer made an improper comment and that some limited and questionable evidence exists to show that another person may have been present during the crime do not detract from the overwhelming evidence that supports Clarence Brandley as the prime suspect in the murder of Cheryl Ferguson.

John C. Skelton

This case involves the murder of Joe Neal on April 24, 1982, by explosives.[65] A simple bomb constructed of dynamite and a six-volt battery was attached to Neal's truck, below the driver's-side floorboard, with horseshoe magnets. The bomb was connected to the backup lights of the pickup, so that it would explode when the truck was placed in reverse. The six-volt battery was used as a backup power source in case the electrical system in the truck failed; it did not.

John Skelton was implicated in the murder based on the following circumstantial evidence. First, he had a motive. Several witnesses testified that he was angry with Neal, a former employee whom he had accused of stealing from the company before firing him. Lacking the requisite proof of Neal's guilt, Skelton had concocted a scheme to frame Neal and other former employees so that they would be sent to prison, a scheme that he failed to follow through with. The new owner, to whom Skelton had sold his steam-cleaning business, told him that the former employees would likely just receive probation. He had also threatened to harm and kill Neal during previous discussions with various witnesses.

The evidence at trial showed that Skelton had also described the manner in which he would kill Neal, through the use of explosives and with the help of one of the witnesses. Just before the murder, Skelton had arranged for a former employee to bring him four magnets from the steam-cleaning business. He had also purchased dynamite and blasting caps from another source just a couple of weeks earlier. Experts from the DPS crime lab testified that the paper the dynamite was wrapped in was consistent with that purchased by John Skelton and that the paint on the magnets found at the scene was identical to that on those given to Skelton by his ex-employee. After the murder, Skelton called the former employee and a neighbor and asked about the death of Neal. He also indicated before the murder that something "spectacular" was about to happen that would make the newspapers. Evidence also showed that he had previously bragged to the same employee about his plan to firebomb a competitor's business; a few days later the business was bombed.

Skelton's alibi was that he was not present when the killing occurred, but that he was in Springfield, Missouri, and therefore could not have been involved in the crime. He produced alibi witnesses at trial that placed him in Missouri on the afternoon on the day of the killings. Phone records confirm that he made calls from a motel in Springfield on the afternoon of the murder, and a Springfield pharmacist testified that he had filled prescriptions for him that evening. When questioned about the whereabouts of the dynamite, which Skelton claimed to have bought to blow up tree stumps on his farm, he stated that it had been stolen out of his truck in Springfield.

Skelton's alibi, however, does not completely exclude the possibility that the he could have been present at the time the bomb was set, probably during the night of the 23rd or the early morning of the 24th. It would have been possible to make the 800-mile drive in time to arrive in Springfield on the afternoon of the day of the murder. This would clash with the testimony of only one witness, a female physician, identified as a "friend" of Skelton's, who said that he had spent the evening of the 23rd with her and had breakfast with her on the morning of the 24th. The evidence also does not exclude the possibility that Skelton acted in tandem with another person who may have actually set the bomb.

However, after reviewing the evidence, the Court of Criminal Appeals reversed this case after finding "no evidence which connects the appellant with the actual setting of the bomb, nor is there any evidence showing that he solicited, encouraged, directed, aided or attempted to aid another to place the bomb."[66] The majority noted that although they did not "relish the thought of reversing the conviction in this heinous case and ordering an acquittal," they were nevertheless compelled by law to do so, since the evidence was purely circumstantial. The level of proof that would have been required to sustain Skelton's conviction in this case was quite demanding, as seen in the following statement by the majority:

> Although the evidence against appellant leads to a strong suspicion or probability that appellant committed this capital offense, we cannot say that it excludes to a moral certainty every other reasonable hypothesis except the appellant's guilt.[67]

Although Skelton, like McManus, may not be considered legally guilty, given the strength of the circumstantial evidence presented at trial, the likelihood that Skelton did not commit, or at least was not party to, the crime is slight.

Federico M. Macias

This case involves the burglary or robbery and murder of Robert and Naomi Haney on December 7, 1983, in El Paso.[68] When the Haneys were found, their feet and hands were bound, and they had been murdered execution-style with a machete. Guns, coins, a watch, a wallet, a green athletic bag, a machete, and $8,000 in cash had been taken from the residence. Most of these items were later retrieved from the yard of nineteen-year-old Pedro Luevanos. An eyewitness also identified him as one of two men driving by the place in a car that day. Luevanos implicated Macias as his coperpetrator and the actual killer. He received a twenty-five-year sentence in exchange for his testimony. Macias was convicted of the murder and sentenced to death.

The U.S. District Court for the Western District of Texas reversed the conviction, holding that Macias had been denied effective assistance of counsel. In its findings, the Court emphasized that the defense attorney was underpaid, that he was an Anglo, and that he was a former prosecutor who failed to put on much of a defense. Macias's plight became a local cause célèbre in El Paso because it involved the murder of an Anglo couple by two Hispanics. These circumstances generated criticism of, and accusations of bias against, the El Paso prosecutor's office and the entire local justice system. After the reversal, the prosecutor's office was unsuccessful in obtaining a grand jury indictment in the case.

The evidence against the defendant consisted mainly of the testimony of Pedro Luevanos, his accomplice; the testimony of Edward Parker, a jailhouse informant who overheard Macias discussing the details of the crime with his cellmate; the testimony of nine-year-old Jennifer Flores, a neighbor girl who claimed to have seen Macias at his home with blood on his hands and shirt on that day; and three pieces of circumstantial evidence. The three items of circumstantial evidence included a bloody shoeprint that matched the style of shoe that Macias was alleged to have worn that day (positioned by the body as the killer likely would have been standing when hacking the victim to death), his flight from El Paso to California the next day, and his history of working for the Haneys as a handy man.

The U.S. magistrate judge found ineffective assistance of counsel for the following reasons: 1) the attorney failed to call witnesses to rebut Jennifer Flores's testimony; 2) the attorney failed to call witnesses to support the defendant's alibi; and 3) the attorney failed to develop mitigating evidence at the punishment phase. When analyzed further, however, the trial attorney had arguably strong reasons for the "failures." As opposed to a situation in which defendant's counsel is either lazy or oblivious of this type of rebuttal evidence, Macias's attorney, a former prosecutor, found the testimony of the two alibi witnesses, Macias's wife and her employer, to be inconsistent and unbelievable. Also, by making the claim that the defendant did not commit this offense, Macias's counsel would be opening the door to rebuttal evidence that the defendant had committed a similar unrelated offense during the previous year in California.

The magistrate judge disagreed with the trial attorney's strategy in this instance, and argued that the attorney could have successfully prevented the introduction of impeachment evidence concerning the previous offense because it was dissimilar enough from the current offense that it failed to contain those "distinguishing characteristics" that would have led to its admissibility under Texas case law. The magistrate judge argued that the following dissimilarities were enough for defendant's counsel to rely upon in distinguishing the two situations: 1) proximity in time and place—the previous crime had occurred during the previous year in California, not Texas; 2) mode of dress—it is unknown what the defendant was wearing during the previous offense; and 3) method of committing the two crimes—in the California crime, the defendant had used a ball peen hammer to bludgeon the victim, but in the present case the weapon was a machete.

Although the magistrate judge found many differences between the two crimes, from a layperson's point of view the similarities between the previous offense and the one for which the defendant was sentenced to death were striking. The 1982 California offense involved the aggravated robbery and attempted murder of a Mr. Kolenberg. Just as in the current offense, Kolenberg was an older man known to have a large amount of cash on hand; he had employed the defendant to clean up around his property; the offense was committed at the victim's home; and the victim's wife, although not harmed, was present at the time of the offense. Kolenberg was bludgeoned nearly to death, but not killed, by the defendant and a younger accomplice, who used an object found on the premises, although it was a ball peen hammer instead of a machete. As in the current case, the crime scene, although extremely bloody, failed to yield any usable fingerprints or any of the perpetrators' bloody clothing. In each case, the defendant was having problems with his wife before the crime; left town after the offense, leaving his codefendants "holding the bag"; and refused to turn himself in to the police after finding out he was wanted in connection with the crimes. Another ironic similarity is that the defendant in the California case also claimed to have been wrongly accused; a change in the testimony of his accomplice had led to his release.

In condemning defense counsel's failure to develop mitigating evidence for the punishment phase of the trial, the magistrate pointed out that the defendant's good character could have been brought out through family witnesses. Most of the magistrate's critique, however, focused on the attorney's failure to introduce evidence from the California Rehabilitation Center, where Macias had spent most of his youth. This, the magistrate argued, could have shifted the burden of Macias's crimes to the state, which had failed to rehabilitate him, and could also have shown that he was not dangerous while incarcerated. The magistrate stated that there was "a 'reasonable probability' that, had this evidence been presented, Petitioner would have received a sentence of life in prison."[69] The reason that the trial attorney gave for not raising this evidence during the punishment stage was that it would have magnified Macias's drug abuse, his being a heroin addict, and his multitude of bad acts during those years, which resulted in his return to the center twice. Macias's previous juvenile record included twenty-one arrests, plus another six arrests between the ages of eighteen and nineteen. These previous arrests included numerous burglaries and simple robberies, along with an armed robbery.

Although this case is touted as a "miscarriage of justice," it appears that the true miscarriage was the failure of the state of California either to rehabilitate or to effectively incapacitate Macias for the crimes he had committed in the past, as well as the failure of defense attorneys to defend a capital-murder case zealously enough to ensure that an overly active federal magistrate judge could not overturn the case.

Muneer Deeb

Dubbed the "Lake Waco Murders" because of the crime's physical proximity to the lake, this case involved the brutal murder of two teenage girls and their male companion.[70] Evidence showed that the girls had been raped, stabbed, and beaten. Three suspects, David Spence, Gilbert Melendez, and Anthony Melendez, were convicted of the crime. The Melendez brothers received life sentences after pleading guilty; David Spence, who led the abduction, rape, and murder, was sentenced to death, and then executed on April 3, 1997.

Muneer Deeb was implicated in the crime as a coconspirator. Deeb had promised to pay David Spence $5,000 if Spence would kill Deeb's girlfriend, Gayle, who was living in a nearby youth home for troubled teens and who was also an employee at Deeb's convenience store. In addition to being angry with her for seeing another guy, Deeb had just purchased a life insurance policy on her, listing himself as the beneficiary. Ironically, the hired hit man murdered the wrong girl. The actual victim was similar in appearance to Gayle, was with the young man that Gayle was supposedly seeing, and had a similar name, Jill. Under the doctrine of transferred intent, Deeb was convicted for his role in the botched assassination and sentenced to death. His conviction was reversed because of the improper admission of evidence at trial. At his subsequent retrial, the testimony of three witnesses who testified during the first trial was unavailable, and Deeb was acquitted.

While the "exoneration" in this case came about as a result of the Court of Criminal Appeals' reversal on direct review, and the subsequent acquittal, comments made by those involved in the case suggest that Deeb was not "innocent." The Court of Criminal Appeals reversed the verdict in the case because the testimony of a jailhouse informant, who had testified about discussions with his cellmate, David Spence (who, in turn, had outlined in detail his "deal" with Deeb), was hearsay, and therefore should have been excluded from the trial. According to the Court of Criminal Appeals, the trial court had erred in allowing the testimony under the coconspirator exception to the hearsay rule; the statements made in prison were not in furtherance of the conspiracy, which had been quashed by that time. Because the state's opening and closing arguments at the guilt and punishment phases of the trial emphasized the jailhouse informant's testimony as conclusive proof of Deeb's guilt, the Court could not "conclude beyond a reasonable doubt that the admission of [the informant's] testimony did not contribute to the conviction or punishment."[71]

While this amounted to reversible error, the court did say of the remaining evidence that "this is enough evidence to conclude beyond a reasonable doubt that appellant took part in the conspiracy with David Wayne Spence." The court further stated:

> The evidence set out above serves as a sufficient basis for the fact finder's determination that the appellant hired David Wayne Spence to kill Gayle Kelley for remuneration and the promise of remuneration, and that Spence caused the death of Jill Montgomery while acting pursuant to that agreement. Even if [the informant's] testimony was excluded, there would be sufficient evidence to justify this conclusion.[72]

The court enumerated the other evidence that supported Deeb's guilt. The appellant had recently taken out an insurance policy for $20,000 on the life of the intended victim, Gayle Kelley, listing himself as the beneficiary. He told the wife of his business partner that if something happened to Kelley, he would receive the money. Deeb's business partner testified that he heard Deeb ask Spence if he could find someone to kill Kelley; he heard an affirmative response from Spence; and he heard Deeb's agreement to get Spence money for the job. Several witnesses testified to the fact that Montgomery and Kelley resembled each other. After the murder, Deeb told his business partner that he would be rich if Kelley had been with Franks (the male victim). After making the second insurance payment, he told his business partner, "Wait and see, [Gayle] will die just like them." After the murder, Deeb told Kelley that Franks had gotten what he deserved and that "I did it. I killed them," but immediately retracted the statement saying it was just a joke.[73] Another witness overheard Spence's girlfriend demanding money from Deeb after the murder. One of the accomplices, Gilbert Melendez, testified that Spence had taken him to meet Deeb and later, after the murder, discussed the payment, which Deeb indicated would be forthcoming. He also testified that Spence had referred to Jill, one of the female victims, by the wrong name, but one that was similar to hers, on the night of the murder.

At retrial, the hearsay testimony of the jailhouse informant was obviously not allowed. Gilbert Melendez also refused to testify because the state had reneged on its promise to obtain early parole for him. Deeb's ex–business partner had returned to Jordan and could not be located. What was a difficult case to prove initially because of the nature of the conspiracy became impossible to prove beyond a reasonable doubt without the testimony of these witnesses. The foreman of the jury in the second trial, which resulted in Deeb's acquittal, stated that though they were unable to find him guilty beyond a reasonable doubt, the jurors did not consider him innocent.

Ricardo Aldape Guerra

On July 13, 1982, at approximately 10:00 p.m., in a lower-middle-class Mexican American neighborhood in Houston, George Brown, a pedestrian, informed police officer James Harris that a car had attempted to run down him and his dog only moments earlier.[74] Following the route of the assailants, less than a minute later Harris came upon a car matching Brown's description, stalled in an intersection. He ordered the two occupants to get out of the car, and then put them in "frisking" position on the hood of the squad car. At this point one of the men shot Harris in the head at point-blank range three times with a Browning nine-millimeter pistol. While fleeing, the assailant then shot into a nearby vehicle, killing Jose Armijo, Sr. When police entered a garage where the subjects were hiding, a firefight ensued; Officer Trepagnier was wounded five times. Other officers came to his aid and managed to kill the shooter, Roberto Carrasco Flores, in a brief exchange of gunfire. Under the body of Flores they found the Browning nine millimeter, which was positively identified as the weapon used to kill Jose Armijo, Sr. and was likely the gun used to kill Officer Harris. Tucked in Flores's pants was Harris's service revolver. Ricardo Aldape Guerra was found hiding nearby; next to him, wrapped in a red bandana, was a .45-caliber pistol that had been fired while the defendants were fleeing the shooting of Officer Harris. The surviving defendant, Guerra, was convicted of capital murder and sentenced to death on the basis of eyewitness testimony.

On habeas review, U.S. District Court Judge J. Hoyt found that Guerra was denied a fair trial. Hoyt ruled that the police had violated the defendant's due-process rights by intimidating witnesses and using suggestive pretrial identification procedures. The judge also found that the prosecutors had failed to disclose exculpatory evidence and had used false testimony at trial. In cataloguing the wrongdoings of law enforcement and prosecutors in this case, the judge made a convincing argument that they forced witnesses into supporting a concocted scenario in which Guerra appeared to be the shooter, when nearly all of the available evidence pointed to the deceased, Flores, as the shooter. Their implausible scenario was that Guerra and Flores had picked up each other's weapons in their haste to get out of their car, only to switch them back later after fleeing the scene.

The specific inconsistencies in this case are clear and nearly uncontroverted. Many persons involved with the case, including a former prosecutor and one of the reviewing judges, were convinced that the physical evidence and the initial statements made by witnesses in the immediate aftermath of the shooting pointed to Flores as the shooter. The officials in this case, in their zeal to avenge the death of Harris, made the mistake of attempting to force the facts to fit a scenario that they felt sure would elicit a death sentence. The appropriate response would have been to file capital-murder charges against Guerra as a "party" to the crime, which they failed to do. Even if the jury had not imposed a death sentence at trial, or if Guerra's involvement was later found by appellate courts not to warrant a death sentence, it would have at least ensured a life sentence. Guerra was unquestionably a "party" to the crime under Section 7.02 of the Texas Penal Code.[75]

Along with Flores, who appeared to be the leader of the gang, Guerra and several other undocumented aliens living together near the scene of the crime were under investigation for the robbery of a gun store in which $15,000 worth of guns and ammunition was stolen. While robbing the store, the perpetrators, identified in testimony at Guerra's trial, did not steal money from the store's cash register, nor did they take the wallets or jewelry of customers they had ordered down on the floor. Instead, they took only guns and ammunition, a move that the Court of Criminal Appeals saw as evidence of their intention to commit further criminal acts of violence. Along with Flores, Guerra was carrying a gun in his belt on the day Harris was shot. Rather than try to prevent the crime or to come to the aid of the victims, Guerra fired his own weapon while attempting to flee the scene. Although it is obvious that Guerra did not do what the prosecution wrongly accused him of, and was thus later "exonerated" on habeas review, the prosecutor's tactical error does not absolve Guerra of his obvious involvement in and responsibility for the crime.

Similarities among the Cases

These cases illustrate several troubling issues in crime detection and prosecution. These issues become particularly important when the crime is capital murder and a mistake may result in the execution of an innocent party. The first issue centers on the presence of accomplices. Many of the cases just described either had known coperpetrators, or the evidence suggested the possible presence of a coperpetrator. These situations seriously challenge law enforcement officials and prosecutors because they must sort through the evidence to determine who was "most" culpable in committing the crime. Coperpetrators are often the only available eyewitnesses to a crime, so prosecutors must secure their cooperation, usually by offering some kind of incentive, such as a reduced sentence or even immunity, in exchange for their testimony. Besides the obvious impeachability of a witness who was involved in the crime and who was compensated for his testimony, questions about the veracity of accomplice statements are renewed when the statements change or when the physical evidence does not support the state's theory. The state's case upon retrial can be devastated by a witness who changes his or her testimony or who refuses to testify at all in the retrial.

Another thread that runs through these questionable cases is the presence of procedural irregularities. Some of these were systemic errors that were unforeseeable. For example, two of these cases were reversed because of improper jury-selection procedures. In other cases, the state simply did not preclude all other reasonable hypotheses concerning the guilt of the defendants. More troubling were those cases that involved obvious improprieties by the state during its investigation or prosecution. In each of these cases, safety mechanisms in the court system brought these errors to light, although media publicity and extensive investigation by postconviction counsel often provided the impetus for the courts' decisions.

Reversals by the courts often focused on procedural errors and not on the guilt of the defendants. In nearly all of the cases where the reviewing courts were compelled to reverse because of errors that had occurred, the courts nonetheless expressed their belief in the guilt of the defendant and assumed that a retrial could right the infirmities. Similarly, prosecutors' decisions not to pursue a case, or their failure to secure an indictment or conviction, should not be seen as "exonerating" the defendant. Prosecutors' decisions not to pursue cases were typically based on pragmatic concerns about securing a conviction rather than on a belief that the defendants were innocent. The exclusion of evidence, the refusal of witnesses to testify, changes in witnesses' testimony, or simply the passage of time made it difficult for prosecutors to secure a conviction in these cases. Negative publicity also likely played a role both in prosecutors' unwillingness to bring charges and in the refusal of grand juries to indict, or petit juries to convict, in these cases.

Far from being hapless victims of a wrongful prosecution, many of these defendants were granted a reprieve, escaping their just deserts because of procedural improprieties that led to their release. Certainly some of these cases were clear instances of wrongful prosecution or prosecutorial misconduct, and the convictions could not have been secured had it not been for these violations. In other cases, however, the guilt of the individual was equally clear, and had it not been for the blunders of investigators, the overzealousness of prosecutors, or the incompetence of their defense attorneys, these defendants would have been justly executed. In this sense, the true injustice is to the victims of the crimes, since those responsible for the proper execution of the laws failed to honor the safeguards of the criminal-justice system, and the defendant was thereby able to escape responsibility for his actions.

Is it possible that an innocent person was executed in the past, or will be executed in the future? Of course. No criminal justice system is foolproof. Whether the omnipresent possibility that an innocent person will be executed should lead one to reject the death penalty is a value judgment that must be answered by each person. However, no activity comes without some kind of risk. As supporter of capital punishment Ernest van den Haag points out, ambulances have been involved in fatal collisions while trying to save lives, yet society agrees that the benefits outweigh the risks. Although an imperfect analogy, the point remains that the choice to pursue any policy option will always involve some risk. The key is to minimize it as much as possible. Regardless of whether some of the defendants above were actually "innocent," these cases do serve as a powerful reminder of the need for vigilance when the stakes are so high.

The Costs of Execution and Life Imprisonment

The cost of capital punishment was not an issue before the modern era. Before 1924, the cost of executions in Texas typically only involved building a gallows, purchasing a length of rope, and paying a hangman. Even these costs could be spared by finding a tree with a strong limb, borrowing a rope—as the counties adjacent to Bexar County (San Antonio) did around the turn of the century—and using a local law-enforcement official to perform the execution. The capital-murder trial was no more lengthy or complicated than a regular murder trial, and the time spent by the defendant in the county jail awaiting execution was minimal.

The procedure changed slightly in 1924 with the advent of the electric chair. The use of the electric chair required that the execution procedure become centralized because the electric chair itself was housed in the state prison at Huntsville. This change in procedure affected the cost of execution only minimally. While those sentenced to death had to be transported to the state prison for electrocution, the legal authority for the sanction still rested with the county. The state charged counties a nominal fee that covered the cost of burial expenses. Time spent in prison increased slightly: execution dates set by county judges after cases were affirmed by the Court of Criminal Appeals were typically stayed for thirty days so that the governor's office could review the case for issues that might warrant a commutation to life in prison. Regardless of these changes, the process was still expeditious enough that the minimal costs associated with electrocution never amounted to an issue.

In the late 1960s, however, legal challenges ground executions to a halt. By 1972, death rows across the United States, which were typically used only to house a handful of prisoners temporarily, were now holding over six hundred inmates awaiting execution; Texas housed forty-seven inmates on its death row. Although no one calculated the cost then, the combined cost to the state of litigating appeals and housing inmates in secure confinement for several years while they awaited execution would likely have approached the cost of "life" in prison by the early 1970s. This would certainly be true in Texas, considering that "life" in prison amounted to about ten years spent in productive work on a prison farm before being paroled.

When *Furman* invalidated all the death penalty systems in the United States, it also prompted a spike in the cost of capital punishment. After the reenactment of capital punishment, condemned inmates had long waits on death row while courts determined whether these new statutes were constitutional. In Texas, nearly a decade passed from the reactivation of the death penalty in January 1974 to the execution of Charlie Brooks in December 1982. Even after executions had resumed in the 1980s, defendants mounted successful challenges against the procedures used to implement capital punishment. In resolving these legal issues, the state released three times as many death row inmates during this period as it executed. Capital-murder trials, now conducted in separate guilt and penalty phases and requiring the time-consuming individual voir dire of potential jurors, became much costlier than simple murder trials. The appellate process, particularly at the federal level, had become a quagmire as the courts responded to claims raised concerning each detail in the newly implemented state death-penalty schemes. Since the condemned served many years before execution, and the majority of death sentences were overturned, and retrials and resentencings drove up costs, and most death-row inmates ended up serving a life sentence anyway rather than being executed, the efficiency of the system of capital punishment in Texas and elsewhere came into question.

It was during this tumultuous time that the initial cost studies were conducted. These studies were often commissioned by state legislatures considering reimplementation of the death penalty, most notably in Maryland, New York, and Kansas. These studies invariably found that given the new trial procedures, the lengthy appellate litigation, the rate of reversals, the eventual likelihood of sentence reduction to life, and the amount of time spent on death row for those few eventually executed, the cost of an execution was greater than that of a life sentence. The studies concluded that the cost to the state in maintaining a system of capital punishment would be much more expensive than the alternative maximum sanction of a life sentence. After reviewing these early cost analyses, the Spangenberg Group, in a 1989 law-review article, concluded that "the death penalty is not now, nor has it ever been, a more economical alternative to life imprisonment."[76]

This conclusion, however, somewhat overstates the findings. Historically, capital punishment was at least as cost effective as life imprisonment, and probably even more so. Even the findings for the period after *Furman* must be considered carefully. First, this was a special period of history, when many changes were being implemented. It would be unreasonable to expect any system to be efficient during such dramatic and unguided change. Additionally, the paucity of data from which the original estimates were extrapolated, as well as the questionable assumptions the estimations relied upon, brings into question the reliability of these estimates. The General Accounting Office (known since July 2004 as the Government Accountability Office) presented a report in 1989 to a congressional subcommittee studying the newly implemented federal death penalty. After reviewing the same studies analyzed by the Spangenberg Group, the GAO was somewhat more circumspect in reporting its findings:

> In recent years, studies, articles, and reports have been published on the costs associated with the death penalty at the state level. They have generally concluded that, contrary to what many people believe, death sentence cases cost more than non-death sentence cases. However, we found these conclusions were not adequately supported. Most of the studies did not actually compare death sentence cases with non-death sentence cases, and some of the studies did not contain actual cost data. Further, even in cases where cost data were cited, these data were incomplete.[77]

Although the evidence that the death penalty costs more than life imprisonment was sparse and based on questionable assumptions, these early comparisons, along with similar studies completed during the 1990s, have been uncritically cited so many times that it has now become conventional wisdom that the death penalty costs more than life imprisonment. Probably the most influential disseminator of these cost figures is the Death Penalty Information Center (DPIC), whose executive director, Richard Dieter, is arguably the nation's most prominent abolitionist voice. Publications available on the DPIC Web site, such as *Millions Misspent: What Politicians Don't Say About the High Costs of the Death Penalty,* decry the "exorbitant costs of capital punishment."[78] In March 2003, testifying before a joint legislative committee in Massachusetts, Dieter answered his own question, "How much does the death penalty cost?" with the following examples: North Carolina, $2.16 million more per execution than life imprisonment; Florida, $3.2 million per execution with a cost (including all system expenses) of $24 million per execution carried out to date; Texas, $2.3 million per execution (about three times the cost of imprisonment for life); California, $100 million per execution carried out so far; Indiana, total system cost projection of $51 million (exceeding life-without-parole costs by 38 percent); federal death penalty, defense costs for death cases four times the cost of nondeath cases, and prosecution costs 67 percent higher; counties nationwide, $1.6 billion over fifteen years.[79]

These figures provide a shocking picture of the costs of the death penalty across the nation. However, these studies suffer from many of the same drawbacks of those published in the 1980s. First, the figures are estimated from a small pool of cases, sometimes only the most extreme examples. Second, in many studies the figures do not include an estimate relative to the cost of the alternative sentence of life in prison. Third, the studies quoting "system expenses" inflate the costs of executions by attributing the cost associated with all capital litigation to those few that result in executions. Finally, it appears that some figures are not based on any articulable source, but are simply asserted by the author without any explanation as to how the figures were derived.

Some of the studies are of a higher quality than others. The stronger studies are usually completed by economists rather than newspaper reporters; they rely on experience from the recent rather than the distant past (or on predictions); they include a large pool of typical cases as opposed to a small sample of extreme cases; they provide the cost relative to the alternative sentence (life) at each step in the judicial process; and they provide multiple estimates based on varying assumptions about the future rate of reversals in death-penalty cases. These characteristics are included in the National Center on State Courts' "ideal" methodology, developed in 1986.[80] The more closely a study is able to follow this ideal methodology, the more reliable its estimate of the actual cost of executions in comparison to life sentences.

The first comprehensive examination to estimate the cost of capital punishment was performed by researchers at Duke University in North Carolina.[81] Philip Cook and his colleagues included in their calculations not only the direct costs of litigation, such as fees for public defenders, prosecutors, and judges, but also an hourly "load" rate that would account for the indirect costs associated with trials, as well as appeals and retrials. The researchers performed similar calculations for noncapital trials at which defendants were sentenced to a twenty-year "life" prison sentence. They provided two separate cost estimates. In the first, a capital murder case was found to exceed the cost of a noncapital first-degree murder case by $163,000 ($67,000 over the cost of a noncapital trial plus an additional $262,000 for appeals, minus $166,000 in prison savings).

In a second estimate, the researchers calculated the cost for "successful" capital prosecutions (those resulting in execution), including the costs associated with reversals, resentencing, and ultimately housing for life many of those initially sentenced to death. Assuming a 10 percent successful-execution rate for those cases initially prosecuted as capital murder, the cost per execution was estimated to be $2.16 million. Although this is the figure favored by the DPIC and other abolitionist groups, the researchers admit that the estimate is tenuous and dramatically affected by the percentage of death penalty cases assumed to result in executions. For example, the authors' calculation of cost savings per execution decreases to $780,000 if the hypothetical execution rate is increased to 30 percent.

Their study, however, was completed in 1993, before a major change in the statutory definition of "life." Rather than twenty years, North Carolina inmates convicted of capital murder must now serve the rest of their natural life in prison, with no possibility for parole. Given the average age at entrance to prison and the average life expectancy, it has been estimated that such inmates will serve about forty-seven years behind bars.[82] Including the additional twenty-seven years of confinement, the total cost of a life sentence would be $593,000.[83] Under the current definition of life, the cost associated with a capital-murder case in North Carolina appears to be a bargain, saving the state $264,000 in incarceration costs. Also in recent years, the percentage of death-penalty cases resulting in executions has increased dramatically from the early modern era, lowering the costs associated with unsuccessful capital-murder prosecutions. Given the lack of parole eligibility, the cost savings of life imprisonment essentially washes out when the rate of success in executing death sentences reaches 50 percent.[84]

Another study carried out for the Indiana Criminal Law Study Commission compared the cost of the death penalty to life without parole, both for individual cases and at the system level, including the costs of trial, appeals, and incarceration, projecting these costs over time.[85] Included in trial costs were all out-of-pocket expenses, including attorney's fees, investigations, expert witnesses, jury-related costs, as well as overtime and supplemental costs to prosecuting attorneys, court personnel, and sheriff department personnel. Costs at the appeals stage included mainly staff time incurred by the Public Defender's Office and the Office of the Attorney General. Costs related to executions included the extra pay to all personnel on hand as well as the out-of-pocket expenses involved in procuring chemicals and making funeral arrangements.

In this study, Mark Goodpaster, a senior fiscal analyst of legislative services, found that the death penalty had very high up-front costs, especially the cost of the trial during the first year and the appeals during the ensuing nine years.[86] The cost of life without parole, on the other hand, was spread out over a lengthy incarceration, an average of forty-seven years. Goodpaster also considered the fact that life-without-parole inmates would require much more extensive medical care toward the end of their terms. At the same time, these costs had to be discounted, after adjusting for inflation, because the costs would be borne so far in the future. Cost streams were estimated for both death-sentenced and life-without-parole inmates over this forty-seven-year period.

After making all these adjustments, Goodpaster calculated that the average per capita cost, in present value, for the death penalty was $668,000 and for life without parole, $551,000, a difference of an additional $117,000 for each death-penalty case. He then calculated the total system cost for the entire cohort of offenders sentenced to death in Indiana since 1979, comparing this to the hypothetical cost of life without parole for the same cohort through the expiration of all their sentences by the year 2051. Assuming a future 20 percent death-penalty-reversal rate for cases currently on death row, the total cost of the death penalty was projected to exceed the cost of life without parole by more than one third, $51 million versus $37 million. While one could argue that the 20 percent reversal rate for future cases is a conservative estimate, Goodpaster included in the system-cost difference the much higher rate of reversals that had already resulted from death-penalty cases disposed of during previous years, a rate of nearly 50 percent. Therefore, the study presented a much more liberal estimate of reversal rates than might be apparent at first glance, with the total cost-difference estimate based on reversals for over half of the death penalty cases that had run their course. As in previous studies, assumptions made by the author could tilt the scales toward or away from life without parole.

Nonetheless, findings from the two most comprehensive studies performed to date suggest that costs associated with the death penalty are in the same ballpark as the costs of life sentences. In Texas, a state that has successfully carried out far more executions than any other jurisdiction during the modern era, one could reasonably assume that the costs associated with the death penalty are likely to be lower than in other jurisdictions; frequency of use should result in increased efficiency.

The most widely quoted estimate of the cost of capital punishment in Texas, however, disputes that notion. This estimate comes from a study completed by reporter Christy Hoppe of the *Dallas Morning News*.[87] This study, quoted by Richard Dieter in his testimony before the Massachusetts Legislature's Joint Committee on Criminal Justice, estimates the cost of an execution in Texas to be about $2.3 million on average. Although widely cited in the popular press, on Web sites, and in the academic literature, this estimate, given the many subjective decisions that necessarily entered into its calculation, needs to be carefully reviewed rather than uncritically accepted.

Basing her findings on five Dallas County capital-murder cases in fiscal year 1991, Hoppe reported the average cost of a death-penalty trial, including court personnel, jury panel, defense, prosecution, and judges, to be $266,000. Although based on a limited sample, this figure comports with recent reports of trial costs in other death-penalty cases around the state, including a recent estimate by the Texas Office of Court Administration, which put the cost of a death penalty trial at $200,000 to $300,000.[88] The cost of a death penalty trial alone is not enough to determine the cost effectiveness of capital punishment, even at the trial stage. Cost effectiveness can be determined only through a comparison of the costs incurred in death-penalty cases relative to those in which the alternative sentence was sought. As shown in the studies described earlier, trial costs associated with life sentences will offset to some degree the costs associated with capital-murder trials. Even though these expenses could have been estimated in the same manner as the costs of death sentences, by extrapolating from a number of cases tried in Dallas County where the death penalty was not sought, Hoppe failed to include any such estimate in her cost analysis.[89]

Hoppe estimated the cost of state appeals at $94,000, including costs related to defense, prosecution, reproduction of the trial record, and Court of Criminal Appeals time. Based on payments to the now defunct Texas Resource Center, Hoppe found defense costs for federal appeals to be $92,000, but the estimated cost to the attorney general's office was only $20,000. Taken together, Hoppe's estimates of state and federal appeals expenditures, amounting to about $200,000 on average, also appear to be reasonable.[90] Again, Hoppe made no attempt to compare these costs to those associated with life-sentence appeals.

The last component of the cost breakdown provided by Hoppe values the "estimate of [federal] appellate court costs and outlays associated with the death penalty" at $1.7 million. While this figure accounts for the bulk of Hoppe's overall estimate, there is no explanation of how this figure was derived. A 1989 report from the General Accounting Office is listed as the source of this estimate.[91] A search of government documents and secondary sources did not turn up this report. The only 1989 GAO report that refers to the cost of capital punishment, *Criminal Justice: Limited Data Available on Costs of Death Sentences, Report to the Chairman, Subcommittee on Civil and Constitutional Rights, Committee on the Judiciary, House of Representatives,* did not include any discussion of federal outlays on the death penalty. In fact, the first caption in the report states, "Federal Data on the Cost of the Death Penalty Are Nonexistent." Although not explicitly included among Hoppe's cost breakdown, the other $137,000 needed to round out the $2.317 million figure presumably comes from the cost of confining a death-sentenced inmate for an average 7.5 years while awaiting execution.

Hoppe concluded that the $2.3 million cost of a death sentence was more than three times the estimated $750,000 cost of the alternative "life" sentence, forty years in prison. Her estimates for the cost of time served by death-sentenced and life-sentenced inmates were derived by multiplying the state's average daily cost to keep an inmate housed by the amount of time they are to be housed.[92] These estimates based on the average daily cost of confinement, however, do not take into account the cost of new construction or other capital outlays which would likely be necessary to house additional lifers not sentenced to death. Nor do her estimates take into consideration the additional cost of health care and the special facilities required by the elderly while in prison and, if eventually released, in the community (those sentenced after September 1, 2005, must serve life without the possibility of parole). It is highly unlikely that at that stage in their lives, parolees will be able to obtain employment and earn an income. Having been in prison for forty years, these inmates will not have been able to save up for retirement. The median age of those committing capital offenses is twenty-four, so being released after serving a forty-year sentence would put them back into the community at about retirement age. Since the average life expectancy is seventy-seven, the state will likely end up paying living and health-care expenses for released life-sentenced inmates during their final twelve or so golden years.

Even assuming for the sake of argument that all of Hoppe's verifiable figures are reasonable estimates of the costs associated with a death sentence or a sentence of life imprisonment, it becomes clear that the question of whether a death or life sentence costs more hinges completely on the inclusion of the $1.7 million for federal-court outlays. Excluding this unfathomable "per capita" estimate, Hoppe's total estimated cost for the death penalty would be just over $600,000, far short of the estimated cost of life imprisonment at $750,000. In sum, the most widely cited estimate of the cost of capital punishment in Texas is groundless. The verifiable information contained in the *Dallas Morning News* study shows the death penalty to be cheaper than life imprisonment.

Any attempt to evaluate the cost of the death penalty against the cost of a life sentence is going to face serious obstacles: many figures related to the costs of processing capital cases in Texas are either unidentifiable or unavailable. In perhaps the most comprehensive study of a state's capital punishment system ever completed, the Illinois Governor's Commission on Capital Punishment decided that "undertaking a detailed study with respect to the costs associated with the death penalty in Illinois was beyond the capacity of the Commission, and in light of the inherent problems associated with studying the cost issue, initiating research is [*sic*] this area seemed unwise."[93] Nonetheless, after reviewing the most reliable studies performed in other states and critically analyzing the only study that has yet to be completed in Texas, the evidence suggests that the costs associated with the death penalty are similar to those associated with life sentences.

Conclusion

Several issues regarding the administration of capital punishment have caused many to question the fairness and efficiency of maintaining this system of punishment. Specifically, questions about the fair and unbiased implementation of capital punishment, about the possibility of executing innocent individuals, and about the cost of capital punishment versus life imprisonment have been persuasive issues in the debate over capital punishment. Many of these problems or concerns, however, are more applicable to the early post-*Furman* period than to more recent years, particularly in Texas, and presumably in any other state that regularly utilizes capital punishment.

In the immediate aftermath of *Furman,* states were left with little guidance in reimplementing the death-penalty statutes. Although the *Furman* court invalidated capital punishment and expressed concerns regarding potential racial bias, the plurality opinion did not tell the states how to address these concerns. The states therefore went through a period of trial and error, in which the Supreme Court defined the constitutional limits of statutes through its review of specific cases. It was during this period of flux that many of the above concerns came to light.

As these issues were raised, courts, legislatures and executives responded. Many states, such as Texas, where the social and political climate has always been very supportive of capital punishment, made dedicated efforts to address these concerns: for example, making the process more fair by providing greater resources for defense, more certain by providing for postconviction DNA testing, and more efficient by streamlining appeals. The process has been one of constant refinement, sometimes because of specific court cases and sometimes *sua sponte*.

This process has resulted in a change in what used to be common knowledge regarding the death penalty. First, evidence of racial disparity has all but disappeared. The only significant race effects found in this analysis do not fit the expected pattern, and are likely due to other case characteristics, such as the heinousness of the crime and the perceived culpability of the defendant. Second, the danger of executing a truly innocent individual has been exaggerated. Of the few Texas defendants who have been labeled "exonerated," most were in fact guilty of the crime or were participants in the crime, but prosecutorial misconduct or procedural errors led to their release. Finally, the process itself has become more efficient: capital punishment in Texas is at least as cost efficient as life imprisonment, and perhaps even more so.

Critics charge that recent changes either do not go far enough or are not carried out as intended.[94] For example, while additional resources have been provided to defense attorneys, monetary caps discourage vigorous defense. Further, compensation, like the qualifications for defense counsel, varies widely across jurisdictions. The law providing for DNA testing has been so narrowly interpreted by the Texas Court of Criminal Appeals that many condemned inmates are actually unable to take advantage of its provisions. The streamlining of appeals is also fraught with problems. State habeas petitions often must be submitted before the direct review has even occurred. Further, many meritorious claims are "cut off" from being heard because the issues were not raised in the initial petition. Throughout the process, anecdotes of professional incompetence abound.

No system is perfect, particularly in criminal justice. Some have come to the conclusion that as long as there is any possibility, no matter how remote, that an innocent person might be executed or that a person might be denied his constitutional rights, the state should not have in place a method of punishment that is so final. However, for those who take a more social utilitarian approach, these administrative concerns should now cause less reason for hesitation than at any other point in history.

This is not to imply that further changes might not be warranted or useful. It is necessary to remain vigilant, to improve the process whenever possible, and to ensure that those who are responsible for its administration are held accountable for failing to perform their duties. Most system failures are the result of a participant's failure to perform his or her duty, such as prosecutors or law enforcement officials withholding exculpatory evidence or encouraging false testimony, or defense attorneys failing to diligently defend clients. Although safety mechanisms built into the system have shown that they catch many of these wrongs, numerous instances can be detailed where those currently on death row, and even those executed, suffered certain procedural injustices.[95] When the stakes are so high, procedural justice must be enforced with a policy of zero tolerance. Doing so would not only help prevent abuses, but it would also strengthen Texans' confidence in the justice system generally, and in capital punishment in particular.

CHAPTER 6

Conclusion

A man had to answer for the wicked that he done.
Take all the rope in Texas, find a tall oak tree,
Round up all of them bad boys, hang them high in the street,
For all the people to see that
Justice is the one thing you should always find.
TOBY KEITH AND SCOTT EMERICK, "BEER FOR MY HORSES"

Capital punishment is supposed to serve the purposes of social defense and retribution. The argument that it deters or incapacitates dangerous offenders was not conclusively supported, and analysis of data herein failed to provide solid evidence for the death penalty as a mechanism of social defense. Comparative analysis could not show that the death penalty reduces homicide rates any more successfully than life imprisonment. Still, it is possible that the death penalty acts as a general deterrent, preventing others from committing homicides, but it may simply be impossible to empirically measure the effect of an event that did not occur. It was also difficult to show the necessity of the death penalty for incapacitating dangerous offenders. Although it is certain that without the death penalty some capital murderers would commit violent acts in the future, only a small percentage of those who have been given a second chance have actually committed further violent acts, particularly murder. And the existence of the death penalty has not completely prevented capital murderers from committing further acts of violence or murder.

The strongest argument in favor of retaining capital punishment lies in its retributive purpose. Whether capital punishment is a legitimate way to punish offenders is a moral issue that is in many ways beyond the bounds of empirical research and the scope of this work. Nonetheless, numerous indicators support the use of the death penalty for retribution. First, public-opinion data indicate that Texans favor the use of capital punishment, even if it is shown not to serve the purposes of social defense. Second, Texans seated as jurors in capital cases have been willing to impose the death penalty in a vast majority of the cases. Third, the types of cases subject to the death penalty have been narrowly circumscribed by statute and prosecutorial charging practices. With few exceptions, the death penalty is targeted to the most heinous murders. It is regularly demanded and imposed in these cases, but seldom in other, less severe cases. As a result, the death penalty has been shown to follow the principles of proportionality, meaning its application is predictable, not arbitrary or capricious.

In support of the populist notion that the electorate is capable of making policy decisions regarding the proper sanctioning of its citizens, members of all three branches of Texas government have worked together to ensure that the will of the people in maintaining a functioning capital-punishment system is recognized, and that this system is implemented in a constitutionally acceptable manner. Numerous procedural refinements have been made as problems concerning the use of the sanction have come to light. Some of these include specifically directing jurors to consider mitigating evidence, informing jurors of the meaning of a life sentence, limiting successive appeals, providing defendants with counsel throughout the appellate process, increasing professional standards and compensation for counsel, and providing for the reanalysis of DNA evidence. Through this process of continuous refinement, the state has been successful in sustaining an efficient system of capital punishment. Not only has this routinization of the process made the death penalty cost effective in Texas—unlike the situation in many other states not yet able to fully implement their death-penalty schemes—but, simultaneously, the procedure is also becoming immune to many of the criticisms historically leveled against capital punishment.

That this diligence in refining the process has met with successful results is illustrated by three trends occurring in the implementation of the death penalty in Texas during the modern era. First is the increased likelihood that the death penalty will actually be carried out on those sentenced to death. The rate of appellate reversal and other releases from death row have continuously decreased throughout the modern era. As shown in Figure 6.1, reversals routinely outnumbered executions through the mid-1980s. During the late 1980s, the ratio between the number of executions and reversals was 1:1. Only in the 1990s, when many roadblocks were removed and a wave of executions was carried out, did executions begin to outpace reversals. By the mid-1990s, the ratio of executions to reversals had increased to 2:1. By 1999, the number of executions exceeded reversals at a ratio exceeding 10:1.

Just as in other states, Texas has experienced ebbs and flows in perform-

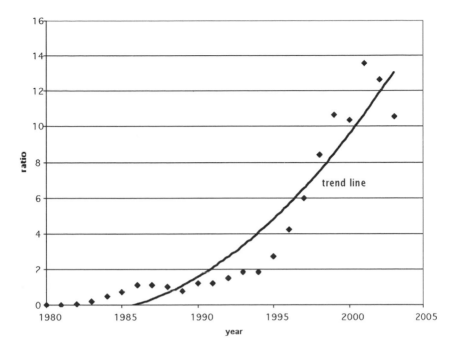

Figure 6.1. Ratio of executions to reversals in Texas, 1980–2003

ing executions. Challenges to procedures have resulted in changes, which in turn have spurred additional challenges to the newly enacted procedures. For instance, criticisms about the lengthy appeals process led to limits on appeals in 1995. This limiting of appeals was challenged, naturally, and during the pendency of these challenges, executions were put on hold. This resulted in a mini-moratorium in 1996, a year in which only three executions were carried out. However, the cases that had built up awaiting the decision by the Court of Criminal Appeals were disposed of in 1997, creating a small wave of executions. These types of challenges will be likely to occur in the future as a natural and necessary part of the process. However, such challenges are likely to affect smaller, more specific groups, as opposed to resulting in a statewide moratorium. Currently, for instance, juvenile executions have been stayed pending the U.S. Supreme Court's decision on the constitutionality of executing juveniles. This is quite different from challenges to the death-penalty system overall, which halts the executions of all offenders. Regardless, it appears that the current flow will continue to outstrip any minor ebbs that should occur in the future.

In addition to the increased likelihood that executions will be carried out,

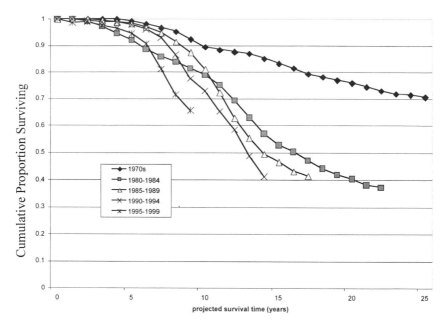

Figure 6.2. Predicted survival rates and time on death row prior to execution for five Texas death-row cohorts

executions are also being carried out more swiftly.[1] The most appropriate way to gauge a possible trend in the amount of time it takes for a condemned inmate to be executed is to examine the time to execution for cohorts of condemned inmates. In Figure 6.2, survival analysis was used to chart the rate of survival for condemned prisoners grouped by their year of entrance to death row. The survival curves show a combination of the actual proportion and the projected proportion of each group surviving through the end of its observation periods.[2] The first series shows that over 70 percent of the condemned prisoners received on death row during the 1970s are likely to survive through their twenty-fifth year. This can be compared to the most recent series, which shows that for the group entering in the late 1990s, only 63 percent of the condemned are predicted to survive through their eighth year on death row. The median time to execution has steadily decreased from sixteen years for the early 1980s cohort, to fourteen years for the late 1980s cohort, to under thirteen years for the early 1990s cohort. These figures provide evidence that the time to execution has been sharply decreasing throughout the modern era.

The median time to execution for the cohort entering death row in the late 1990s is not yet possible to calculate with certainty. However, since only 63 percent of this group is predicted to survive up through their eighth year, and

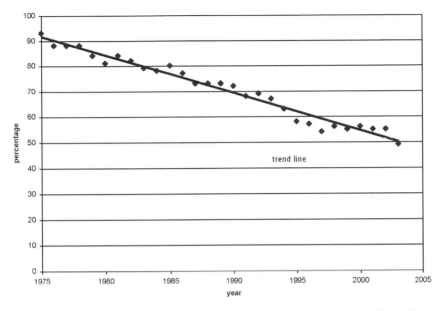

Figure 6.3. Percentage of death-sentenced cases in Texas involving white victims, 1975–2003

given the steepness of the survival curve relative to the earlier series, this group will probably spend an average of about a decade on death row before execution. If appeals were processed more efficiently, it is possible that this average time could ultimately decrease to about seven years. Of course, for those few death-sentenced inmates who choose to forgo appeals, the time to execution can be less than a year.[3]

The routinization of the death penalty has led to additional benefits beyond economy. Most importantly, when the death penalty is routinely sought in cases that fit a particular fact pattern, the potential influence of improper extralegal factors is likely to decrease. The most obvious extralegal factor found to influence death sentencing historically has been race. Although little evidence of offender-based racial disparity has been found in the modern era, numerous studies have found evidence of victim-based racial disparities. The lower likelihood of the death penalty being pursued against killers of blacks has also been documented herein. Figure 6.3, however, demonstrates one of the most dramatic shifts in the imposition of the death penalty in Texas during the modern era: the race of the victim has not had a constant influence on case processing, but has changed dramatically since 1974. Death-penalty cases decided in the immediate aftermath of *Furman* involved white victims over 90 percent of the time, but this percentage steadily declined to less than 50 percent by 2003.

This trend shows that the death penalty is currently being pursued on behalf of minorities at much higher rates than in the past, providing them with the power to mobilize the most extreme criminal-justice resource at an unprecedented level. In 2003, fully 28 percent of the condemned inmates entering death row had killed black victims, and another 28 percent had killed Hispanic victims. These figures are very close to the percentage of homicides involving victims of these racial and ethnic groups. Throughout the modern era, the proportion of victims among overall homicides has remained about one-third each for Hispanics, whites, and blacks. This parity in death sentencing will come at another cost, however, because most homicides are intraracial. Sentencing more defendants to death for killing minorities means that more minorities will be sentenced to death.

The moral question of whether the state should ever have the right to take a life can never be answered conclusively. Everyone has personal views on the issue and personal reasons supporting those views. The analysis of data described herein is not likely to change anyone's view on the death penalty. The goal of this study was to provide facts about the implementation of the death penalty at the turn of the millennium in the nation's most active death-penalty jurisdiction. A secondary goal might be for this empirical examination of the death penalty in practice to be of use to those engaging in the deeper normative debate over capital punishment.

Appendix

Table A. Actual versus estimated changes in Texas homicides, based on adjusted U.S. homicides, 1996–1997

Month	U.S. homicides	Actual TX homicides	Est. TX homicides	Act.-Est.	t stat	Texas executions
Jan. 1996	−.0468	−.1088	−.0980	−.0108	−.0800	0
Feb. 1996	.0436	−.1367	.0514	−.1881	−1.3882	2
Mar. 1996	−.1023	−.2273	−.1897	−.0375	−.2771	0
Apr. 1996	−.1879	−.3796	−.3312	−.0484	−.3572	0
May 1996	−.0445	.1880	−.0942	.2822	**2.0824**	0
June 1996	−.0243	−.1597	−.0607	−.0990	−.7307	0
July 1996	−.1009	−.2635	−.1874	−.0761	−.5617	0
Aug. 1996	−.1641	−.1273	−.2918	.1646	1.2146	0
Sep. 1996	−.1432	−.0859	−.2573	.1713	1.2643	1
Oct. 1996	−.1220	−.0076	−.2222	.2147	1.5841	0
Nov. 1996	−.0908	−.2047	−.1707	−.0340	−.2511	0
Dec. 1996	−.0587	.0672	−.1176	.1847	1.3634	0
Jan. 1997	−.0737	−.2137	−.1424	−.0713	−.5265	0
Feb. 1997	−.1331	−.1917	−.2406	.0489	.3609	1
Mar. 1997	.0502	.1961	.0624	.1337	.9867	1
Apr. 1997	−.0611	.2000	−.1215	.3215	**2.3729**	6
May 1997	−.1177	−.3291	−.2152	−.1139	−.8408	8
June 1997	−.0839	−.0496	−.1592	.1096	.8091	8
July 1997	−.0521	−.0407	−.1066	.0660	.4870	1
Aug. 1997	−.1141	−.0278	−.2092	.1814	1.3389	0
Sep. 1997	−.0622	−.0171	−.1234	.1063	.7845	4
Oct. 1997	−.0623	−.3130	−.1235	−.1894	−1.3981	3
Nov. 1997	−.0503	.0000	−.1037	.1037	.7651	4
Dec. 1997	−.1046	−.1748	−.1936	.0187	.1382	1

Note: Figures in the second, third, and fourth columns represent proportional changes in U.S. homicides, in actual Texas homicides (compared to figures from the same month of the previous year), and in estimated Texas homicides; the fifth column shows the difference between actual and estimated Texas homicides. Significant *t* statistics are in boldface.

Table B. Predicted cumulative Texas homicides, 1996–1997, based on adjusted U.S. homicides

Month	Act.-Est.	Homicides 1 yr. earlier	Additional homicides	Cumulative homicides
Jan. 1996	−.0108	147	−1.59	−1.59
Feb. 1996	−.1881	139	−26.15	−27.74
Mar. 1996	−.0375	132	−4.96	−32.69
Apr. 1996	−.0484	137	−6.63	−39.32
May 1996	.2822	133	37.53	−1.79
June 1996	−.0990	144	−14.26	−16.05
July 1996	−.0761	167	−12.71	−28.76
Aug. 1996	.1646	165	27.16	−1.60
Sep. 1996	.1713	128	21.93	20.33
Oct. 1996	.2147	132	28.33	48.66
Nov. 1996	−.0340	127	−4.32	44.34
Dec. 1996	.1847	134	24.75	69.09
Jan. 1997	−.0713	131	−9.35	59.74
Feb. 1997	.0489	120	5.87	65.61
Mar. 1997	.1337	102	13.64	79.25
Apr. 1997	.3215	85	27.33	106.58
May 1997	−.1139	158	−18.00	88.58
June 1997	.1096	121	13.27	101.85
July 1997	.0660	123	8.12	109.97
Aug. 1997	.1814	144	26.12	136.09
Sep. 1997	.1063	117	12.44	148.53
Oct. 1997	−.1894	131	−24.82	123.71
Nov. 1997	.1037	101	10.47	134.18
Dec. 1997	.0187	143	2.68	136.86

Note: **Act.-Est.**: Difference between the actual and estimated number of homicides in Texas, expressed as a proportional change (from Table A). **Additional homicides**: Additional homicides predicted by multiplying the "Act.-Est." proportion by the actual number of homicides from the same month of the previous year.

Table C. Predicted cumulative Texas homicides, 1996–1997, based on Texas violent crimes

Month	TXVi	AcTXHom	EsTXHom	Act.-Est.	t stat	Cum. Hom.
Jan. 1996	.0000	−.1208	−.0417	−.0791	−.5683	−11.79
Feb. 1996	.0208	−.1304	−.0164	−.1140	−.8192	−27.53
Mar. 1996	−.0247	−.2273	−.0717	−.1556	−1.1178	−48.07
Apr. 1996	.0185	−.3750	−.0193	−.3557	**−2.5554**	−96.45
May 1996	.0334	.1955	−.0011	.1966	1.4123	−70.30
June 1996	.0371	−.1736	.0034	−.1770	−1.2715	−95.79
July 1996	−.0100	−.2663	−.0538	−.2125	−1.5263	−131.69
Aug. 1996	−.0219	−.1325	−.0683	−.0642	−.4613	−142.35
Sep. 1996	−.0159	−.1000	−.0610	−.0390	−.2803	−147.42
Oct. 1996	−.0676	−.0150	−.1238	.1088	.7813	−133.02
Nov. 1996	−.0420	−.2109	−.0927	−.1182	−.8495	−148.16
Dec. 1996	−.0284	.0672	−.0762	.1434	1.0299	−128.95
Jan. 1997	−.0747	−.2137	−.1324	−.0813	−.5842	−139.60
Feb. 1997	−.0795	−.1917	−.1382	−.0535	−.3842	−146.02
Mar. 1997	.0557	.1961	.0259	.1701	1.2223	−128.66
Apr. 1997	−.0862	.2000	−.1464	.3464	**2.4883**	−99.22
May 1997	−.0544	−.3270	−.1078	−.2193	−1.5752	−134.08
June 1997	−.0005	−.0336	−.0423	.0087	.0621	−133.05
July 1997	−.0446	−.0403	−.0958	.0555	.3986	−126.17
Aug. 1997	−.0372	−.0278	−.0869	.0591	.4246	−117.66
Sep. 1997	−.0604	−.0171	−.1150	.0979	.7035	−106.20
Oct. 1997	−.0577	−.3130	−.1118	−.2012	−1.4453	−132.56
Nov. 1997	−.0677	.0000	−.1239	.1239	.8900	−120.05
Dec. 1997	−.0987	−.1748	−.1615	−.0133	−.0957	−121.96

Note: **TXVi**: proportional change in Texas's violent crime rate over the same month from the previous year. **AcTXHom**: actual proportional change in Texas homicides over the same month of the previous year. **EsTXHom**: estimated proportional change in Texas homicides based on the regression model, in the absence of an execution. **Act.-Est.**: difference between the actual and estimated number of homicides in Texas, expressed as a proportional change. **Cum. Hom.**: cumulative number of homicides over the amount predicted by the regression model. Significant *t* statistics are in boldface. This figure was derived by multiplying "Act.-Est." in Table C by the figure for "Homicides 1 yr. earlier" from Table B to obtain "additional homicides" (omitted here), which were then summed to obtain the final cumulative homicide totals.

Notes

Note: The full text of most Supreme Court cases can be found on FindLaw.com. Recent cases from other federal appellate courts, U.S. district courts, and some state appellate courts are also available there.

Chapter 1

1. Dan Reid and John Gurwell, *Eyewitness* (Houston: Cordovan Press, 1973), 230.

2. Michael Meltsner, *Cruel and Unusual: The Supreme Court and Capital Punishment* (New York: Random House, 1973).

3. *Furman v. Georgia,* 408 U.S. 238 (1972).

4. *Branch v. Texas,* 408 U.S. 238 (1972).

5. Charles Ehrhardt and L. Harold Levinson, "Florida's Legislative Response to *Furman*: An Exercise in Futility?" 64 *Journal of Criminal Law and Criminology* 10 (1973).

6. Audiotape: Public Hearing on HB 200, 63rd Legislature, held by the House Committee on Criminal Jurisprudence, tapes 1–3 (Feb. 6, 1973).

7. The concerns of House bill advocates, though quelled when the Supreme Court upheld the Florida statute in *Profitt v. Florida,* 428 U.S. 242 (1976), were partially vindicated when the Court held in *Ring v. Arizona,* 536 U.S. 584 (2002), that the jury must be the ultimate arbiter of capital sentencing.

8. The Sharpstown stock-fraud scandal was a fraud-and-bribery investigation carried on by both the federal and state government against the governor, the Speaker of the House, the former state attorney general, the former state insurance commissioner, and others. Civil suits were also filed. When all was said and done, the incumbent governor was deemed an unindicted coconspirator and lost his bid for reelection; the incumbent Speaker of the House and others were convicted of felonies; and half of the members of the legislature either decided not to run for reelection or were voted out of office. Running on a "reform" platform, Dolph Briscoe and William Hobby were elected governor and lieutenant governor, respectively, and a series of far-reaching reform laws were passed. See *The Handbook of Texas Online,* s.v. "Sharpstown Stock-Fraud Scandal,"

available at http://www.tsha.utexas.edu/handbook/online/articles/view/SS/mqsi.html (last accessed March 22, 2005).

The public's and Hobby's support for capital punishment was confirmed in a telephone interview with Senator Bill Meier on Oct. 25, 2002.

9. For discussion, see Michael Kuhn, "House Bill 200: The Legislative Attempt to Reinstate Capital Punishment in Texas," 11 *Houston Law Review* 410 (1974); Texas House, bill file, HB 200, 63rd Leg., 1973.

10. *Texas Penal Code Annotated*, sec. 19.03 (West 2001).

11. The details of the conference committee's deliberations that resulted in this unique legislative enactment were not recorded, so it is not possible to know exactly how or why the specific wording of the special issues arose. In a recent interview, Senator Bill Meier, chair of the conference committee, stated that his greatest concern was predominantly pragmatic; he wanted to come up with a bill that would pass both the House and the Senate (Meier interview, Oct. 25, 2002). Meier credited Terry Doyle, a member of the House, with developing the specific wording of the special issues; the *Austin American-Statesman* (May 28, 1973) credited Rep. Bob Maloney. Neither party was available for interview, however, so the exact methods and reasoning used to come up with the questions cannot be known with certainty. It appears that the first and third special issues could be considered an amalgamation of the mitigating factors raised in the Senate version of the bill, whereas the second special issue addressed the issue of dangerousness, a major concern of House delegates. Further, the language regarding dangerousness and the idea of basing sentences on a determination of dangerousness, although eschewed by the American Law Institute, were supported by the Council of Judges of the National Council on Crime and Delinquency in their Model Sentencing Act, which was being widely distributed at that time (Council of Judges of the National Council on Crime and Delinquency, "Model Sentencing Act: Second Ed.," 18 *Crime and Delinquency* 335, 341 [1972]).

For the wording of the three special issues, see *Texas Code of Criminal Procedure Annotated*, art. 37.071b (West 2001)

12. *Texas Code of Criminal Procedure Annotated*, art. 37.071g (West 2001).

13. *Woodson v. North Carolina*, 428 U.S. 280 (1976); *Roberts v. Louisiana*, 428 U.S. 325 (1976).

14. *Gregg v. Georgia*, 428 U.S. 153 (1976); *Profitt*, 428 U.S. 242; *Jurek v. Texas*, 428 U.S. 262 (1976).

15. See Charles Black, "Due Process for Death: *Jurek v. Texas* and Companion Cases," 26 *Catholic University Law Review* 1 (1976); David Crump, "Capital Murder: The Issues in Texas," 14 *Houston Law Review* 532 (1977); Peggy C. Davis, "Texas Capital Sentencing Procedures: The Role of the Jury and the Restraining Hand of the Expert," 69 *Journal of Criminal Law and Criminology* 300 (1978); George E. Dix, "Administration of the Texas Death Penalty Statutes: Constitutional Infirmities Related to the Prediction of Dangerousness," 55 *Texas Law Review* 1343 (1977); Giles R. Scofield, "Due Process in the United States Supreme Court and the Death of the Texas Capital Murder Statute," 8 *American Journal of Criminal Law* 1 (1980).

16. *Jurek*, 428 U.S. at 272–274.

17. *Penry v. Lynaugh*, 492 U.S. 302 (1989).

18. This is not surprising given that the original first and third questions were largely redundant; the fact that a defendant has been convicted of first-degree murder typically

warrants an affirmative answer to those questions. Had deliberateness been lacking or sufficient provocation been present, the jury most likely would have convicted the defendant of a lesser degree of homicide.

19. This question is raised most often in cases involving accomplices charged under the felony-murder doctrine, meaning that if someone is killed during the course of a felony, the accomplice is guilty of murder regardless of whether he or she intended to commit a murder, because murder was a foreseeable outcome. The Supreme Court had not accepted the imposition of the death penalty under the same theory of accomplice liability and had given clear instructions about when the death penalty could be imposed in such cases. Texas adopted the more restrictive standard set forth by the Court in *Edmund v. Florida*, 458 U.S. 782 (1982)—holding that those who did not kill or did not intend to kill could not be sentenced to death—even though the Court had loosened these rules in *Tison v. Arizona*, 481 U.S. 137 (1987), by upholding a death sentence where the defendant had a mental state of "reckless indifference" to human life.

20. *Texas Code of Criminal Procedure Annotated*, art. 37.071, sec. 2(b)(1)(2) (West 2001). The question involving accomplice liability is asked only if a defendant is found guilty as a party under secs. 7.01 and 7.02 of the penal code (*Texas Penal Code Annotated*, sec. 7.01 [West 2001]).

21. *Texas Code of Criminal Procedure Annotated*, art. 37.071, sec. 2(c)(2) (West 2001).

22. *Report of the Commission to Investigate and Report the Most Humane and Practical Method of Carrying into Effect the Sentence of Death in Capital Cases*, New York, Jan. 17, 1888, cited in Amnesty International, *Lethal Injection: The Medical Technology of Execution* (Jan. 1998), available at http://web.amnesty.org/library/Index/engACT500011998 (last accessed March 22, 2005).

23. Claudia Feldman, "Estelle Supports Change in Method of Execution," *Houston Chronicle*, May 6, 1977.

24. Ibid.

25. Ibid.

26. Audiotape: Public Hearing on HB 945, 65th Legislature, held by the House Committee on Criminal Jurisprudence, tapes 1–3 (March 1, 1977).

27. Feldman, "Estelle Supports Change."

28. Rob Wood, "Injections Don't Faze Death Row," *Austin American-Statesman*, Jun. 12, 1977, B13.

29. Ibid.

30. Audiotape of public hearing on HB 945.

31. Ibid.

32. "Member of ACLU Critical of Texas' Injection Death Bill," *Houston Chronicle*, May 6, 1977.

33. Audiotape of public hearing on HB 945.

34. *Texas Statutes and Codes Annotated*, ch. 138, art. 43.14 at 288 (West 1977).

35. *Ex parte Granviel*, 561 S.W.2d 503, 507–508 (Tex. Crim. App. 1978).

36. *Ex parte Granviel*, 561 S.W.2d 503.

37. *Adams v. Texas*, 448 U.S. 38 (1980), in accordance with *Witherspoon v. Illinois*, 391 U.S. 510 (1968).

38. The Court ruled that capital defendants had to be given a Miranda warning before being examined by a state psychiatrist if the psychiatrist was going to testify in the punishment phase of a capital trial (*Estelle v. Smith*, 451 U.S. 454, 466–469 [1981]). Fur-

ther, the examination was considered a "critical stage" in the proceedings, and therefore the defendant was entitled to counsel (469–471). Violations of this rule, however, were later subject only to harmless-error analysis (*Satterwhite v. Texas*, 486 U.S. 249 [1988]).

39. Dick J. Reavis, "Charlie Brooks' Last Words," *Texas Monthly*, Feb. 1983, 101.

40. Since 1997, the average annual number of inmates sentenced to death has been about thirty-six; the average annual number of executions has been just under thirty.

41. This information is based on a personal interview with an original member of the execution team.

42. With the exception of Nebraska, all current death-penalty jurisdictions have adopted lethal injection. Some states still list their former method of execution as an option for those sentenced to death before the switch to lethal injection (Thomas P. Bonczar and Tracy L. Snell, *Capital Punishment, 2002*, Bureau of Justice Statistics Bulletin, U.S. Department of Justice [Washington, D.C., 2003]).

43. Although these rates are not perfectly indicative of the level of success, since they include death row cases that have not been fully litigated, reversal rates have shown a similar pattern, being quite low in Texas cases and nearing the all-jurisdiction low in Virginia in recent years.

Chapter 2

1. *Civil Rights Act of 1965*, Public Law 101-576, *U.S. Statutes at Large* 104:2838 (codified as amended in scattered sections of *U.S. Code* 2, *U.S. Code* 28, and *U.S. Code* 42); *Roe v. Wade*, 410 U.S. 113 (1973).

2. The actual index crime rate rose from an average of 1,938 per 100,000 during 1960–1962 to 4,037 during 1970–1972 (Michael Maltz, *Uniform Crime Reports*, available at *http://bjsdata.ojp.usdoj.gov/dataonline/Search/Crime/State/StatebyState.cfm* [last visited Oct. 30, 2003]).

3. See L. Thomas Winfree, "Attica," in *Encyclopedia of American Prisons*, ed. Marilyn D. McShane and Frank P. Williams III, 43 (New York: Garland Press, 1996).

4. *Furman*, 408 U.S. 238; *McGautha v. California*, 402 U.S. 183 (1971).

5. *Furman*, 408 U.S. at 345.

6. See *The Handbook of Texas Online*, s.v. "Sharpstown Stock-Fraud Scandal," http://www.tsha.utexas.edu/handbook/online/articles/view/SS/mqs1.html (last accessed March 22, 2005).

7. The debates surrounding HB 200 were transcribed by the authors from recordings made at the public hearings. Audiotapes: Public Hearing on HB 200.

8. Hugo A. Bedau, ed., *The Death Penalty in America* (New York: Doubleday Anchor, 1967); *Furman*, 408 U.S. at 372; Thorsten Sellin, *Capital Punishment* (New York: Harper and Row, 1967) and *The Penalty of Death* (Philadelphia: American Law Institute, 1959).

9. See John K. Cochran et al., "Deterrence or Brutalization? An Impact Assessment of Oklahoma's Return to Capital Punishment," 32 *Criminology* 107 (1994); William C. Bailey, "Disaggregation in Deterrence and Death Penalty Research: The Case of Murder in Chicago," 74 *Journal of Criminal Law and Criminology* 827 (1983); William Bowers and Glenn Pierce, "Deterrence or Brutalization: What is the Effect of Executions?" 26 *Crime and Delinquency* 453 (1980).

10. See Sellin, *Capital Punishment* and *Penalty of Death;* Karl F. Schuessler, "The Deterrent Effect of the Death Penalty," 284 *Annals of the American Academy of Political and Social Science* 54 (1952).

11. In many states, statutes include "heinous, atrocious, and cruel" in the criteria for death-eligible murders. See James R. Acker and Charles S. Lanier, "Beyond Human Ability? The Rise and Fall of Death Penalty Legislation," in *America's Experiment with Capital Punishment,* ed. Acker et al., 77, 92 (Durham, N.C.: Carolina Academic Press, 1998). Unlike the narrowly focused statutory criteria in Texas, this statutory language allows prosecutors a wide range of discretion when deciding what charges to bring against a defendant. In a study of St. Louis County, Missouri, for example, the prosecutor charged all of those eventually convicted of some degree of murder with first-degree (capital) murder. Each case was deemed to contain some circumstance that would have made the case death-eligible, had the state chosen to pursue it (Jon Sorensen and Donald H. Wallace, "Prosecutorial Discretion in Seeking Death: An Analysis of Racial Disparity in the Pretrial Stages of Case Processing in a Mid-Western County," 16 *Justice Quarterly* 559 [1999]).

12. One category of murder that fits this criterion is murder that occurs during the course of a felony, such as robbery-murder or rape-murder. The only available measure, however, that contains information on the characteristics of homicides for jurisdictions across the United States, the Supplemental Homicide Reports (SHR), has many flaws (Michael G. Maxfield, "Circumstances in Supplementary Homicide Reports: Variety and Validity," 27 *Criminology* 671 [1989]). Over 80 percent of all homicides are reported in this database, but reporting levels by state are not uniform. Besides suffering from this uneven reporting, the SHR database is missing the circumstances of about one-fourth of the homicides reported. Studies have found that this missing information is not spread equally across crime categories, but rather most often occurs in stranger-murders and murders involving felonies (See Marc Riedel et al., *The Nature and Pattern of American Homicide* [Washington, D.C., 1985]).

Even in cases where the details surrounding a homicide are complete, this information is often suspect because of inconsistent reporting practices across jurisdictions. For example, some jurisdictions are quick to report murders suspected of involving a contemporaneous robbery as robbery-murder, yet other jurisdictions do not report any murder as involving a robbery without prior confirmation. Therefore, an analysis of felony murder across jurisdictions may not yield reliable results.

13. See *Roberts v. Louisiana,* 431 U.S. 633 (1977).

14. This rate was calculated by aggregating the number of sworn police officers (in 2000) in all states within each category (abolitionist or retentionist), dividing that total by the annual average number of police killings (for each jurisdictional category) during 1999–2001 (4.667/76,552 in abolitionist states versus 46.667/574,402 in retentionist), and then multiplying by 100,000. All jurisdictions with the death penalty on the books during this period were considered retentionist. The results vary only slightly when the analysis is restricted to those states that actually executed prisoners during this period.

15. See William C. Bailey and Ruth D. Peterson, "Police Killings and Capital Punishment: The Post-*Furman* Period," 25 *Criminology* 1 (1987); Albert P. Cardarelli, "An Analysis of Police Killed in Criminal Action: 1961–1963," 59 *Journal of Criminal Law, Criminology, and Police Science* 447 (1968).

16. Please note that New Hampshire's death penalty status is purely *de jure*: in the

post-*Furman* era, New Hampshire has neither sentenced a defendant to death nor executed any defendants (Tracy L. Snell and Laura M. Maruschak, *Capital Punishment, 2001,* Bureau of Justice Statistics Bulletin, U.S. Department of Justice [Washington, D.C., 2002]).

17. Admittedly, this measure is only a rough indicator of risk, but is at least as dependable as those employed recently by economists studying the death penalty. Most econometric studies include measures of the likelihood of arrest, the likelihood of conviction, and the likelihood of execution (see, for example, Hashem Dezhbakhsh et al., "Does Capital Punishment Have a Deterrent Effect? New Evidence from Postmoratorium Panel Data," 5 *American Law and Economics Review* 344 (2003), available at http://aler.oupjournals.org/cgi/reprint/5/2/344; last accessed March 23, 2005).

Estimation procedures in the literature have become exceedingly complex, yet their estimations rely on a number of assumptions. They assume a constant level of death-eligible murders relative to homicides. They include figures for convictions and executions that are lagged a number of years from the point of arrest, and rely on the average number of years from arrest to conviction and from conviction to sentence. This is much more problematic than the authors of these studies seem to admit, because the average number of years from conviction to execution is not the same across the United States. It varies broadly across and within jurisdictions. Jurisdictions shepherd cases through the appellate process to final resolution at different rates, and within retentionist jurisdictions, pile-ups on death row occur because of pending legal decisions that involve classes of offenders or all death-row inmates. These pile-ups are often followed by a purging, of one sort or another, after the successful end to such litigation. It seems that Oklahoma experienced a purging during 1999–2001, while Louisiana experienced a pile-up.

18. Ruth D. Peterson and William C. Bailey, "Is Capital Punishment an Effective Deterrent for Murder? An Examination of Social Science Research," in Acker, *America's Experiment,* 157, 177.

19. See Sellin, *Capital Punishment* and *Penalty of Death.*

20. This occurred during 1907–1917 (Stuart Banner, *The Death Penalty: An American History* [Cambridge, Mass.: Harvard Univ. Press, 2002], 219–221).

21. Ibid., 222–223. More recently, Massachusetts, a state in which no executions had occurred in over fifty years, nearly reimplemented capital punishment in 1997 following the brutal murder of ten-year-old Jeffrey Curley. Both the House and Senate gave initial approval to the death penalty bill. The bill ultimately failed, however, because Rep. John Slattery (D-Peabody), who had initially voted for the death-penalty bill, changed his mind during the two weeks the bill was in a conference committee. See the Background section of *Issue: Death Penalty 2003,* Massachusetts Politics and Policy Online, available at http://o2133.org/issue.cfm?ID=115 (last accessed March 23, 2005).

22. Analyses limited to specific subcategories of death-eligible murder, such as the killing of a police officer, are not possible over time within a jurisdiction because of the rarity of such occurrences overall. Data limitations make it impossible to disaggregate other types of capital murder, such as robbery-murder, over this period (1960–2002). The SHR data have been collected only since 1976 and suffer from numerous problems (see n. 12 to this chapter and related text). However, because the trends in these types of murders have been found to track those of homicides generally, overall homicides may be used as a reasonable proxy for death-eligible murder (see the references in n. 15 to this chapter).

23. Twenty-two executions were carried out during 1985–1987, an average of just

over seven a year. While twenty-two executions over three years would not be considered an execution wave by today's standards, it was the first substantial purging of death-row inmates by execution in over two decades. This is part of the natural ebb and flow in the processing of death-penalty cases. A backlog of cases had built up pending the resolution of current legal challenges. Supreme Court decisions in the early 1980s—see *Adams*, 448 U.S. 38, and *Estelle*, 451 U.S. 454—cleared the way for death-penalty cases to move through the system to final disposition in the mid-1980s.

24. See, for example, Don Feder, "Capital Punishment Foes Dead Wrong" (*Boston Herald.com*, Jan. 10, 2001), available at http://www.prodeathpenalty.com/Feder.htm (last accessed March 22, 2005).

25. Typically referred to as the coefficient of determination, R^2, a squared correlation coefficient, is derived through a comparison of the distance of intersecting points (x, y) from the regression line, relative to the total distance from the mean of the dependent variable. When summed, the measure yields the proportion of variance in the dependent variable that is explained by the model.

The regression coefficient (b) is simply the slope of the line. In the general equation of a straight line, $y = a + bx$, a is the y-intercept, y is the predicted value of the dependent variable, and x is the independent variable; the value for b represents the predicted increase in y for each unit increase in x. The mathematical formula and a more detailed explanation can be found in Hubert M. Blalock, Jr., *Social Statistics*, 2nd ed. (New York: McGraw-Hill, 1979), 408.

26. Before the regression model to measure the influence of executions on homicides could be calculated, it was necessary to make some corrections in order to provide the best unbiased linear equation. First, the years analyzed were restricted to 1977–2001 so that the regression assumptions of linearity of the data and normality of the data distributions could be maintained. Including all of the moratorium years would have resulted in a cluster of data points at zero on the x-axis, making the fitting of a regression line problematic and biasing the resulting regression coefficients.

Second, adjustments had to be made to the equation because the data violated the regression assumption of independence. Ordinary least-squares regression assumes that the value of any given observation is not influenced by the value on any other observation and that none are repeated measures. In this case, the assumption is violated because the value of an observation in any given year is influenced by the observation from a previous year. This problem, referred to as autocorrelation, is inherent in longitudinal designs. The Durbin Watson (DW) statistic tests whether the autocorrelation is large enough to warrant corrections. In this case, the DW test indicated a significant problem of autocorrelation (DW = 1.05, $p < .01$), meaning that the number of homicides in any given year tended to be related to the number occurring in previous years. The standard method of correction involves including a lag of the dependent variable on the right-hand side of the equation. In this case, the number of homicides from the previous year, in addition to the number of executions, was included as a predictor of the number of homicides in a given year. This solved the problem of autocorrelation (DW = 1.728; n.s.) and, with an R^2 of .839 ($p < .001$) and a t-value for executions of -2.742 ($p < .01$; one-tailed), produced the following linear equation:

$$\text{Predicted Homicides} = 684.242 - 11.250 \text{ (executions)} + .707 \text{ (previous year's homicides)}$$

The intercept of 684.242 suggests that in the absence of any executions or any homicides during a previous year, the estimated number of homicides in a given year would be approximately 684. The final coefficient suggests that one may expect a .707 increase in homicides for each of the previous year's homicides.

27. To test for time priority, an equation was formulated in which murders and executions were lagged by one year before regressing them against each other. By lagging each of the variables of interest and then treating them as dependent variables, it is possible to see whether the predicted direction of the relationship holds. Finding that executions predict homicides during the following year would suggest the appropriate time priority and thus provide support for the deterrence argument. Finding that homicides are as successful at predicting executions during the following year as executions are at predicting homicides would suggest that time priority is questionable in this case.

To perform an analysis that provides a fair test of the influence of one variable, it was necessary to delete the years before the first execution; thus, the sample was restricted to 1982–2001. When all these years were included, the DW statistic indicated a high degree of autocorrelation; correcting for this would have required the inclusion of lagged versions of the dependent variables on the right-hand side of each of the equations, making the proposed test for causal order impossible. The actual findings show that executions were only slightly more successful at predicting homicides (R^2 = .561; p < .001) than homicides were at predicting executions (R^2 = .500; p < .001). The coefficients in each of these models were significant and negative: execution lag = -26.608 (p < .001) and homicide lag = -.020 (p < .001), respectively.

The first equation, showing that increased executions in one year reduced homicides during the next, is quite plausible, but the second equation, showing that increased homicides during one year reduced executions during the next, is not plausible. Logic excludes the alternative causal ordering, but the tests show that simultaneous changes cannot be ruled out.

28. These variables were percentage of population living in metropolitan area, percentage of population age 18 to 34, unemployment rate, physician rate, conviction rate, incarceration rate, percentage of population on AFDC, percentage of homicides involving guns, and high and low homicide seasons (Jon Sorensen et al. "Capital Punishment and Deterrence: Examining the Effect of Executions on Murder in Texas," 45 *Crime and Delinquency* 481 [1999]).

29. Regression was used to model the relationship between the two trends in Figure 2.3, and showed that U.S. homicide rates predicted Texas homicide rates nearly 60 percent (R^2 = .599) better than chance. See n. 58 to this chapter and related text.

30. Homicide rates increased from an average of 4.8 per 100,000 during 1960–1962 to 9.5 during 1990–1992. The rate of violent crime increased from 160 to 749 during the same period (Maltz, *Uniform Crime Reports*).

31. U.S. Department of Justice, Bureau of Justice Statistics, *Homicide Trends in the United States: Trends by City Size*, available at http://www.ojp.usdoj.gov/bjs/homicide/city.htm (last accessed March 22, 2005).

32. See Bedau, *Death Penalty in America;* Sellin, *Capital Punishment* and *Penalty of Death.*

33. Isaac Ehrlich, "The Deterrent Effect of Capital Punishment: A Question of Life or Death," 65 *American Economic Review* 397 (1975).

34. *Fowler v. North Carolina,* 428 U.S. 904 (1976). In *Gregg,* 428 U.S. 168, the Court considered deterrence to be one of the social purposes served by capital punishment. They were undoubtedly swayed by Ehrlich's study, which was the only available evidence supporting the deterrence hypothesis, whereas numerous other studies refuted the proposition. The Court stated that "[a]lthough some of the studies suggest that the death penalty may not function as a significantly greater deterrent than lesser penalties, there is no convincing empirical evidence either supporting or refuting this view" (185). Finding the statistical evidence to be inconclusive, the Court relied on a commonsense approach in support of deterrence:

> We may nevertheless safely assume that there are murderers, such as those who act in passion, for whom the threat of death has little or no deterrent effect. But for many others the death penalty undoubtedly is a significant deterrent. There are carefully contemplated murders, such as murder for hire, where the possible penalty of death may well enter into the cold calculus that precedes the decision to act. (185–186).

35. See David C. Baldus and James W. L. Cole, "A Comparison of the Work of Thorsten Sellin and Isaac Ehrlich on the Deterrent Effect of Capital Punishment," 85 *Yale Law Journal* 170 (1975); William J. Bowers and Glenn Pierce, "The Illusion of Deterrence in Isaac Ehrlich's Research on Capital Punishment," 85 *Yale Law Journal* 187 (1975); Lawrence R. Klein et al., "The Deterrent Effect of Capital Punishment: An Assessment of Estimates," in *Deterrence and Incapacitation: Estimating the Effects of Criminal Sanctions on Crime Rates,* ed. Alfred Blumstein et al. (Washington, D.C.: National Academy of Sciences, 1978), 331.

36. Isaac Ehrlich, "Capital Punishment and Deterrence: Some Further Thoughts and Additional Evidence," 85 *Journal of Political Economy* 741 (1977).

37. See D. Beyleveld, "Ehrlich's Analysis of Deterrence," 22 *British Journal of Criminology* 101 (1982); Arnold Barnett, "The Deterrent Effect of Capital Punishment: A Test of Some Recent Studies," 29 *Operations Research* 341 (1981); Lawrence M. Friedman, "The Use of Multiple Regression Analysis to Test for a Deterrent Effect of Capital Punishment: Prospects and Problems," in *Criminology Review Yearbook,* ed. S. Messinger and E. Bittner (Beverly Hills, Calif.: Sage, 1979); Richard M. McGahey, "Dr. Ehrlich's Magic Bullet: Economic Theory, Econometrics, and the Death Penalty," 26 *Crime and Delinquency* 485 (1980).

38. Finding no evidence for deterrence were William C. Bailey, "Murder and Capital Punishment: Some Further Evidence," 45 *American Journal of Orthopsychiatry* 669 (1975); William C. Bailey, "Imprisonment vs. the Death Penalty as a Deterrent to Murder," 1 *Law and Human Behavior* 239 (1977); Brian Forst, "The Deterrent Effect of Capital Punishment: A Cross-State Analysis of the 1960s," 61 *Minnesota Law Review* 743 (1977); Peter Passell, "The Deterrent Effect of the Death Penalty: A Statistical Test," 28 *Stanford Law Review* 61 (1975). Finding evidence in support of the deterrence hypothesis were Dale Cloninger, "Deterrence and the Death Penalty: A Cross-Sectional Analysis," 6 *Journal of Behavioral Economics* 87 (1977); and James Yunker, "Is the Death Penalty a Deterrent to Homicide? Some Time Series Evidence," 5 *Journal of Behavioral Economics* 45 (1976). Cloninger's work was discredited by William J. Boyes and Lee R. McPheters, "Capital Punishment as a Deterrent to Violent Crime: Cross-Sectional

Evidence," 6 *Journal of Behavioral Science* 67 (1977); and by McGahey, "Ehrlich's Magic Bullet," 497–499. Yunker's work was discredited by James A. Fox, "The Identification and Estimation of Deterrence: An Evaluation of Yunker's Model," 6 *Journal of Behavioral Economics* 225 (1977); and by Michael Sesnowitz and David L. McKee, "On the Deterrent Effect of Capital Punishment," 6 *Journal of Behavioral Economics* 217 (1977).

39. See Dale Cloninger, "Capital Punishment and Deterrence: A Portfolio Approach," 24 *Applied Economics* 645 (1992); Steve Layson, "Homicide and Deterrence: A Reexamination of the United States Time-Series Evidence," 52 *Southern Economic Journal* 68 (1985); Yunker, "Death Penalty a Deterrent?" For a review of econometric studies up to that time, see Samuel Cameron, "A Review of the Econometric Evidence on the Effects of Capital Punishment," 23 *Journal of Socio-Economics* 197 (1994). But see also this work by a sociologist: Steven Stack, "Publicized Executions and Homicide, 1950–1980," 52 *American Sociological Review* 532 (1987).

40. See Layson, "Homicide and Deterrence"; James A. Yunker, "A New Statistical Analysis of Capital Punishment Incorporating Post-Moratorium Data," 82 *Social Science Quarterly* 297 (2001); and Cloninger, "Capital Punishment and Deterrence."

41. For a critique of Layson, "Homicide and Deterrence," see James A. Fox and Michael Radelet, "Persistent Flaws in Econometric Studies of the Deterrent Effect of the Death Penalty," 23 *Loyola of Los Angeles Law Review* 29 (1989); for a challenge to Stack, "Publicized Executions," see William C. Bailey and Ruth D. Peterson, "Murder and Capital Punishment: A Monthly Time-Series Analysis of Execution Publicity," 54 *American Sociological Review* 722 (1989).

42. See Peterson and Bailey, "An Effective Deterrent?"; Joan Petersilia, "Death Penalty Resolution Debated and Endorsed," 15 *Criminologist* 1 (1990).

43. Yunker, "New Analysis of Capital Punishment"; Dezhbakhsh et al., "Deterrent Effect? New Evidence"; Hashem Dezhbakhsh and Joanna M. Shepherd, "The Deterrent Effect of Capital Punishment: Evidence from a 'Judicial Experiment,'" July 2003, available at http://people.clemson.edu/~jshephe/CaPuJLE_submit.pdf (last accessed March 23, 2005; revised and resubmitted to the *Journal of Law and Economics*); Zhiqiang Liu, "Capital Punishment and the Deterrence Hypothesis: Some New Insights and Empirical Evidence," 30 *Eastern Economic Journal* 237 (2004); H. Naci Mocan and R. Kaj Gittings, "Getting Off Death Row: Commuted Sentences and the Deterrent Effect of Capital Punishment," 46 *Journal of Law and Economics* 453 (2003); Joanna M. Shepherd, "Murders of Passion, Execution Delays, and the Deterrence of Capital Punishment," 30 *Journal of Legal Studies* 283 (2004); Paul R. Zimmerman, "State Executions, Deterrence, and the Incidence of Murder," 7 *Journal of Applied Economics* 163 (2004).

44. Richard A. Berk, "New Claims about Executions and General Deterrence: Déjà Vu All Over Again?" *Journal of Empirical Legal Studies* (forthcoming), available at http://preprints.stat.ucla.edu/396/JELS.pap.pdf (last accessed March 23, 2005).

45. Dale Cloninger and Roberto Marchesini, "Execution and Deterrence: A Quasi-Controlled Group Experiment," 33 *Applied Economics* 569 (2001).

46. *Ex parte Davis,* 947 S.W.2d 216 (Tex. Crim. App. 1996).

47. Cloninger, "Capital Punishment and Deterrence"; Dale Cloninger and Roberto Marchesini, "Crime Betas: A Portfolio Measure of Criminal Activity," 76 *Social Science Quarterly* 634 (1995).

48. Cloninger and Marchesini, "Crime Betas," 637–638.

49. The general formula is $CR_j = a_j + b_j(CR_I) + e$, where CR_j is the percentage change in a particular crime and CR_I is the percentage change in the crime index. The slope of the line, b_j, is the crime beta, a_j is the intercept, and e is the error term. Here, the term "beta" denotes a standardization of the units of measure for the independent and dependent variables in terms of percentage change, rather than the usual social-science meaning of standardizing b coefficients by the variables' standard deviations (see Blalock, *Social Statistics*, 477–482).

50. The specific formula was expressed thus: $\delta H_{tx} = a + b(\delta H_{us}) + e$; where δH_{tx} and δH_{us} were the twelve-month percentage changes in the number of homicides in Texas and the United States, respectively; a was the intercept, b was the slope of the line (or beta), and e was the error term.

51. Stephen J. Brown and Jerold B. Warner, "Measuring Security Price Performance," 8 *Journal of Financial Economics* 205 (1980).

52. This resulted in the following equation: $\delta H_{tx} = -0.0249 + 1.419(\delta H_{us}) + e$, with an R^2 of 0.432 and standard error of the estimate of 0.141. The beta of 1.419 was statistically significant ($t = 7.3$). According to Cloninger and Marchesini, "In the sampled period, the derived beta coefficient indicates that homicide changes in Texas vary 1.42 times the corresponding U.S. changes. In other words, the changes in homicide in Texas are 1.42 times greater than those for the US and move in the same direction" ("Execution and Deterrence," 570).

53. They did this by inserting the actual twelve-month percentage changes in U.S. homicides into the equation as δH_{us}. Solving the equation resulted in the estimated percentage changes in Texas homicides (δH_{tx}) during the twenty-four-month period from January 1996 through December 1997. Cloninger and Marchesini then subtracted the estimated from the actual percentage changes in Texas homicides and used a t-test to determine whether the actual changes in Texas homicides were significantly different from those expected, relative to the changes in U.S. homicides.

54. To illustrate this calculation, May 1996 figures are taken from Table 1 of Cloninger and Marchesini, "Execution and Deterrence," 571. The actual percentage change in U.S. homicides (USHo) from May 1995 to May 1996 was -0.1640 (a 16.4 percent reduction). Substituting this figure into the equation resulted in the following expected percentage change in Texas homicides for May 1996: $\delta H_{tx} = -0.0249 + 1.419(-0.1640) + e$ = -0.2577. That is, given the prior relationship between homicides in the United States and homicides in Texas during 1989–1995, as well as the actual reduction of 16.4 percent in U.S. homicides from May 1995 to May 1996, Cloninger and Marchesini expected a reduction of 25.77 percent in Texas homicides during the same period. This estimated percentage change in Texas homicides (EsTXHo) was then subtracted from the actual change in Texas homicides (AcTXHo) from May 1995 to May 1996, which was 0.1880 (an 18.8 percent increase), resulting in a difference of 0.4457 (Act—Exp). To Cloninger and Marchesini, this indicated that Texas homicides were 44.57 percent higher than expected during the second month of the moratorium. With a t value of 3.170, it was also the largest difference between actual and expected twelve-month percentage changes in Texas homicides during the twenty-four months of the 1996–1997 series.

55. This figure comes from Cloninger and Marchesini, "Execution and Deterrence," 575, Table 5, which shows an additional cumulative 223.64 homicides occurring from April 1996 through December 1996, to which were added 30.67 expected from January through March (not tabled).

56. These rates represent the number of homicides per 100,000 population, and are calculated as follows: actual rates (1,476 homicides/19,128,000 population x 100,000 = 7.716) versus expected rates (1,222/19,128,000 x 100,000 = 6.388).

57. Unlike the estimation procedure used by Cloninger and Marchesini for 1997, which readjusted for the actual number of Texas homicides in 1996 (N = 1,476), this calculation derived estimated decreases in Texas homicides for 1997 from the expected figures for 1996 (N = 1,222). Using this method, the number of Texas homicides for 1997 was expected to decrease to 1,099, for a rate of 5.7 (1,099 homicides/19,439,000 population x 100,000 = 5.653).

58. This resulted in the following equation; δH_{tx} = -0.0066 + 1.180(δH_{us}) + e, with an R^2 of 0.599 and a standard error of the estimate of 0.0602. The beta coefficient of 1.180 was statistically significant (t = 7.0; p < .001) and shows that for every percentage change in U.S. homicides over the thirty-five-year period, Texas homicides changed 1.18 percent in same direction. Similarly stated, for every 10 percent change in the occurrence of U.S. homicides, there was a corresponding change of nearly 12 percent in the number of Texas homicides. Solving the equation by entering the actual changes in U.S. homicides into it produced the following estimated changes in Texas homicides: EsTXHo 1996, δH_{tx} = -0.0066 + 1.180(-0.0907) + e = -0.1136; EsTXho 1997, δH_{tx} = -0.0066 + 1.180(-0.0733) + e = -0.0913.

59. Cloninger and Marchesini, "Execution and Deterrence," 570.

60. Cloninger and Marchesini supplied the authors with their monthly homicide data.

61. For the estimated total number of homicides, see Maltz, *Uniform Crime Reports*. The percentage distribution of homicides by month was obtained from Table 2.3 in the *Crime in the United States* series. Since the percentage distributions were presented only to the first decimal place, the derived monthly homicides figures, when summed, may differ slightly from the FBI's total estimated homicides for the year.

62. This resulted in the following equation: δH_{tx} = -0.0206 + 1.653(δH_{us}) + e, with an R^2 of 0.473 and a standard error of the estimate of 0.1355. The beta coefficient of 1.653 (t = 7.9; p < .001) represents an even larger fluctuation in Texas homicides relative to U.S. homicides than Cloninger and Marchesini's beta of 1.419. For every 10 percent change in the number of U.S. homicides, there was a corresponding 16.5 percent change in the number of Texas homicides during 1989–1995.

63. Cochran, "Deterrence or Brutalization?"; Bailey, "Disaggregation in Deterrence"; Bowers and Pierce, "Deterrence or Brutalization."

64. Cloninger, "Capital Punishment and Deterrence."

65. Cloninger and Marchesini, "Execution and Deterrence."

66. For the exercise carried out herein, the FBI's violent-crime index was determined to be a more appropriate composite for predicting changes in Texas homicides during the same period. The total-crime index proved inappropriate for modeling changes in Texas homicides during 1989–1995; changes in overall index crimes during this period bore little relationship to changes in homicides (R^2 = .114). Regressing the percentage change in Texas homicides against the percentage change in Texas violent crimes during 1989–1995 resulted in the following equation: δH_{tx} = -0.0417 + 1.214(δV_{tx}) + e, with an R^2 of 0.442 and a standard error of the estimate of 0.1392. In this model, the beta coefficient of 1.214 (t = 7.451; p < .001) indicates that Texas homicides fluctuate 12 percent for every 10 percent change in Texas violent crimes.

Again, necessary adjustments were made to the model. Adjustment for autocorrelation was not necessary (DW = 1.934; n.s.), but the normality assumption may have been violated by two outliers having studentized residuals greater than 3.0. Excluding these outliers from the model resulted in the following equation: δH_{tx} = -0.0498 + 1.004(δV_{tx}) + e. Making this correction had little effect on the number of additional homicides: the cumulative total would change from -121.96 (as presented) to -94.16 (using the outlier-excluding model).

67. Audiotapes: Public Hearing on HB 200.

68. See John E. Conklin, *Why Crime Rates Fell* (Boston: Allyn and Bacon, 2003); Alfred Blumstein and Joel Wallman, eds., *The Crime Drop in America* (New York: Cambridge Univ. Press, 2000).

Chapter 3

1. Audiotapes: Public Hearing on HB 200.

2. Kim Smith, "Serial Killer Lives with Murderous Past," *Odessa American*, Feb. 1, 1999; available at http://www.oaoa.com/twentieth/century1970a.htm (last accessed March 22, 2005).

3. *Furman*, 408 U.S. 238.

4. Audiotapes: Public Hearing on HB 200.

5. "There is no disputing that this Court's decision in *Eddings* requires that in capital cases 'the sentencer . . . not be precluded from considering, as a mitigating factor, any aspect of a defendant's character or record and any of the circumstances of the offense that the defendant proffers as a basis for a sentence less than death.' *Eddings*, supra, at 110 (quoting *Lockett*, supra, at 604 (plurality opinion of BURGER, C. J.)) (emphasis in original). Equally clear is the corollary rule that the sentencer may not refuse to consider or be precluded from considering 'any relevant mitigating evidence.' 455 U.S. at 114." *Skipper v. South Carolina*, 476 U.S. 1, 4–5 (1986).

6. Mark D. Cunningham and Thomas J. Reidy, "Don't Confuse Me with the Facts: Common Errors in Violence Risk Assessment at Capital Sentencing," 26 *Criminal Justice and Behavior* 20 (1999).

7. *Texas Code of Criminal Procedure Annotated*, art. 37.071 (West 1985); *Oregon Revised Statutes*, sec. 163.150 (1997). Oregon adopted the Texas format in 1984. Since 1977, prosecutors in Virginia have been given the option of presenting the jury with a question on the defendant's potential for future dangerousness *or* the heinousness of the offense:

> In assessing the penalty of any person convicted of an offense for which the death penalty may be imposed, a sentence of death shall not be imposed unless the court or jury shall (1) after consideration of the past criminal record of convictions of the defendant, find that there is a probability that the defendant would commit criminal acts of violence that would constitute a continuing threat to society *or* that his conduct in committing the offense for which he stands charged was outrageously or wantonly vile, horrible or inhuman in that it involved torture, depravity of mind or an aggravated battery to the victim; and (2) recommend that the penalty of death be imposed.

Virginia Code Annotated, SEC. 19.2-264.2 (MICHIE 1999; EMPHASIS ADDED)

8. *Texas Code of Criminal Procedure Annotated,* art. 37.071, sec. 2(b)(1) (West 2001).

9. Sally Costanzo and Mark Costanzo, "Life or Death Decisions: An Analysis of Capital Jury Decision-Making under the Special Issues Sentencing Framework," 18 *Law and Human Behavior* 151 at 168 (1994). See also Craig Haney et al., "Deciding to Take a Life: Capital Juries, Sentencing Instructions, and the Jurisprudence of Death," 50 *Journal of Social Issues* 149 (1994).

10. James Marquart et al., "Gazing into the Crystal Ball: Can Jurors Accurately Predict Dangerousness in Capital Cases?" 23 *Law and Society Review* 449 (1989).

11. See Deon Brock et al., "Tinkering with the Machinery of Death: An Analysis of the Impact of Legislative Reform on the Sentencing of Capital Murderers in Texas," 28 *Journal of Criminal Justice* 343 (2000).

12. See *Penry,* 492 U.S. 302; *Barefoot v. Estelle,* 463 U.S. 880 (1983); *Jurek,* 428 U.S. 262.

13. See Grant Wardlaw and David Biles, *The Management of Long-Term Prisoners in Australia* (Canberra: Australian Institute of Criminology, 1980).

14. Timothy J. Flanagan, "Time Served and Institutional Misconduct: Patterns of Involvement in Disciplinary Infractions among Long-Term and Short-Term Inmates," 8 *Journal of Criminal Justice* 357 (1980).

15. A. P. Merillat, *Future Danger?* 2nd ed. (Austin: Texas District and County Attorneys Association, 2000), 32–33.

16. James Marquart and Jon Sorensen, "A National Study of the *Furman*-Commuted Inmates: Assessing the Threat to Society from Capital Offenders," 23 *Loyola of Los Angeles Law Review* 5 (1989).

17. James Marquart and Jon Sorensen, "Institutional and Post-Release Behavior of *Furman*-Commuted Inmates in Texas," 26 *Criminology* 677 (1988).

18. "Kenneth Allen McDuff (USA)," The New Criminologist, available at http://www.thecriminologist.com/new_criminologist/volume1/portrait_serial/portrait_serial.asp (last accessed March 22, 2005).

19. "Executed Offenders," Texas Department of Criminal Justice, available at http://www.tdcj.state.tx.us/stat/executedoffenders.htm (last updated March 16, 2005).

20. ([21/470] x 100). Mark D. Cunningham and Thomas J. Reidy, "Integrating Base Rate Data in Violence Risk Assessments at Capital Sentencing," 16 *Behavioral Sciences and the Law* 71 (1998), referring to Marquart and Sorensen, "Post-Release Behavior."

21. See Cunningham and Reidy, "Violence Risk Assessments"; Marquart and Sorensen, "Post-Release Behavior."

22. See Marquart, "Crystal Ball." Two prisoners were directly released from death row into the outside community.

23. This figure is not directly comparable to that of the *Furman*-commuted inmates reported in Marquart and Sorensen, "Post-Release Behavior," however, because of a more restrictive inclusion of only acts of serious violence and the exclusion of other serious rule violations that did not result in a violent outcome.

24. Merillat, *Future Danger?*

25. For example, assaults such as throwing food at a guard or an inmate were not included as assaults in previous studies, although inmates are often written up as having "assaulted" someone by doing this. The definition of assault can significantly impact reported rates of violence. Starting in March 2001, the Texas Department of Criminal Justice (TDCJ) began disaggregating the broad category of staff assaults, separating

those that resulted in injuries that required treatment beyond first aid. Of the 4,381 disciplinary convictions for staff assaults in 2002, only 54 resulted in treatment beyond first aid (TDCJ, "Executive Services—September 2003," cited in Mark D. Cunningham, Jon R. Sorensen, and Thomas J. Reidy, "Revising Future Dangerousness Revisited: Response to DeLisi and Munoz," 15 *Criminal Justice Policy Review* 365 [2004]).

26. *Beltran v. State*, 728 S.W.2d 382 (Tex. Crim. App. 1987).

27. The provision including inmates killing other inmates was not added to the statute until 1993. See *Texas Penal Code Annotated*, sec. 19.03(a)(6), Historical and Statutory Notes, Acts 1993, 73rd Leg., ch. 715 (West 1993).

28. *Texas Penal Code Annotated*, sec. 19.03(a)(3) (Vernon 1974).

29. *Beltran v. State*, No. 70,888 (Tex. Crim. App., Apr. 28, 1993; not designated for publication).

30. *Stogsdill v. State*, 552 S.W.2d 481 (Tex. Crim. App. 1977).

31. Merillat, *Future Danger?*, 7.

32. Ibid. See also TDCJ, "Executed Offenders"; and TDCJ, "Offenders on Death Row," available at http://www.tdcj.state.tx.us/stat/offendersondrow.htm (last updated March 23, 2005).

33. Jon Sorensen and James Marquart, "Working the Dead," in *Facing the Death Penalty: Essays on Cruel and Unusual Punishment*, ed. Michael Radelet (Philadelphia: Temple Univ. Press, 1989), 169.

34. TDCJ, "Death Row Facts," available at http://www.tdcj.state.tx.us/stat/drowfacts.htm (last updated Dec. 19, 2003).

35. TDCJ, "Offenders No Longer on Death Row," available at http://www.tdcj.state.tx.us/stat/permanentout.htm (last updated Feb. 9, 2005).

36. "Texas Seven Murder Case," *CourtTV.com*, available at http://www.courttv.com/trials/texas7 (Courtroom Television Network, LLC, 2002) (last accessed March 23, 2005).

37. American Correctional Association, "Survey Summary: Riots, Disturbances, Violence, Assaults, and Escapes," 27 *Corrections Compendium* 6, 19 (2002).

38. John Monahan, *Predicting Violent Behavior: An Assessment of Clinical Techniques* (Beverly Hills, Calif.: Sage, 1981).

39. Cunningham and Reidy, "Don't Confuse Me."

40. The hypothetical is necessary because defendants may not want to be interviewed, knowing that anything they say to a state psychiatrist can be used against them in the punishment phase of a capital trial. See *Estelle*, 451 U.S. 454.

41. *Boulware v. Texas*, No. 52,139 (Tex. Crim. App. 1991 [1974]).

42. *Rodriguez v. Texas*, No. 62,274 (Tex. Crim. App. 1978).

43. Cited in Ron Rosenbaum, "Travels with Dr. Death," *Vanity Fair*, May 1990, 166.

44. Gregg Barak, "Media, Crime, and Justice: A Case for Constitutive Criminology," in *Cultural Criminology*, ed. Jeff Ferrell and Clinton R. Sanders (Boston: Northeastern Univ. Press, 1995), 142.

45. See David J. Cooke, "The Development of the Prison Behavior Rating Scale," 25 *Criminal Justice and Behavior* 482 (1998); Kevin S. Douglas and Christopher D. Webster, "The HCR-20 Violence Risk Assessment Scheme: Concurrent Validity in a Sample of Incarcerated Offenders," 26 *Criminal Justice and Behavior* 3 (1999).

46. John Monahan, "Violence Prediction: The Past Twenty and the Next Twenty Years," 23 *Criminal Justice and Behavior* 107 (1996).

47. Paul Meehl, *Clinical vs. Statistical Prediction: A Theoretical Analysis and a Review of the Evidence* (Minneapolis: Univ. of Minnesota Press, 1954), 3–4.

48. See Robert P. Cooper and Paul D. Werner, "Predicting Violence in Newly Admitted Inmates: A Lens Model Analysis of Staff Decision Making," 17 *Criminal Justice and Behavior* 431 (1990); Jon L. Proctor, "Evaluating a Modified Version of the Federal Prison System's Inmate Classification Model: An Assessment of Objectivity and Predictive Validity," 21 *Criminal Justice and Behavior* 256 (1994).

49. See *Pugh v. Locke*, 406 F.Supp. 318 (D. Ala. 1976); *Ramos v. Lamm*, 485 F.Supp. 122 (D. Colo. 1979).

50. Paul Gendreau et al., "Predicting Prison Misconducts," 24 *Criminal Justice and Behavior* 414 (1997); John D. Wooldredge, "Correlates of Deviant Behavior among Inmates of U.S. Correctional Facilities," 14 *Journal of Crime and Justice* 1–25 (1991).

51. Texas Senate, SB 145, 60th Leg., ch. 659, 1967.

52. William Bowers and Ben Steiner, "The Pernicious Illusion of Early Release for First Degree Murderers Not Sentenced to Death," a paper presented at the annual meeting of the American Society of Criminology (Chicago 1996).

53. Haney, "Deciding to Take a Life."

54. Costanzo and Costanzo, "Life or Death Decisions."

55. *Texas Government Code Annotated*, sec. 508.145(b) (Vernon 2002).

56. *Texas Legislature Online*, available at http://www.capitol.state.tx.us/cgi-bin/db2www/tlo/billhist/actions.d2w/report?LEG=77&SESS=R&CHAMBER=S&BILLTYPE=B&BILLSUFFIX=00085 (last accessed March 22, 2005).

57. *Simmons v. South Carolina*, 512 U.S. 154, 163 (1994).

58. *Brown v. Texas*, 118 S.Ct. 366 (1997).

59. *Texas Code of Criminal Procedure Annotated*, art. 37.071, sec. 2(e)(2)(B) (West 2001).

60. Kathleen Maguire and Ann L. Pastore, *Sourcebook of Criminal Justice Statistics, 1996*, U.S. Department of Justice, Office of Justice Programs, Bureau of Justice Statistics (Washington, D.C., 1997).

61. American Correctional Association, "Riots, Disturbances, Violence," 7.

62. FBI, *Crime in the United States, 2000*, Table 1, available at http://www.fbi.gov/ucr/oocius.htm (last accessed March 22, 2005).

63. FBI, *Law Enforcement Officers Killed and Assaulted*, available at http://www.fbi.gov/ucr/ucr.htm#leoka (last accessed March 22, 2005).

64. Jon Sorensen and Robert Wrinkle, "No Hope for Parole: Disciplinary Infractions among Death-Sentenced and Life-without-Parole Inmates," 23 *Criminal Justice and Behavior* 542, 548 (1996); Wendy P. Wolfson, "The Deterrent Effect of the Death Penalty upon Prison Murder," in *The Death Penalty in America*, 3rd ed., ed. Hugo Bedau (New York: Oxford Univ. Press, 1982), 168; Marquart and Sorensen, "*Furman*-Commuted Inmates," 5, 19–21; Thomas J. Reidy et al., "From Death to Life: Prison Behavior of Former Death Row Inmates in Indiana," 28 *Criminal Justice and Behavior* 62, 70 (2001).

65. Reidy, "Death to Life," 73; Jon Sorensen et al., "Patterns of Rule-Violating Behaviors and Adjustment to Incarceration among Murderers," 78 *Prison Journal* 222, 228–229 (1998).

66. Since Texas does not prosecute those under seventeen as capital defendants, only inmates who were at least seventeen when entering prison were included in the sample.

Those convicted of manslaughter were excluded from the sample as well, but they were used to test the validity of the prediction instrument. Also, only those murderers who entered prison from January 1990 through December 1998 were included. Inmates incarcerated before 1990 were excluded for two reasons. First, the best-behaved prisoners in the earlier cohort could have been released from confinement, resulting in sample-selection bias. Second, the reliability of computerized information on disciplinary infractions occurring before the TDCJ's coming online in 1989 is questionable. Inmates entering prison in 1999 were not included so that a minimum follow-up period of three months would be possible. Inmates sentenced to death were excluded from the sample because they were housed under more stringent conditions than most of the other murderers serving time in the TDCJ.

67. If a weapon was involved, the offense was considered violent because of the imminent possibility that injury could occur, even when no serious bodily injuries were sustained. Some level 1 rule violations were specified generically as any act defined by Texas law as a felony. In these instances, inmate folders were consulted to determine the exact nature of the offense. Conviction data were also examined, since the standard practice of the TDCJ is to prosecute and convict inmates for further assaultive offenses committed while confined. See David Eichenthal and James B. Jacobs, "Enforcing the Criminal Law in State Prisons," 8 *Justice Quarterly* 283 (1991). Unspecified level 1 rule violations and convictions were generally assaults on guards. Together, these official records were used to determine the extent of violent acts perpetrated against the staff at the Institutional Division (ID) of the TDCJ.

68. Personal characteristics included military service, branch of military served in, type of discharge from the military, gang membership, IQ score, educational attainment score, educational level, sex, race, ethnicity, citizenship, marital status, religion, and age. Criminal history included the number of arrests, convictions, juvenile confinements, probated sentences, TDC confinements, other prison confinements, and total prior prison terms. Offense-related information included the number of victims; the presence of contemporaneous attempted murders, assaults, burglaries, robberies, sexual assaults, arsons, or drug crimes; the involvement of alcohol or drugs; the county of conviction; and the degree of the murder conviction. Offense information on the following variables was available for a subsample of inmates: the cause of death (gunshot, stabbing, bludgeoning, strangulation, or other), the number of perpetrators, the age and sex of the victims, and the relation of the victim to the offender.

69. Table 3.1 includes violent acts committed by capital and noncapital murderers. Analyzing the incidence of violence separately for capital murderers versus murderers showed that capital murderers were less likely than murderers to be involved in violence (7.2 percent versus 8.6 percent, $\psi^2 = 1.90$, $p = .168$), though the difference was not statistically significant. This counterintuitive finding is consistent with the frequency of violence as well, with a mean of .09 for capital murderers and .12 for murderers ($t = 1.83$, $p = .068$). As noted in Table 3.2, the differences in prison violence between capital and noncapital murderers are due to factors unrelated to their crime of conviction, although some elements of capital murder, such as a contemporaneous robbery (or burglary) or the killing of multiple victims, are influential determinants.

70. Figure 3.1 was plotted using a Cox regression model, which held constant all other factors found to be significantly related to violence. Cox regression is a procedure within the broader category of survival analysis, which generates estimates of the prob-

ability of surviving based on the characteristics and patterns of those failing and the length of time to fail.

71. This probability was estimated using information on murderers received at the TDCJ-ID during 1985–1989. Their likelihood of committing a violent act during their first five years of incarceration was estimated to be .079, based on the behavior of those serving their first five years during the 1990s. The observed probability of violence among those inmates serving their sixth through fifteenth years of incarceration during the 1990s was .127. These figures are not additive, however, since a number of inmates committing acts during the 1990s were repeat-offending.

After estimating recidivism at 33.1 percent from the 1990s data, the rate of new violence among those who served their sixth through fifteenth years during the 1990s can be estimated to be .085 (.127 x .669). By adding .085, the probability that violence will occur during the sixth through fifteenth years, to .079, the estimated probability that violence will occur during the first five years, the estimated likelihood of violence occurring during the fifteen years of incarceration becomes .164. This is an extremely liberal estimate of violence occurring over a fifteen-year term because the best-behaved murderers incarcerated in the late 1980s have been released from prison.

It is nearly impossible to use the data on those incarcerated longer than fifteen years because of sample-selection bias inherent in the sample. However, given the effects of aging, institutional controls for violence, and general trends observed elsewhere, the odds of an inmate becoming involved in an initial act of violence after being incarcerated for fifteen years is extremely low. Given that the previous fifteen-year estimate was constructed liberally, and the rarity of inmates being initiated into violence after fifteen years, the estimate of .164 will be used for the entire forty-year term.

72. This model was estimated using logistic regression ($-2LL$ Change = 280.940; $p < .001$). The percentages, more correctly referred to as predicted proportional changes, were calculated from the logistic regression coefficients in an effort to make them more easily interpreted. The predicted proportional change is derived from Petersen's formula: $\exp(L_1)/[1 + \exp(L_1)] - \exp(L_0)/[1 + \exp(L_0)]$, where L_0 is the logit before the unit change in x_j; $L_1 = L_0 + B_j$ and is the logit after the unit change in x_j (Trond Petersen, "A Comment on Presenting Results from Logit and Probit Models," 50 *American Sociological Review* 130, 131 [1985]). The expected proportion of inmates' involvement in violence was chosen as the comparison point before and after adding the effects of the parameters; hence, L_0 is calculated using the formula $\ln[p/(1-p)]$, where $p = .164$.

The unstandardized regression coefficients were as follows: robbery/burglary, .464; multiple victims, .365; attempted murder/assault, .265; gang membership, .622; prior prison term, .346; age less than 21, .359; age 26 through 30, -.454; age 31 through 35, -.635; and age over 35, -.819. The results from the Cox regression model used to estimate Figure 3.1 were essentially similar to those presented in Table 3.2 in magnitude and significance. The estimates from logistic regression are preferred in calculating the actuarial model; the concern is with the concept of failure, or the commission of a violent act, a dichotomous variable, rather than the time to failure, a continuous variable that is modeled by Cox regression.

73. Projected probabilities were estimated, essentially doubled, from their actual incidence of engaging in violence over an average time served of 4.5 years. See n. 71 to this chapter and the accompanying text.

74. Michael Radelet and James Marquart, "Assessing Non-Dangerousness during Penalty Phases of Capital Trials," 54 *Albany Law Review* 845 (1990).

Chapter 4

1. Audiotape of public hearing on HB 945.
2. *Gregg*, 428 U.S. 153.
3. *Furman*, 408 U.S. 238.
4. *Sourcebook of Criminal Justice Statistics, 2002*, ed. Kathleen Maguire and Ann L. Pastore, available at http://www.albany.edu/sourcebook/ (last accessed March 23, 2005). The corresponding figures for 1966 were 47 percent answering "no, not in favor" and 11 percent having "no opinion"; in 1972 the figures were 41 percent answering "no, not in favor" and 9 percent having "no opinion."
5. Dennis Longmire and Scott Vollum, "Attitudes about Crime and Criminal Justice Policy in Texas: Special Legislative Report—*2003 Texas Crime Poll Special Legislative Survey*," available at http://www.shsu.edu/~icc_drl/2003_Legislative_Report.html (last accessed March 22, 2005).
6. *Sourcebook of Criminal Justice Statistics, 2002*.
7. *Furman*, 408 U.S. at 310.
8. Ibid. at 253.
9. In order to meet the demands of the Court, states reenacting capital punishment statutes in the wake of *Furman* sought to make the application of the death penalty consistent, either by mandating death upon conviction for certain offenses or by guiding the discretion of jurors. In a series of cases decided in 1976, the Court struck down mandatory statutes, holding that sentencers must be allowed to consider the individual circumstances of the crime and the culpability of the defendant in making their punishment determination (*Roberts*, 428 U.S. 325; *Woodson*, 428 U.S. 280). The Court upheld guided-discretion statutes, reasoning that these statutes would prevent the arbitrary imposition of the death penalty while still allowing for individualized consideration. See *Profitt*, 428 U.S. 242; *Jurek*, 428 U.S. 262; *Gregg*, 428 U.S. 153.

In a series of cases, the Court has held that jurors must be allowed to consider and give weight to any evidence that could be considered mitigating. This mandate that statutes allow for individualized consideration, and yet apply the death penalty consistently, has been a source of major tension in post-*Furman* jurisprudence. See Justice Blackmun's dissent from certiorari in *Callin v. Collins*, 510 U.S. 1141 (1994). Nonetheless, the Court has remained involved in refining the appropriateness of capital punishment for particular types of crimes and defendants' particular circumstances. The Court has also categorically excluded crimes involving particular circumstances and defendants with certain characteristics from eligibility for the death penalty. For instance, the Court has held that imposing the death penalty for raping but not murdering an adult woman was excessive (*Coker v. Georgia*, 433 U.S. 584 [1977]).

10. Although the Court viewed this procedure favorably in *Gregg*, they have not required it of states (*Pulley v. Harris*, 465 U.S. 37 [1984]).
11. See Baldus et. al, *Equal Justice and the Death Penalty: A Legal and Empirical Analysis* (Boston: Northeastern Univ. Press, 1990).

12. Jordan Steiker and Carol Steiker, "Judicial Developments in Capital Punishment Law," in Acker, *America's Experiment*, 157, 177.

13. Samuel R. Gross and Robert Mauro, "Patterns of Death: An Analysis of Racial Disparities in Capital Sentencing and Homicide Victimization," 37 *Stanford Law Review* 27 (1984).

14. The pool of homicides used in this analysis was restricted to those committed since the statutory definition of capital murder last changed, effective at the beginning of 1994. To allow for enough follow-up time for determining whether the cases actually resulted in death, the pool was further limited to those murders committed through 2000. Ideally, the pool of arrests should also have been restricted to those that could conceivably be considered death eligible.

One drawback to using data from the Supplemental Homicide Reports is that they include all homicide arrests, including many that do not necessarily carry the requisite culpability to be considered murder. However, it was possible to identify, in the SHR data, some cases that did not involve intentional homicide, such as negligent manslaughters, other types of accidental deaths, and justifiable homicides (i.e., the killing of felons by police officers and citizens), and remove them from further consideration.

The same problem arises in determining whether the crimes meet the statutory criteria for capital murder, since most categories of capital murder are not readily matched against the categories in the dataset. Again, however, some cases can be removed that are clearly not death eligible. Because Texas law provides for capital punishment only in cases where a defendant is at least seventeen at the time of the offense, all cases of offenders known to be sixteen or younger at the time of the offense were excluded from further analysis.

The SHR data were then aggregated to the level of the incident, with information for multiple offenders and victims combined within each incident. Theoretically, it is possible for any offender-victim combination to result in a death sentence: if there were two offenders and two victims, there could be four death sentences. In practice, however, an incident typically results in only one death sentence, regardless of the number of victims or offenders.

15. By May 30, 2003, thirteen cases had resulted in two death sentences, one case in three death sentences, and one case in four death sentences. Of course, the matching process did not always produce perfect matches. Sometimes the police's classification of a characteristic of a case differed from the description in the prison records from which data were gathered. In these instances, the original coding was rechecked, and alternate sources, such as appellate records and newspaper articles, were used to try to verify the correct code. It was clear that in most instances the police department records were the least complete, having been filled out on the spot, so in most cases of discrepancies, the corrected codes from other sources were inserted. This, of course, raises questions about the validity of the SHR data. Four of the death-sentenced cases involving murders in prison also had to be excluded from this analysis because they had not been reported in the SHR data. Although the TDCJ did not report to the SHR program, some counties did, so institutional murders in county jails were reported. Hence, one death-sentenced case involving a murder in the El Paso County jail was matched to its appropriate record in the SHR.

16. Since the goal is to detect the strength of the relationship between those variables that are legitimately related to the sentence of death, those variables that were not

significant predictors were dropped from the regression analysis. One exception was the decision to include "other cause of death." Although the level of statistical significance was .17 in the reduced model presented in Table 4.2, it was kept in the model because it initially met the .05 level of significance in the full model and because the size of its logit coefficient suggested a strong relationship. Finally, the variable female defendant was dropped from the model because gender, although significant, is not generally considered a case characteristic that may legitimately be considered by prosecutors and jurors in their decision making. Additionally, there were few cases in which female defendants received death sentences, thereby reducing the reliability of findings for those cases.

17. The logistic regression coefficient refers to the log odds change in the dependent variable that results from a unit increase in the predictor variable, and as such is not directly interpretable. Once exponentiated, the logistic coefficient can be roughly interpreted as the simple odds change in the dependent variable for each unit change in the predictor variable. Often simply referred to as the "odds multiplier," this exponentiated logistic regression coefficient is presented in Table 4.2. The overall model was significant ($-2LL$ Change = 1127.751; $p < .001$). The unstandardized logistic regression coefficients and (standard errors) were as follows: robbery/burglary, 3.239 (.225), $p < .001$; sexual assault, 3.914 (.361), $p < .001$; other felony type, 1.834 (.305), $p < .001$; knife/cut, .467 (.238), $p < .05$; strangulation, 1.880 (.322), $p < .001$; bludgeoned, .472 (.234), $p < .05$; other cause of death, .835 (.621), $p = $ n.s.; multiple victims, 2.482 (.225), $p < .001$; multiple offenders .613 (.183), $p < .001$; female victim, .664 (.195), $p < .001$.

18. For example, a case involving a robbery or burglary was assigned a weight of 3.239, a sexual assault was assigned 3.914, and so on, for each successive characteristic present in the case. See the previous note for the unstandardized logistic regression coefficients.

19. The quality of the SHR data varies across jurisdictions, which raises concerns about the reliability of the reported data. This is particularly true for those data fields that leave much discretion to the police, who must make decisions on the spot and without the benefit of investigation or hindsight, such as whether the homicide involved a contemporaneous felony. Further, nearly one-half of the cases are missing information related to the offense circumstances or the offender. During the process of analyzing the SHR data, these missing data must be estimated, or the case must be dropped from the analysis.

20. See Baldus, *Equal Justice*.

21. See Arnold Barnett, "Some Distribution Patterns for the Georgia Death Sentence," 18 *Davis Law Review* 1327, 1352 (1985); Robert Weiss et al., "Death Penalty Charging in Los Angeles County: An Illustrative Data Analysis Using Skeptical Priors," 28 *Sociological Methods and Research* 91 (1999).

22. Because many of the predictor variables were specific to each defendant, the logistic regression analysis was computed for defendants ($N = 243$) rather than cases. The exception is the case of the Texas 7. So that this unique case would not bias the resulting equation, only the main defendant, George Rivas, was included in the analysis. A separate model that included all these defendants ($N = 248$) resulted in a similar equation; each predictor variable, other than "fugitive," had similar coefficients and overall better predictive power for the model as a whole.

The overall model included in Table 4.4 was significant ($-2LL$ Change = 101.928; $p < .001$). The unstandardized logistic regression coefficients and (standard errors) were as follows: robbery, .547 (.836); burglary, .716 (.824); sexual assault, 1.435 (.984); arson, -.404 (1.657); multiple victims 1.794 (.758); child under the age of 6, 1.335 (1.253); remuneration, 2.607 (1.481); police killing, 1.125 (1.379); prison 4.392 (1.788); kidnap, 2.398 (.816); obstruction/retaliation, 1.492 (1.528); gunshot, 2.818 (1.158); stab, -1.469 (1.373); bludgeon, 1.294 (1.025); mutilate, 3.803 (1.735); store, 1.037 (.777); victim/stranger, 1.416 (.786); victim/criminal activity, -1.723 (1.052); accomplice, -1.661 (.743); triggerman, 1.219 (1.238); prior homicide, 1.708 (.874); prior sexual assault, 4.265 (1.046); fugitive, 3.054 (2.311); constant = -7.747.

A reduced model was also calculated to test for the possibility that the full model presented herein was overdetermined. This parsimonious model was chosen from the larger model using a forward conditional selection process. If a given variable did not significantly add to the overall power of the model, it did not enter into the equation. The reduced model (-2LL Change = 121.357; p < .001) included the following unstandardized logistic regression coefficients and (standard errors): multiple victims 1.326 (.564); prison 2.337 (1.390); kidnap, 1.894 (.679); gunshot, 1.759 (.679); victim/stranger, 1.976 (.557); accomplice, -1.479 (.526); prior homicide, 1.825 (.721); prior sexual assault, 3.824 (.856); fugitive, 3.999 (1.875); constant = -4.788.

23. To do so, the coefficients for the predictor variables and the constant were summed for each case. Then, the summed measure was exponentiated to produce the odds of receiving a death sentence. Finally, the odds were transformed into probabilities using the following formula: p = odds/(1 + odds). This final measure is the predicted likelihood that a case with a given set of predictor variables will result in a death sentence.

24. See Richard M. McFall and Teresa A. Treat, "Quantifying the Information Value of Clinical Assessments with Signal Detection Theory," 50 *Annual Review of Psychology* 215 (1999).

25. *Roberts,* 428 U.S. 325; *Woodson,* 428 U.S. 280.

26. *Lockett v. Ohio,* 438 U.S. 586, 604 (1978; plurality opinion).

27. *Jurek,* 428 U.S. 262; *Penry,* 492 U.S. 302.

28. This change in the Texas statute did not occur before Penry's resentencing hearing. The trial judge, in an attempt to meet the Supreme Court's mandate, specifically instructed the jurors to consider Penry's mitigating circumstances. Since the statute had not yet changed, however, the judge told jurors that even if they answered all three special issues in the affirmative, they should change one of these answers to no if they did not believe, considering the mitigating circumstances, that Penry deserved a death sentence. This was indeed a "strange and anomalous" situation, in which the trial judge actually instructed the jury to disobey current law by falsifying a response to one of the special issues. See John Conrad, *Jury Nullification: The Evolution of a Doctrine* (Durham, N.C.: Carolina Academic Press, 1998). This valiant attempt at a remedy was again rejected by the Supreme Court, which held in *Penry v. Johnson,* 532 U.S. 782 (2001), that this instruction did not remedy the constitutional error in Penry's case, and remanded yet again.

29. TDCJ, "Offenders on Death Row."

30. *Atkins v. Virginia,* 536 U.S. 304 (2002).

31. The 2003 Gallup Poll showed that only 13 percent of respondents believed that the mentally retarded should be subject to executions (*Sourcebook of Criminal Justice Statistics, 2002*).

32. *Atkins,* 536 U.S. 304.

33. In only sixteen of the nineteen states that have passed legislation since *Penry* did the measure actually become law, bringing the number of death-penalty jurisdictions that ban the execution of the mentally retarded to eighteen. Nineteen jurisdictions still allowed the execution of the mentally retarded at the time of *Atkins.*

34. *Atkins,* 536 U.S. 304.

35. Death Penalty Information Center (DPIC) list, cited in *Atkins,* 536 U.S. at n. 20.

36. Veto proclamation for HB 236.

37. *Texas Code of Criminal Procedure Annotated,* art. 46.02(1)(A)(a) (West 2001).

38. Under the M'Naghten test, mentally disabled persons are exonerated from criminal responsibility. The court must consider under this test whether the defendant suffers from a defect of reason or from a disease of the mind that either prevents him from knowing the nature and quality of his acts or that clouds his judgment to such a degree that he is unaware that what he is doing is wrong. Though this test is used mainly in the area of insanity, it is equally applicable to mental retardation. See David Rumley, "A License to Kill: The Categorical Exemption of the Mentally Retarded from the Death Penalty," 24 *St. Mary's Law Journal* 1299, 1308, 1310 (1993); *Texas Penal Code Annotated,* sec. 8.01 (West 1994).

39. This level of intent is not required in cases of felony murder (*Texas Penal Code Annotated,* sec. 19.02b [West 1994]).

40. *Texas Code of Criminal Procedure Annotated,* art. 37.071 (West 2001).

41. *Ford v. Wainwright,* 477 U.S. 399 (1986); *Texas Code of Criminal Procedure Annotated,* art. 46.05(h) (West 2001).

42. DPIC list, cited in *Atkins* (see n. 35 above).

43. Rumley, "License to Kill," 1299, 1322.

44. Ibid., 1334–1336.

45. Ibid., 1338.

46. *Atkins,* 536 U.S. at 353–354.

47. American Association on Mental Retardation, *Mental Retardation: Definition, Classification, and Systems of Supports,* 9th ed. (Washington, D.C.: American Association on Mental Retardation, 1992), 5.

48. R. G. Ratcliffe, "Two Inmates on Death Row Given Reprieves," *Houston Chronicle,* March 13, 2004.

49. Sixty-nine percent of respondents indicated they did not favor the death penalty for juveniles; 26 percent said they did (*Sourcebook of Criminal Justice Statistics, 2002*).

50. Texas determinate sentences are part of a broader class of sanctions available to juveniles, generally referred to as blended sentences. Juveniles are sentenced to a number of years by the juvenile court. They serve their sentences in a juvenile-justice facility until they reach their majority, and may then be transferred to the Texas Department of Corrections to serve the remainder of their sentences. However, at a hearing before transfer, a juvenile-court judge determines whether the juvenile should in fact be transferred or be allowed to serve the remainder (the adult portion) of the sentence on parole.

51. Melissa Moon et al., "Putting Kids to Death: Specifying Public Support for Juvenile Capital Punishment," 17 *Justice Quarterly* 663 (2000). N. Finkel et al., "Killing Kids: The Juvenile Death Penalty and Community Sentiment," 12 *Behavioral Sciences and the Law* 5 (1994).

52. *Bell v. Ohio*, 438 U.S. 637 (1978).

53. *Lockett*, 438 U.S. 586, 604.

54. *Eddings v. Oklahoma*, 455 U.S. 104 (1982).

55. *Thompson v. Oklahoma*, 108 S.Ct. 2687 (1988).

56. Justice Kennedy joined the Court after oral arguments were made in this case and did not participate in the decision.

57. *Stanford v. Kentucky*, 492 U.S. 361 (1989).

58. *In re Stanford*, 537 U.S. 968 (2002).

59. *Roper v. Simmons*, 112 S.W.3d 397 (Mo. 2003).

60. Ibid., at 413.

61. The Supreme Court heard arguments in *Roper* on October 13, 2004, and issued its decision on March 1, 2005. The Court held, 5–4, that the "Eighth and Fourteenth Amendments forbid imposition of the death penalty on offenders who were under the age of 18 when their crimes were committed." See the Addendum at the end of this chapter for a discussion of the ruling.

62. *Trop v. Dulles*, 356 U.S. 86 (1958).

63. *Roper*, 112 S.W.3d at 412.

64. Joseph Hoffmann, "On the Perils of Line Drawing: Juveniles and the Death Penalty," 40 *Hastings Law Review* 229, 258 (1989).

65. Texas does not allow the execution of any offender who was younger than seventeen when the offense was committed.

66. "Capital Punishment, Juveniles and the Death Penalty," *#46: Death Penalty Websites*, available at http://www.geometry.net/detail/basic_c/capital_punishment_juveniles_&_death_penalty_page_no_3.html (last accessed March 22, 2005).

67. In February 2002, an appellate court determined that Martinez was not a danger to society and reduced his sentence to life in prison. However, disproportionality still exists in this case: the more culpable Venegas will be eligible for parole in a mere ten years, but Martinez must serve a mandatory minimum of forty years of his life sentence before becoming eligible for parole.

Chapter 5

1. *Furman*, 408 U.S. 238.

2. *Branch v. Texas*, 447 S.W.2d 932 (Tex. Crim. App. 1969).

3. *Furman*, 408 U.S. at 253.

4. Ibid. at 351, quoting Rupert Koeninger, "Capital Punishment in Texas, 1924–1968," 15 *Crime and Delinquency* 132, 141 (1969). For a discussion of racial concerns, see also the opinions of Justice Stewart at 306 and Justice White at 310.

5. Marvin E. Wolfgang and Marc Reidel, "Race, Judicial Discretion, and the Death Penalty," 407 *Annals of the American Academy of Political and Social Science* 119 (1973); Gary Kleck, "Racial Discrimination in Criminal Sentencing: A Critical Evaluation of the Evidence with Additional Evidence on the Death Penalty," 46 *American Sociological Review* 783 (1981).

6. U.S. Department of Justice, Law Enforcement Assistance Administration, National Prisoner Statistics Bulletin, *Capital Punishment, 1971–1972* (Washington, D.C., 1974).

7. James W. Marquart et al., *The Rope, the Chair, and the Needle: Capital Punishment in Texas, 1923–1990* (Austin: Univ. of Texas Press, 1994), 42, 48.

8. *Coker*, 433 U.S. 584.

9. Harold Garfinkel, "Research Note on Inter- and Intra-Racial Homicides," 27 *Social Forces* 369 (1949); Guy B. Johnson, "The Negro and Crime," 217 *Annals of the American Academy of Political and Social Science* 93 (1941).

10. Marquart, *Rope, Chair, and Needle*, 72, 77.

11. Deon Brock et al., "The Influence of Race on Prison Sentences for Murder in Twentieth-Century Texas," in *Practical Applications for Criminal Justice Statistics*, ed. Mark L. Dantzker et al. (Woburn, Mass.: Butterworth-Heinemann, 1998), 211.

12. Marvin E. Wolfgang et al., "Comparison of the Executed and the Commuted among Admissions to Death Row," 53 *Journal of Criminal Law, Criminology, and Police Science* 301 (1958); Elmer H. Johnson, "Selective Factors in Capital Punishment," 36 *Social Forces* 165 (1957).

13. For an overview of post-*Furman* studies up through the 1980s, see U.S. General Accounting Office, *Death Penalty Sentencing: Research Indicates Pattern of Racial Disparities*, Report to Senate and House Committees on the Judiciary (Feb. 1990).

14. See Jon Sorensen et al., "Empirical Studies on Race and Death Penalty Sentencing: A Decade after the GAO Report," 37 *Criminal Law Bulletin* 395 (2002).

15. See *McCleskey v. Kemp*, 481 U.S. 279 (1987; 5–4 decision).

16. Michael Radelet and Glenn Pierce, "Race and Prosecutorial Discretion in Homicide Cases," 19 *Law and Society Review* 587 (1985).

17. Jesse L. Jackson, Sr., and Bruce Shapiro, *Legal Lynching: The Death Penalty and America's Future* (New York: Random House, 2003).

18. James Alan Fox and Marianne W. Zawitz, *Homicide Trends in the United States*, U.S. Department of Justice, Bureau of Justice Statistics, available at http://www.ojp .usdoj.gov/bjs/homicide/homtrnd.htm (last accessed March 22, 2005).

19. William Wilbanks, *The Myth of a Racist Criminal Justice System* (Monterey, Calif.: Brooks-Cole, 1987).

20. Samuel R. Gross and Robert Mauro, "Patterns of Death: An Analysis of Racial Disparities in Capital Sentencing and Homicide Victimization," 37 *Stanford Law Review* 27 (1984); Baldus, *Equal Justice*.

21. The advantage to this method is its breadth, which generally includes the entire state over the course of many years. However, it suffers because of the relatively limited number of control variables available in the SHR. See Marian Williams and Jefferson Holcomb, "Racial Disparity and Death Sentences in Ohio," 29 *Journal of Criminal Justice* 207 (2001).

22. William Bowers and Glenn Pierce, "Arbitrariness and Discrimination under post-*Furman* Capital Statutes," 26 *Crime and Delinquency* 563, 596 (1980).

23. Sheldon Ekland-Olson, "Structured Discretion, Racial Bias, and the Death Penalty: The First Decade After *Furman* in Texas," 69 *Social Science Quarterly* 853 (1988).

24. The figure for blacks who killed whites (BkW) was significantly positive, indicating a predicted proportional increase in likelihood of a capital conviction of 7.5 percent. BkB (the figure for blacks who killed blacks) was significantly negative, as had been found by others performing similar studies, predicting a decrease of 5.1 percent. However, the figure for WkW (whites who killed whites) was the racial combination that had the most influence on capital-murder charging, predicting an increase of

10.5 percent. (This model included three racial combinations, BkW, WkW, and BkB; all other racial combinations served as the reference category). See Jon Sorensen and James Marquart, "Prosecutorial and Jury Decision-Making in Post-*Furman* Texas Capital Cases," 28 *Review of Law and Social Change* 743, 766 (1990–1991).

25. The main drawback to this method is the huge amount of manpower required to search individual case files; this usually results in a much more limited sample for the geographical area covered or the time frame examined. See David Baldus et al., "Racial Discrimination and the Death Penalty in the Post-*Furman* Era: An Empirical and Legal Overview, with Recent Findings from Philadelphia," 83 *Cornell Law Review* 1638 (1998).

26. See Sorensen and Marquart, "Prosecutorial and Jury Decision-Making." Sentencing studies that do not control for earlier charging decisions must be received cautiously, however, because of the potential for sample-selection bias. When less aggravated cases involving select racial categories routinely make it to the sentencing stage, but then result in sentences similar to those imposed on other racial categories, racial disparities resulting from earlier prosecutorial decisions become exacerbated during the sentencing process. Unless the prior probabilities of cases advancing to a given stage of case processing are controlled for, it is more difficult to detect the presence of racial disparities occurring during the sentencing phase or to accurately gauge their effects. In this case, although not statistically significant, the logistic regression coefficients suggested a pattern victim-based racial discrimination. It may well be that this race-of-victim effect would have become more pronounced at sentencing if the likelihood of certain types of cases—notably, killings of whites—reaching the stage of a penalty trial had been taken into consideration.

27. This information is based on the 2000 census. See U.S. Census Bureau, Census 2000 Data for the State of Texas, Texas Redistricting Data, Table 1. Population by Race and Hispanic or Latino Origin, for All Ages and for 18 Years and Over, for Texas: 2000, available at http://www.census.gov/census2000/states/tx.html (last accessed March 22, 2005).

28. This finding should be interpreted with caution because of the small number of such cases resulting in death sentences.

29. In measuring the effects of race on sentence, race is added into the model simultaneously with the other legitimate variables. This allows race variables the greatest possible chance of influencing the results: race variables are allowed to directly compete with the other case characteristics in explaining variance in death sentences, rather than being entered after the other legitimate case characteristics.

30. To estimate the effects of race in the logistic regression equation, a series of dummy variables indicating the presence of particular racial categories for offenders, victims, and offender-victim interactions had to be calculated. In estimating the logistic regression models, it was also necessary to exclude one or more of the racial categories because of the requirement that predictor variables not be perfectly correlated with one another. Including all the dummy variables would have resulted in near perfect multicollinearity among the predictor variables, making the coefficients impossible to interpret. The excluded dummy variables are not completely left out of the model, but instead serve as the referent for those dummy variables explicitly included. Because logistic regression coefficients are not directly interpretable, their exponents, more commonly referred to as odds multipliers, are presented in Table 5.2. They may be interpreted as

the increase in likelihood of a death sentence for a case with a particular characteristic, as compared to a case in the reference category (all other predictor variables in the model held constant).

31. But see, Weiss, "Death Penalty Charging."

32. By necessity, some categories are not explicitly included in the model, either because of the small number of homicide cases or the small number resulting in death for these categories. As such, all categories involving Asian offenders, along with the killing of blacks and Asians by whites, are relegated to the reference category. Cases involving interracial killings between blacks and Hispanics were also added to the reference category to stabilize comparisons among those explicitly included in the model. Although it is preferable to include all main effects and interaction terms (except for the exclusion of one reference category for each) in the model, doing so resulted in small cell sizes, which caused the model to become extremely unstable when attempts were made to include all of these terms. The size of the coefficients changed very little, and the direction of the relationships did not change at all, when main effects were added to the model (or when any particular interaction term was added), although most of the coefficients lost their statistical significance because of an increase in standard errors. This exercise of adding and subtracting main effects and interaction terms to the model confirmed that all significant categories were included and that their coefficients were stable; the model as presented is both optimal and robust.

33. Marc Riedel, "Counting Stranger Homicides: A Case Study of Statistical Prestidigitation," 2 *Homicide Studies* 206 (1998).

34. David Luckenbill, "Criminal Homicide as a Situated Transaction," 25 *Social Problems* 176 (1977); Marvin E. Wolfgang, *Patterns in Criminal Homicide* (Philadelphia: Univ. of Pennsylvania Press, 1958).

35. Harry Kalven and Hans Zeisel, *The American Jury* (Boston: Little, Brown, 1966), 165.

36. The liberation hypothesis has been tested in several studies of racial disparity in death sentencing. Baldus and colleagues found that in the least serious cases, according to their measure of culpability, defendants were not likely to get a death sentence regardless of their race or the race of the victim (*Equal Justice*). Similarly, in highly aggravated cases, prosecutors usually sought the death penalty, and jurors usually imposed it, regardless of the race of the offenders or the victims. It was in the intermediate range of cases, where the likelihood of receiving the death penalty amounted to a coin toss, that racial effects were the strongest. A re-analysis of sentencing in capital-murder cases in Georgia, using a different methodology, similarly found the following:

> Salient differences in the details of the killing of blacks and whites could, to a considerable extent, explain the higher rate of death sentences in the white-victim cases. But in a limited fraction of cases—exemplified by the robbery-killing of a merchant—the race of the victim might matter a great deal.
>
> ARNOLD BARNETT, "SOME DISTRIBUTION PATTERNS FOR THE GEORGIA DEATH SENTENCE," 18 *Davis Law Review* 1327, 1352 (1985).

37. Historically, the Harris County district attorney's office has employed a policy of zero tolerance for police killings, prosecuting all such murders as death-penalty cases.

This measure, which simply subsumes police killings within the category "Other Felony," thus underestimates the influence of this legally relevant case characteristic and identifies a potential weakness of relying on the SHR data.

38. See note 22, Chapter 4.

39. Illinois Governor's Commission on Capital Punishment, *Report of the Governor's Commission on Capital Punishment* (April 15, 2002), available at http://www.idoc.state.il.us/ccp/ccp/reports/index.html (last accessed March 22, 2005).

40. Marvin E. Wolfgang et al., *Delinquency in a Birth Cohort* (Chicago: Univ. of Chicago Press, 1972).

41. "James Hanratty: The Final Verdict," *BBC News* (May 10, 2002), available at http://news.bbc.co.uk/1/hi/wales/1977508.stm (last accessed March 22, 2005).

42. James Liebman et al., "A Broken System: Error Rates in Capital Cases, 1973–1995," available at http://ccjr.policy.net/cjedfund/jpreport/ (last accessed March 22, 2005).

43. See, for example, Talia Harmon, "Predictors of Miscarriages of Justice in Capital Cases," 18 *Justice Quarterly* 949 (2001).

44. Hugo Bedau and Michael Radelet, "Miscarriages of Justice in Potentially Capital Cases," 40 *Stanford Law Review* 21 (1987).

45. Michael Radelet et al., *In Spite of Innocence: Erroneous Convictions in Capital Cases* (Boston: Northeastern Univ. Press, 1992).

46. Stephen Markman and Paul Cassell, "Protecting the Innocent: A Response to the Bedau-Radelet Study," 41 *Stanford Law Review* 121 (1988).

47. Radelet, *In Spite of Innocence*, 18.

48. Ibid., 127.

49. Hugo Bedau and Michael Radelet, "The Myth of Infallibility: A Reply to Markman and Cassell," 41 *Stanford Law Review* 161 (1988).

50. Death Penalty Information Center, *Cases of Innocence: 1973–Present*, available at http://www.deathpenaltyinfo.org/article.php?scid=6&did=109 (last updated March 15, 2005).

51. Ibid.

52. Indiana Criminal Law Study Commission, *The Application of Indiana's Capital Sentencing Law: Findings of the Indiana Criminal Law Study Commission*, 6–7 (Jan. 10, 2002), available at http://www.in.gov/cji/research/ (last accessed March 22, 2005). Also available from the Indiana Criminal Justice Institute, One North Capital, Suite 1000, Indianapolis, Ind. 46204-2038.

53. Sources for this section include *Kleasen v. State*, 560 S.W.2d 938 (Tex. Crim. App. 1977); "Texan Accused in '74 Slayings Dies in London," *Dallas Morning News*, Apr. 22, 2003; Kent Larsen, "U.S. Gun Zealot Alters U.K. Law," *Mormon News*, available at http://www.mormonstoday.com/000514/D2Kleasen01.shtml (last accessed March 22, 2005); reviews for *Evil Among Us: The Texas Mormon Missionary Murders* by Ken Driggs, available at http://www.signaturebooks.com/reviews/evil.htm (last accessed March 22, 2005); "Murder Suspect Died of Heart Disease," *BBC News*, Oct. 15, 2003, available at http://news.bbc.co.uk/2/uk_news/england/humber/3195506.stm (last accessed March 22, 2005).

54. Citations have been omitted.

55. Sources for this section include *McManus v. State*, 591 S.W.2d 505 (Tex. Crim. App. 1979); *Houston Chronicle Publishing Co. v. McMaster*, 598 S.W.2d 864 (Tex. Crim.

App. 1980); Cindy Horswell, "Free McManus Not Excited, Just Wants to be Left Alone," *Houston Chronicle,* Jan. 23, 1987; "McManus Case Draws Mixed Reactions," *Houston Chronicle,* Jan. 25, 1987; "Derese Is Paroled after 10 Years in Prison," *Houston Chronicle,* Sept. 26, 1987.

56. Sources for this section include *Adams v. State,* 577 S.W.2d 717 (Tex. Crim. App. 1979); *Adams,* 448 U.S. 38; *Adams v. State,* 624 S.W.2d 568 (Tex. Crim. App. 1981); *Ex parte Adams,* 768 S.W.2d 281 (Tex. Crim. App. 1989).

57. *Witherspoon* held that jurors could not be excused from capital cases merely because they had "conscientious scruples against or were otherwise opposed to capital punishment." The state's power to exclude jurors was limited to excluding only those "whose beliefs about capital punishment would lead them to violate the law or violate their oaths." The Texas statute, which allowed prosecutors to strike jurors who could not convincingly assert that the mandatory sentence of death or life imprisonment would "not affect deliberations on any issue of fact," was found by the Supreme Court to overstep the limits set by *Witherspoon* (*Witherspoon,* 391 U.S. 510).

58. Adams challenged the governor's right to commute his sentence after it was overturned on appeal, but the Court of Criminal Appeals upheld the move, citing the commutations resulting from *Furman* as precedent. In reversed cases in Texas, the governor has consistently used the power to commute, in consultation with prosecutors.

59. *Ex parte Adams,* 768 S.W.2d at 285.

60. Sources for this section include *Brandley v. State,* 691 S.W.2d 699 (Tex. Crim. App. 1985); *Ex parte Brandley,* 781 S.W.2d 886 (Tex. Crim. App. 1989); *Brandley v. Keeshan,* 64 F.3d 196 (5th Cir. 1995); Cathy Gordon, "Test Backs Innocence of Brandley Co-Worker," *Houston Chronicle,* Apr. 10, 1987; "State Probers Deny New Evidence Clears Brandley," *Houston Chronicle,* Jun. 24, 1987; Cindy Horswell, "Brandley Co-Worker Charged in Sexual Assaults," *Houston Chronicle,* Jan. 24, 1990; Paul McKay, "Brandley's Charges Dropped After Ruling," *Houston Chronicle,* Oct. 2, 1990; John Makeig, "Brandley, Girlfriend Leave Court Together Despite Assault Charge," *Houston Chronicle,* Jun. 14, 1997.

61. *Ex parte Brandley,* 781 S.W.2d at 887.

62. Ibid. at 895.

63. Ibid. at 894 (n. 9).

64. Ibid. at 896.

65. *Skelton v. State,* 795 S.W.2d 162 (Tex. Crim. App. 1989).

66. Ibid. at 167.

67. Ibid. at 169.

68. Sources for this section include *Macias v. State,* 733 S.W.2d 192 (Tex. Crim. App. 1987); *Martinez-Macias v. Collins,* 810 F.Supp. 782 (W.D. Tex. 1991).

69. *Martinez-Macias v. Collins,* 810 F.Supp. at 785.

70. Sources for this section include *Spence v. State,* 795 S.W.2d 743 (Tex. Crim. App. 1990); *Deeb v. State,* 815 S.W.2d 692 (Tex. Crim. App. 1991); Kathy Fair, "Conviction Overturned, Inmate Now Seeks a Job / Deeb Condemned in '82 Waco Killings," *Houston Chronicle,* July 6, 1991.

71. *Deeb v. State,* 815 S.W.2d at 699.

72. Ibid. at 702.

73. Ibid. at 698.

74. Sources for this section include *Guerra v. State,* 771 S.W.2d 453 (Tex. Crim. App.

1988); *Guerra v. Collins,* 916 F.Supp. 620 (S.D. Tex. 1995); *Guerra v. Johnson,* 90 F.3d 1075 (5th Cir. 1996).

75. *Texas Penal Code Annotated,* sec. 7.02 (West 1999): CRIMINAL RESPONSI-BILITY FOR CONDUCT OF ANOTHER.

(a) A person is criminally responsible for an offense committed by the conduct of another if:

(1) acting with the kind of culpability required for the offense, he causes or aids an innocent or non-responsible person to engage in conduct prohibited by the definition of the offense;

(2) acting with intent to promote or assist the commission of the offense, he so-licits, encourages, directs, aids, or attempts to aid the other person to commit the offense; or

(3) having a legal duty to prevent commission of the offense and acting with intent to promote or assist its commission, he fails to make a reasonable effort to prevent commission of the offense.

(b) If, in the attempt to carry out a conspiracy to commit one felony, another felony is committed by one of the conspirators, all conspirators are guilty of the felony actually committed, though having no intent to commit it, if the offense was committed in furtherance of the unlawful purpose and was one that should have been anticipated as a result of the carrying out of the conspiracy.

76. Robert L. Spangenberg and Elizabeth R. Walsh, "Capital Punishment or Life Imprisonment? Some Cost Considerations," 23 *Loyola of Los Angeles Law Review* 45 (1989).

77. U.S. General Accounting Office, *Limited Data Available on Costs of Death Sen-tences,* Report to the Subcommittee on Civil and Constitutional Rights, Committee on the Judiciary, House of Representatives (Sept. 1989).

78. The text of *Millions Misspent* is available on the DPIC Web site at http://www.deathpenaltyinfo.org/article.php?scid=45&did=385 (last accessed March 23, 2005).

79. Richard C. Dieter, "The Costs of the Death Penalty," a paper presented to the Joint Committee on Criminal Justice, Legislature of Massachusetts, March 27, 2003.

80. National Center for State Courts, *Does the Death Penalty Impose Additional Costs on the Criminal Justice System? A Research Design* (Arlington, Va., 1986).

81. Philip J. Cook and Donna B. Slawson, "The Costs of Processing Murder Cases in North Carolina" (May 1993), available at http://www-pps.aas.duke.edu/people/faculty/cook/comnc.pdf (last accessed March 23, 2005).

82. Mark Goodpaster, "Cost Comparison between a Death Penalty Case and a Case Where the Charge and Conviction Is Life without Parole," in *Application of Indiana's Capital Sentencing Law,* 122A–122FF.

83. Based on an operating cost, in 1991 dollars, of $15,819 a year to house inmates in minimum security, the additional twenty-seven years would cost $427,000 (which, when added to the $166,000 in savings for the twenty years, brings the total to $593,000). See Cook, "Costs of Processing Murder Cases," 72.

84. Based on a recalculation of the authors' "Summing Up the Costs" (Cook, "Costs of Processing Murder Cases," 77–79).

85. *Application of Indiana's Capital Sentencing Law.*

86. Goodpaster, "Cost Comparison."

87. Christy Hoppe, "Executions Cost Texas Millions," *Dallas Morning News,* Mar. 8, 1992, available at http://www.tcadp.org/costs.html (last accessed March 23, 2005).

88. Russell Gold, "Counties Struggle with High Cost of Prosecuting Death-Penalty Cases," *Wall Street Journal,* Jan. 9, 2002, available at http://www-unix.oit.umass .edu/~leg485/cost2.htm (last accessed March 23, 2005). The three capital murder trials in Jasper County arising from the dragging death of James Byrd cost just over $1 million in 1999 (an average cost of $340,000 for each trial). The cost of retrying John Paul Penry was estimated to exceed $200,000.

89. Similarly, Hoppe failed to take into consideration the costs of unsuccessful death-penalty trials. Expenditures on death-penalty trials that do not result in execution must be absorbed by those trials that do. In two instances, expenditures on death-penalty trials could be considered wasted: when the trials result in sentences other than death and when death sentences are overturned on appeal. Currently, more than 80 percent of death-penalty trials result in death sentences, and about 90 percent of these will result in execution (see Chapter 1). This "success" rate of 72 percent requires that nearly 1.4 death-penalty trials take place for each one that ultimately results in an execution; this increases the cost estimate for a "successful" death penalty trial from $266,000 to $372,400.

90. The estimate of state appellate costs includes expenditures for both the direct appeal and the state habeas corpus proceeding. After the defendant is sentenced, his case is automatically appealed to the Court of Criminal Appeals, where issues related to the record (errors occurring during trial) can be raised. At the same time, the trial court holds state habeas corpus proceedings to determine if any constitutional errors occurred (typically, these are procedural errors related to the processing of the defendant's case by the police, prosecutor, or defense attorneys). The state of Texas now reimburses defense attorneys up to $25,000 for their time and investigations at the habeas stage; however, attorneys' fees seldom approach this cap. See Texas Defender Service, *Lethal Indifference: The Fatal Combination of Incompetent Attorneys and Unaccountable Courts in Texas Death Penalty Appeals* (2002), available at http://www.texasdefender.org/front.pdf (last accessed March 23, 2005).

Federal habeas proceedings arising in Texas involve three stages of appeals, including an appeal to the U.S. district court having jurisdiction, an appeal to the Court of Appeals for the Fifth Circuit, and a certiorari petition to the U.S. Supreme Court. The state, through the attorney general's office, bears the monetary costs for the prosecution; defense counsel is paid by the federal courts. The cost varies by case and level of review, but the U.S. district court currently caps defense payments at $35,000 and expenses related to experts and investigation at $7,500 (telephone interview with Philip Wischkaemper, capital assistance attorney, Texas Criminal Defense Lawyers Association [February 2004]).

91. In an e-mail communication, Hoppe stated that she no longer retained background materials for that story, but did recall that the figures were presented to a congressional subcommittee by the General Accounting Office and that she had "found out about its existence through a printed article on the subcommittee hearing" (e-mail correspondence with Christy Hoppe, reporter for the *Dallas Morning News* [November 5, 2003]).

92. For death-sentenced inmates, she based her estimate on 7.5 years, the average

time for the appeals process to run its course. However, one could insist on factoring in additional time for those inmates whose cases have been reversed and retried. In the modern era, the average time served on death row before execution has been 10.43 years (TDCJ Web site, "Death Row Facts"). Further, the cost of housing death-row inmates has increased since their move to the Terrell/Polunsky Unit. Multiplied by the average per diem cost of housing one of these inmates, the total estimated cost of housing a death-sentenced prisoner before execution is $234,592 ($61.58 per day x 365.25 days per year x 10.43 years; 2002 dollars). This figure is somewhat higher than that proffered by Hoppe; however, one could argue the overall mean of 10.43 years is too high, skewed by a few older cases that have had to meander through all the immediate post-*Furman* roadblocks, whereas cases currently resulting in death sentences can be expected to result in execution much faster.

Hoppe's estimate for life-sentenced inmates is based on the assumption that the inmate will be housed for forty years in TDCJ in a single cell at the highest security level. In other studies, the authors assume that life-sentenced inmates will serve some portion of their time in a lower security setting. Recent studies of the behavior of life-sentenced inmates have clearly shown that they do not present an extreme threat to the prison population and can be housed in lower security levels of confinement if the system allows.

One way of calculating the difference in housing costs between death-row and life-sentenced inmates is to assume that the costs for life-sentenced inmates will be similar to those for death-sentenced inmates during the initial years of incarceration, but that life-sentenced inmates will then be housed at a lower security level. If the cost of housing life-sentenced inmates rivals that of death-sentenced inmates for the average period up to execution (10.43 years)—considering the first decade a wash between death-sentenced and life-sentenced inmates also provides a rough control for potential cost differences between straight lifers and those initially sentenced to death but later given a life sentence—the cost of housing a lifer for the first decade is $234,592, the same as for a death-sentenced prisoner. Assuming that lifers are spread across security levels for the remaining three decades puts the average cost at $475,327 ($44.01 per day x 365.25 days per year x 29.57 years) for a total housing cost of approximately $710,000 per lifer.

93. Illinois Governor's Commission on Capital Punishment, *Report of the Commission*, 11.

94. Texas Defender Service, *Lethal Indifference*.

95. Ibid.

Chapter 6

1. The average time to execution in the modern era has been ten and a half years. The overall figures show that this time to execution has increased since the early modern era. Such figures, however, are deceiving, for two related reasons. First, the executions in the 1980s included only a small portion of condemned inmates' cases; the figures include only the first cases from the 1970s cohort to result in execution, so the time to execution reflects only the small number of cases that were processed quickest. This, then, cannot be considered an "average" time to execution for those sentenced to death during a given period, but an average only for those few cases that were most speedily

processed. Second, recent executions have included many of the remaining cases that were adjudicated in the earlier part of the modern era and have finally been resolved, in addition to more recently adjudicated cases that have been more speedily processed. The time served by the former prisoners inflates the overall estimates of time served to execution among more recent cohorts of death-sentenced inmates.

2. Survival analysis uses data regarding how long it took to execute inmates in the past in order to estimate how long it will take to execute the remaining death-sentenced inmates (those who have survived through Dec. 31, 2003). Of course, survival through Dec. 31, 2003, should not be construed literally; rather, it means only that condemned inmates had not been executed by then. Survivors include all inmates who were on death row on that date, as well as all condemned inmates who had been released from death row, even if they later were released from prison or died from causes other than the execution. Inmates who died while on death row from causes other than execution are not considered survivors. It is unknown whether they would have been executed or not. As such, they were considered successful survivors up to the time of their death, at which time their cases were censored. For a detailed technical discussion of survival analysis, see Douglas A. Luke and Sharon M. Homan, "Time and Change: Using Survival Analysis in Clinical Assessment and Treatment Evaluation," 10 *Psychological Assessment* 360 (1998).

3. The only mandatory appeal is direct review by the Court of Criminal Appeals. Inmates who waive their remaining appeals can be executed within a year. For example, Joe Gonzales was executed 252 days after his arrival on death row.

References

Books, Journals, and Web Sites

Acker, James R., and Charles S. Lanier. "Beyond Human Ability? The Rise and Fall of Death Penalty Legislation." In *America's Experiment with Capital Punishment: Reflections on the Past, Present, and Future of the Ultimate Penal Sanction,* edited by James R. Acker, Robert M. Bohm, and Charles S. Lanier. (Durham, N.C.: Carolina Academic Press, 1998).

American Association on Mental Retardation. *Mental Retardation: Definition, Classification, and Systems of Supports.* 9th ed. Washington, D.C.: American Association on Mental Retardation, 1992.

American Correctional Association. "Survey Summary: Riots, Disturbances, Violence, Assaults, and Escapes." 27 *Corrections Compendium* 6, 19 (2002).

Amnesty International. *Lethal Injection: The Medical Technology of Execution* (Jan. 1998). Available at http://web.amnesty.org/library/Index/engACT500011998 (last accessed March 22, 2005).

Atlas, Scott. "How Can We Be Sure?" 29 *Litigation* 1 (2003).

Bailey, William C. "Disaggregation in Deterrence and Death Penalty Research: The Case of Murder in Chicago." 74 *Journal of Criminal Law and Criminology* 827 (1983).

———. "Imprisonment vs. the Death Penalty as a Deterrent to Murder." 1 *Law and Human Behavior* 239 (1977).

———. "Murder and Capital Punishment: Some Further Evidence." 45 *American Journal of Orthopsychiatry* 669 (1975).

Bailey, William C., and Ruth D. Peterson. "Murder and Capital Punishment: A Monthly Time-Series Analysis of Execution Publicity." 54 *American Sociological Review* 722 (1989).

———. "Police Killings and Capital Punishment: The Post-*Furman* Period." 25 *Criminology* 1 (1987).

Baldus, David C., and James W. L. Cole. "A Comparison of the Work of Thorsten Sellin and Isaac Ehrlich on the Deterrent Effect of Capital Punishment." 85 *Yale Law Journal* 170 (1975).

Baldus, David C., George Woodworth, and Charles A. Pulaski, Jr. *Equal Justice and the Death Penalty: A Legal and Empirical Analysis* (Boston: Northeastern Univ. Press, 1990).

Baldus, David C., George Woodworth, David Zuckerman, Neil Alan Weiner, and Barbara Broffitt. "Racial Discrimination and the Death Penalty in the Post-*Furman* Era: An Empirical and Legal Overview, with Recent Findings from Philadelphia." 83 *Cornell Law Review* 1638 (1998).

Banner, Stuart. *The Death Penalty: An American History*. Cambridge, Mass.: Harvard Univ. Press, 2002.

Barak, Gregg. "Media, Crime, and Justice: A Case for Constitutive Criminology." In *Cultural Criminology*, ed. Jeff Ferrell and Clinton R. Sanders. Boston: Northeastern Univ. Press, 1995.

Barnett, Arnold. "The Deterrent Effect of Capital Punishment: A Test of Some Recent Studies." 29 *Operations Research* 341 (1981).

———. "Some Distribution Patterns for the Georgia Death Sentence." 18 *Davis Law Review* 1327 (1985).

Bedau, Hugo A., ed. *The Death Penalty in America: An Anthology*. Garden City, N.Y.: Anchor Doubleday, 1967.

Bedau, Hugo A., and Michael Radelet. "Miscarriages of Justice in Potentially Capital Cases." 40 *Stanford Law Review* 21 (1987).

———. "The Myth of Infallibility: A Reply to Markman and Cassell." 41 *Stanford Law Review* 161 (1988).

Berk, Richard A. "New Claims about Executions and General Deterrence: Déjà Vu All Over Again?" *Journal of Empirical Legal Studies* (forthcoming, 2005), available at http://preprints.stat.ucla.edu/396/JELS.pap.pdf (last accessed March 23, 2005).

Beyleveld, D. "Ehrlich's Analysis of Deterrence." 22 *British Journal of Criminology* 101 (1982).

Black, Charles. "Due Process for Death: *Jurek v. Texas* and Companion Cases." 26 *Catholic University Law Review* 1 (1976).

Blalock, Hubert M., Jr. *Social Statistics*. 2nd ed. New York: McGraw-Hill, 1979.

Blumstein, Alfred, and Joel Wallman, eds. *The Crime Drop in America*. New York: Cambridge Univ. Press, 2000.

Bonczar, Thomas P., and Tracy L. Snell. See U.S. Department of Justice.

Bowers, William, and Glenn Pierce. "Arbitrariness and Discrimination under Post-*Furman* Capital Statutes." 26 *Crime and Delinquency* 563 (1980).

———. "Deterrence or Brutalization: What Is the Effect of Executions?" 26 *Crime and Delinquency* 453 (1980).

———. "The Illusion of Deterrence in Isaac Ehrlich's Research on Capital Punishment." 85 *Yale Law Journal* 187 (1975).

Bowers, William, and Ben Steiner. "The Pernicious Illusion of Early Release for First Degree Murderers Not Sentenced to Death." Paper, annual meeting of the American Society of Criminology, Chicago, 1996.

Boyes, William J., and Lee R. McPheters. "Capital Punishment as a Deterrent to Violent Crime: Cross-Sectional Evidence." 6 *Journal of Behavioral Science* 67 (1977).

Brock, Deon, Jonathan Sorensen, and James Marquart. "The Influence of Race on Prison Sentences for Murder in Twentieth-Century Texas." In *Practical Applications for Criminal Justice Statistics,* ed. Mark L. Dantzker, Arthur J. Lurigio, Magnus J. Seng, and James M. Sinacore. Woburn, Mass.: Butterworth-Heinemann, 1998.

————. "Tinkering with the Machinery of Death: An Analysis of the Impact of Legislative Reform on the Sentencing of Capital Murderers in Texas." 28 *Journal of Criminal Justice* 343 (2000).

Brown, Stephen J., and Jerold B. Warner. "Measuring Security Price Performance." 8 *Journal of Financial Economics* 205 (1980).

Cameron, Samuel. "A Review of the Econometric Evidence on the Effects of Capital Punishment." 23 *Journal of Socio-Economics* 197 (1994).

"Capital Punishment, Juveniles, and the Death Penalty." *#46: Death Penalty Websites.* Available at http://www.geometry.net/detail/basic_c/capital_punishment_juveniles _&_death_penalty_page_no_3.html (last accessed March 22, 2005).

Cardarelli, Albert P. "An Analysis of Police Killed in Criminal Action, 1961–1963." 59 *Journal of Criminal Law, Criminology, and Police Science* 447 (1968).

Carrington, Frank G. *Neither Cruel nor Unusual: The Case for Capital Punishment.* New Rochelle, N.Y.: Arlington House, 1978.

Cloninger, Dale. "Capital Punishment and Deterrence: A Portfolio Approach." 24 *Applied Economics* 645 (1992).

————. "Deterrence and the Death Penalty: A Cross Sectional Analysis." 6 *Journal of Behavioral Economics* 87 (1977).

Cloninger, Dale, and Roberto Marchesini. "Crime Betas: A Portfolio Measure of Criminal Activity." 76 *Social Science Quarterly* 634 (1995).

————. "Execution and Deterrence: A Quasi-Controlled Group Experiment." 33 *Applied Economics* 569 (2001).

Cochran, John K., Mitchell B. Samlin, and Mark Seth. "Deterrence or Brutalization? An Impact Assessment of Oklahoma's Return to Capital Punishment." 32 *Criminology* 107 (1994).

Conklin, John E. *Why Crime Rates Fell.* Boston: Allyn and Bacon, 2003.

Conrad, John. *Jury Nullification: The Evolution of a Doctrine.* Durham, N.C.: Carolina Academic Press, 1998.

Cook, Philip J., and Donna B. Slawson. "The Costs of Processing Murder Cases in North Carolina." May 1993. Available at http://www.pps.aas.duke.edu/people/ faculty/cook/comnc.pdf (last accessed on March 23, 2005).

Cooke, David J. "The Development of the Prison Behavior Rating Scale." 25 *Criminal Justice and Behavior* 482 (1998).

Cooper, Robert P., and Paul D. Werner. "Predicting Violence in Newly Admitted Inmates: A Lens Model Analysis of Staff Decision Making." 17 *Criminal Justice and Behavior* 431 (1990).

Costanzo, Sally, and Mark Costanzo. "Life or Death Decisions: An Analysis of Capital Jury Decision-Making under the Special Issues Sentencing Framework." 18 *Law and Human Behavior* 151 (1994).

Council of Judges of the National Council on Crime and Delinquency. "Model Sentencing Act: Second Ed." 18 *Crime and Delinquency* 335, 341 (1972).

CourtTV.com. "Texas Seven Murder Case." Available at http://www.courttv.com/ trials/texas7 (Courtroom Television Network, LLC 2002; last accessed March 23, 2005).

Crump, David. "Capital Murder: The Issues in Texas." 14 *Houston Law Review* 532 (1977).

Cunningham, Mark D., and Thomas J. Reidy. "Don't Confuse Me with the Facts: Common Errors in Violence Risk Assessment at Capital Sentencing." 26 *Criminal Justice and Behavior* 20 (1999).

———. "Integrating Base Rate Data in Violence Risk Assessments at Capital Sentencing." 16 *Behavioral Science and the Law* 71 (1998).

Cunningham, Mark D., Jon R. Sorensen, and Thomas J. Reidy. "Revising Future Dangerousness Revisited: Response to DeLisi and Munoz." 15 *Criminal Justice Policy Review* 365 (2004).

Davis, Peggy C. "Texas Capital Sentencing Procedures: The Role of the Jury and the Restraining Hand of the Expert." 69 *Journal of Criminal Law and Criminology* 300 (1978).

Death Penalty Information Center. *Cases of Innocence, 1973 – Present*. Available at http://www.deathpenaltyinfo.org/article.php?scid=6&did=109 (last updated March 5, 2005).

Dezhbakhsh, Hashem, Paul H. Rubin, and Joanna M. Shepherd. "Does Capital Punishment Have a Deterrent Effect? New Evidence from Postmoratorium Panel Data." 5 *American Law and Economics Review* 344 (2003). Available at http://aler.oupjournals.org/cgi/reprint/5/2/344 (last accessed March 23, 2005).

Dezhbakhsh, Hashem, and Joanna M. Shepherd. "The Deterrent Effect of Capital Punishment: Evidence from a 'Judicial Experiment.'" July 2003. Available at http://people.clemson.edu/~jshephe/CaPuJLE_submit.pdf (last accessed March 23, 2005). Revised and resubmitted to the *Journal of Law and Economics*.

Dieter, Richard C. "The Costs of the Death Penalty." Paper presented to the Joint Committee on Criminal Justice, Legislature of Massachusetts, March 27, 2003.

Dix, George E. "Administration of the Texas Death Penalty Statutes: Constitutional Infirmities Related to the Prediction of Dangerousness." 55 *Texas Law Review* 1343 (1977).

Douglas, Kevin S., and Christopher D. Webster. "The HCR-20 Violence Risk Assessment Scheme: Concurrent Validity in a Sample of Incarcerated Offenders." 26 *Criminal Justice and Behavior* 3 (1999).

Driggs, Ken. *Evil Among Us: The Texas Mormon Missionary Murders*. Salt Lake City, Utah: Signature Books, 2000. Reviews of the book available at http://www.signaturebooks.com/reviews/evil.htm (last accessed March 22, 2005).

Ehrhardt, Charles, and L. Harold Levinson. "Florida's Legislative Response to *Furman*: An Exercise in Futility?" 64 *Journal of Criminal Law and Criminology* 10 (1973).

Ehrlich, Isaac. "Capital Punishment and Deterrence: Some Further Thoughts and Additional Evidence." 85 *Journal of Political Economy* 741 (1977).

———. "The Deterrent Effect of Capital Punishment: A Question of Life or Death." 65 *American Economic Review* 397 (1975).

Eichenthal, David, and James B. Jacobs. "Enforcing the Criminal Law in State Prisons." 8 *Justice Quarterly* 283 (1991).

Ekland-Olson, Sheldon. "Structured Discretion, Racial Bias, and the Death Penalty: The First Decade after *Furman* in Texas." 69 *Social Science Quarterly* 853 (1988).

Finkel, N. J., K. C. Hughes, S. F. Smith, and M. L. Hurabiell. "Killing Kids: The Juvenile Death Penalty and Community Sentiment." 12 *Behavioral Sciences and the Law* 5 (1994).

Flanagan, Timothy J. "Time Served and Institutional Misconduct: Patterns of Involvement in Disciplinary Infractions among Long-Term and Short-Term Inmates." 8 *Journal of Criminal Justice* 357 (1980).

Forst, Brian. "The Deterrent Effect of Capital Punishment: A Cross-State Analysis of the 1960s." 61 *Minnesota Law Review* 743 (1977).

Fox, James A. "The Identification and Estimation of Deterrence: An Evaluation of Yunker's Model." 6 *Journal of Behavioral Economics* 225 (1977).

Fox, James A., and Michael Radelet. "Persistent Flaws in Econometric Studies of the Deterrent Effect of the Death Penalty." 23 *Loyola of Los Angeles Law Review* 29 (1989).

Fox, James Alan, and Marianne W. Zawitz. See U.S. Department of Justice.

Friedman, Lawrence M. "The Use of Multiple Regression Analysis to Test for a Deterrent Effect of Capital Punishment: Prospects and Problems." In *Criminology Review Yearbook,* ed. Sheldon L. Messinger and Egon Bittner. Beverly Hills, Calif.: Sage, 1979.

Garfinkel, Harold. "Research Note on Inter- and Intra-Racial Homicides." 27 *Social Forces* 369 (1949).

Gendreau, Paul, Claire Goggin, and M. A. Law. "Predicting Prison Misconducts." 24 *Criminal Justice and Behavior* 414 (1997).

Goodpaster, Mark. "Cost Comparison between a Death Penalty Case and a Case Where the Charge and Conviction Is Life without Parole." In *The Application of Indiana's Capital Sentencing Law: Findings of the Indiana Criminal Law Study Commission* (2002), 122A–122FF.

Gross, Samuel R., and Robert Mauro. "Patterns of Death: An Analysis of Racial Disparities in Capital Sentencing and Homicide Victimization." 37 *Stanford Law Review* 27 (1984).

Handbook of Texas Online. "Sharpstown Stock-Fraud Scandal." At http://www.tsha .utexas.edu/handbook/online/articles/view/SS/mqs1.html (last accessed March 22, 2005).

Haney, Craig, Lorelei Sontag, and Sally Costanzo. "Deciding to Take a Life: Capital Juries, Sentencing Instructions, and the Jurisprudence of Death." 50 *Journal of Social Issues* 149 (1994).

Harmon, Talia. "Predictors of Miscarriages of Justice in Capital Cases." 18 *Justice Quarterly* 949 (2001).

Hoffman, Joseph. "On the Perils of Line Drawing: Juveniles and the Death Penalty." 40 *Hastings Law Review* 229 (1989).

Hoppe, Christy. "Executions Cost Texas Millions." *Dallas Morning News,* Mar. 8, 1992. Available at http://www.tcadp.org/costs.html (last accessed March 23, 2005).

Illinois Governor's Commission on Capital Punishment. *Report of the Governor's Commission on Capital Punishment,* April 15, 2002. Available at http://www.idoc.state .il.us/ccp/ccp/reports/index.html (last accessed March 22, 2005).

Indiana Criminal Law Study Commission. *The Application of Indiana's Capital Sentencing Law: Findings of the Indiana Criminal Law Study Commission* (Jan. 10, 2002). Available at http://www.in.gov/cji/research/ (last accessed March 22, 2005). Also available from the Indiana Criminal Justice Institute, One North Capital, Suite 1000, Indianapolis, Ind. 46204-2038.

Jackson, Jesse L., Sr., and Bruce Shapiro. *Legal Lynching: The Death Penalty and America's Future*. New York: Random House, 2003.

Johnson, Elmer H. "Selective Factors in Capital Punishment." 36 *Social Forces* 165 (1957).

Johnson, Guy B. "The Negro and Crime." 217 *Annals of American Academy of Political and Social Science* 93 (1941).

Kalven, Harry, and Hans Zeisel. *The American Jury*. Boston: Little, Brown, 1966.

Kleck, Gary. "Racial Discrimination in Criminal Sentencing: A Critical Evaluation of the Evidence with Additional Evidence on the Death Penalty." 46 *American Sociological Review* 783 (1981).

Klein, Lawrence R., Brian Forst, and Viktor Filatov. "The Deterrent Effect of Capital Punishment: An Assessment of Estimates." In *Deterrence and Incapacitation: Estimating the Effects of Criminal Sanctions on Crime Rates*, ed. Alfred Blumstein, Jacqueline Cohen, and Daniel Nagin, 331–360. Washington, D.C.: National Academy of Sciences, 1978.

Koeninger, Rupert. "Capital Punishment in Texas, 1924–1968." 15 *Crime and Delinquency* 132 (1969).

Kuhn, Michael. "House Bill 200: The Legislative Attempt to Reinstate Capital Punishment in Texas." 11 *Houston Law Review* 410 (1974).

Layson, Steve. "Homicide and Deterrence: A Reexamination of the United States Time-Series Evidence." 52 *Southern Economic Journal* 68 (1985).

Liebman, James S., Jeffrey Fagan, and Valerie West. "A Broken System: Error Rates in Capital Cases, 1973–1995." 2000. Available at http://ccjr.policy.net/cjedfund/jpreport/ (last accessed March 22, 2005).

Liu, Zhiqiang. "Capital Punishment and the Deterrence Hypothesis: Some New Insights and Empirical Evidence." 30 *Eastern Economic Journal* 237 (2004).

Longmire, Dennis, and Scott Vollum. "Attitudes about Crime and Criminal Justice Policy in Texas: Special Legislative Report—*2003 Texas Crime Poll Special Legislative Survey*." Available at http://www.shsu.edu/~icc_drl/2003_Legislative_Report.html (last accessed March 22, 2005).

Luckenbill, David. "Criminal Homicide as a Situated Transaction." 25 *Social Problems* 176 (1977).

Luke, Douglas A., and Sharon M. Homan. "Time and Change: Using Survival Analysis in Clinical Assessment and Treatment Evaluation." 10 *Psychological Assessment* 360 (1998).

Markman, Stephen, and Paul Cassell. "Protecting the Innocent: A Response to the Bedau-Radelet Study." 41 *Stanford Law Review* 121 (1988).

Marquart, James, Sheldon Ekland-Olson, and Jon Sorensen. "Gazing into the Crystal Ball: Can Jurors Accurately Predict Dangerousness in Capital Cases?" 23 *Law and Society Review* 449 (1989).

———. *The Rope, the Chair, and the Needle: Capital Punishment in Texas, 1923–1990*. Austin: Univ. of Texas Press, 1994.

Marquart, James, and Jon Sorensen. "Institutional and Post-Release Behavior of *Furman*-Commuted Inmates in Texas." 26 *Criminology* 677 (1988).

———. "A National Study of the *Furman*-Commuted Inmates: Assessing the Threat to Society from Capital Offenders." 23 *Loyola of Los Angeles Law Review* 5 (1989).

Massachusetts Politics and Policy Online. *Issue: Death Penalty 2003*. Available at http://o2133.org/issue.cfm?ID=115 (last accessed March 23, 2005).

Maxfield, Michael G. "Circumstances in Supplementary Homicide Reports: Variety and Validity." 27 *Criminology* 671 (1989).

McFall, Richard M., and Teresa A. Treat. "Quantifying the Information Value of Clinical Assessments with Signal Detection Theory." 50 *Annual Review of Psychology* 215 (1999).

McGahey, Richard M. "Dr. Ehrlich's Magic Bullet: Economic Theory, Econometrics, and the Death Penalty." 26 *Crime and Delinquency* 485 (1980).

Meehl, Paul. *Clinical vs. Statistical Prediction: A Theoretical Analysis and a Review of the Evidence*. Minneapolis: Univ. of Minnesota Press, 1954.

Meltsner, Michael. *Cruel and Unusual: The Supreme Court and Capital Punishment*. New York: Random House, 1973.

Merillat, A. P. *Future Danger?* 2nd ed. Austin: Texas District and County Attorneys Association, 2000.

Mocan, H. Naci, and R. Kaj Gittings, "Getting Off Death Row: Commuted Sentences and the Deterrent Effect of Capital Punishment." 46 *Journal of Law and Economics* 453 (2003).

Monahan, John. *Predicting Violent Behavior: An Assessment of Clinical Techniques*. Beverly Hills, Calif.: Sage, 1981.

———. "Violence Prediction: The Past Twenty and the Next Twenty Years." 23 *Criminal Justice and Behavior* 107 (1996).

Moon, Melissa, John Paul Wright, Francis T. Cullen, and Jennifer Pealer. "Putting Kids to Death: Specifying Public Support for Juvenile Capital Punishment." 17 *Justice Quarterly* 663 (2000).

National Center for State Courts. *Does the Death Penalty Impose Additional Costs on the Criminal Justice System? A Research Design*. Final report. Arlington, Va., 1986.

New Criminologist. "Kenneth Allen McDuff (USA)." Available at http://www.thecriminologist.com/new_criminologist/volume1/portrait_serial/portrait_serial.asp (last accessed March 22, 2005).

Passell, Peter. "The Deterrent Effect of the Death Penalty: A Statistical Test." 28 *Stanford Law Review* 61 (1975).

Petersilia, Joan. "Death Penalty Resolution Debated and Endorsed." 15 *Criminologist* 1 (1990).

Peterson, Ruth D., and William C. Bailey. "Is Capital Punishment an Effective Deterrent for Murder? An Examination of Social Science Research." In Acker, *America's Experiment with Capital Punishment*, 157–182.

Proctor, Jon L. "Evaluating a Modified Version of the Federal Prison System's Inmate Classification Model: An Assessment of Objectivity and Predictive Validity." 21 *Criminal Justice and Behavior* 256 (1994).

Radelet, Michael, Hugo Bedau, and Constance Putnam. *In Spite of Innocence: Erroneous Convictions in Capital Cases*. Boston: Northeastern Univ. Press, 1992.

Radelet, Michael, and James Marquart. "Assessing Non-Dangerousness during Penalty Phases of Capital Trials." 54 *Albany Law Review* 845 (1990).

Radelet, Michael, and Glenn Pierce. "Race and Prosecutorial Discretion in Homicide Cases." 19 *Law and Society Review* 587 (1985).

Reavis, Dick J. "Charlie Brooks' Last Words." *Texas Monthly,* Feb. 1983.

Reid, Don, and John Gurwell. *Eyewitness.* Houston: Cordovan Press, 1973.

Reidy, Thomas J., Mark D. Cunningham, and Jon R. Sorensen. "From Death to Life: Prison Behavior of Former Death Row Inmates in Indiana." 28 *Criminal Justice and Behavior* 62 (2001).

Riedel, Marc. "Counting Stranger Homicides: A Case Study of Statistical Prestidigitation." 2 *Homicide Studies* 206 (1998).

Rosenbaum, Ron. "Travels with Dr. Death." *Vanity Fair,* May 1990.

Rumley, David. "A License to Kill: The Categorical Exemption of the Mentally Retarded from the Death Penalty." 24 *St. Mary's Law Journal* 1299 (1993).

Schuessler, Karl F. "The Deterrent Effect of the Death Penalty." 284 *Annals of the American Academy of Political and Social Science* 54 (1952).

Scofield, Giles R. "Due Process in the United States Supreme Court and the Death of the Texas Capital Murder Statute." 8 *American Journal of Criminal Law* 1 (1980).

Sesnowitz, Michael, and David L. McKee. "On the Deterrent Effect of Capital Punishment." 6 *Journal of Behavioral Economics* 217 (1977).

Sellin, Thorsten. *Capital Punishment.* New York: Harper and Row, 1967.

——. *The Death Penalty.* Philadelphia: American Law Institute, 1959.

Shepherd, Joanna M. "Murders of Passion, Execution Delays, and the Deterrence of Capital Punishment." 33 *Journal of Legal Studies* 283 (2004).

Sorensen, Jon, and James Marquart. "Prosecutorial and Jury Decision-Making in Post-*Furman* Texas Capital Cases." 18 *Review of Law and Social Change* 743 (1990–1991).

——. "Working the Dead." In *Facing the Death Penalty: Essays on Cruel and Unusual Punishment,* ed. Michael Radelet. Philadelphia: Temple Univ. Press, 1989.

Sorensen, Jon, and Donald H. Wallace. "Prosecutorial Discretion in Seeking Death: An Analysis of Racial Disparity in the Pretrial Stages of Case Processing in a Mid-Western County." 16 *Justice Quarterly* 559 (1999).

Sorensen, Jon, Donald H. Wallace, and Rocky L. Pilgrim. "Empirical Studies on Race and Death Penalty Sentencing: A Decade after the GAO Report." 37 *Criminal Law Bulletin* 395 (2002).

Sorensen, Jon, and Robert Wrinkle. "No Hope for Parole: Disciplinary Infractions among Death-Sentenced and Life-without-Parole Inmates." 23 *Criminal Justice and Behavior* 542 (1996).

Sorensen, Jon, Robert Wrinkle, Victoria Brewer, and John Marquart. "Capital Punishment and Deterrence: Examining the Effect of Executions on Murder in Texas." 45 *Crime and Delinquency* 481 (1999).

Sorensen, Jon, Robert Wrinkle, and A. Gutierrez. "Patterns of Rule-Violating Behaviors and Adjustment to Incarceration among Murderers." 78 *Prison Journal* 222 (1998).

Spangenberg, Robert L., and Elizabeth R. Walsh. "Capital Punishment or Life Imprisonment? Some Cost Considerations." 23 *Loyola of Los Angeles Law Review* 45 (1989).

Stack, Steven, "Publicized Executions and Homicide, 1950–1980." 52 *American Sociological Review* 532 (1987).

Steiker, Jordan, and Carol Steiker. "Judicial Developments in Capital Punishment Law." In Acker, *America's Experiment with Capital Punishment.*

Texas Defender Service. *Lethal Indifference: The Fatal Combination of Incompetent Attorneys and Unaccountable Courts in Texas Death Penalty Appeals* (2002). Available at http://www.texasdefender.org/front.pdf (last accessed March 23, 2005).

Texas Department of Criminal Justice. "Death Row Facts." Available at http://www .tdcj.state.tx.us/stat/drowfacts.htm (last updated Dec. 19, 2003).

——. "Executed Offenders." Available at http://www.tdcj.state.tx.us/stat/executed offenders.htm (last updated March 16, 2005).

——. "Offenders No Longer on Death Row." Available at www.tdcj.state.tx.us/stat/ permanentout.htm (last updated Feb. 9, 2005).

——. "Offenders on Death Row." Available at http://www.tdcj.state.tx.us/stat/ offendersondrow.htm (last updated March 23, 2005).

Texas Legislature. House. Bill file, HB 200. 63rd Leg., 1973.

——. House. Committee on Criminal Jurisprudence. Public Hearing on HB 200. 63rd Leg., Feb. 6, 1973 (audiotapes 1–3).

——. House. Committee on Criminal Jurisprudence. Public Hearing on HB 945. 65th Leg., March 1, 1977 (audiotapes 1–3).

Texas Legislature. Senate. SB 85. 77th Leg., 2001. History of action on the bill available at *Texas Legislature Online,* http://www.capitol.state.tx.us/cgi-bin/db2www/tlo/ billhist/actions.d2w/report?LEG=77&SESS=R&CHAMBER=S&BILLTYPE=B &BILLSUFFIX=00085 (last accessed March 22, 2005).

——. Senate. SB 145. 60th Leg., 1967.

"They Shoot Horses, Don't They?" *Time,* Oct. 8, 1973.

U.S. Bureau of the Census. Census 2000 Data for the State of Texas, Texas Redistricting Data, Table 1. Population by Race and Hispanic or Latino Origin, for All Ages and for 18 Years and Over, for Texas: 2000. Available at http://www.census.gov/ census2000/states/tx.html (last accessed March 22, 2005).

U.S. Department of Justice. Bureau of Justice Statistics. *Capital Punishment, 2001,* by Tracy L. Snell and Laura M. Maruschak. Washington, D.C., 2002.

——. Bureau of Justice Statistics. *Capital Punishment, 2002* by Thomas P. Bonczar and Tracy L. Snell. Washington, D.C., 2003.

——. Bureau of Justice Statistics. *Crime Trends—State Level: State-by-State and National Trends.* Available at http://bjsdata.ojp.usdoj.gov/dataonline/Search/Crime/ State/StatebyState.cfm (last accessed March 25, 2005).

——. Bureau of Justice Statistics. *Homicide Trends in the United States* by James Alan Fox and Marianne W. Zawitz. Available at http://www.ojp.usdoj.gov/bjs/homicide/ homtrnd.htm (last accessed March 22, 2005).

——. Bureau of Justice Statistics. *Homicide Trends in the United States: Trends by City Size.* Available at http://www.ojp.usdoj.gov/bjs/homicide/city.htm (last accessed March 22, 2005).

——. Bureau of Justice Statistics. *Sourcebook of Criminal Justice Statistics, 1996,* ed. Kathleen Maguire and Ann L. Pastore. Washington, D.C., 1997.

——. Bureau of Justice Statistics. *Sourcebook of Criminal Justice Statistics, 2002,* ed. Kathleen Maguire and Ann L. Pastore. Available at http://www.albany.edu/source book/ (last accessed March 23, 2005).

————. Federal Bureau of Investigation. *Crime in the United States, 2000.* Available at http://www.fbi.gov/ucr/ucr.htm#cius (last accessed on March 22, 2005).

————. Federal Bureau of Investigation. *Law Enforcement Officers Killed and Assaulted.* Available at http://www.fbi.gov/ucr/ucr.htm#leoka (last accessed March 22, 2005).

————. Law Enforcement Assistance Administration. National Prisoner Statistics Bulletin. *Capital Punishment, 1971–1972.* Washington, D.C., 1974.

————. National Institute of Justice. *The Nature and Patterns of American Homicide,* by Marc Reidel, Margaret A. Zahn, and Lois Mock. Washington, D.C., 1985.

U.S. General Accounting Office. *Death Penalty Sentencing: Research Indicates Pattern of Racial Disparities.* Report to Senate and House Committees on the Judiciary. Washington, D.C., 1990.

————. *Limited Data Available on Costs of Death Sentences.* Report to the Subcommittee on Civil and Constitutional Rights, Committee on the Judiciary, House of Representatives. Washington, D.C., 1989.

Wardlaw, Grant, and David Biles. *The Management of Long-Term Prisoners in Australia.* Canberra: Australian Institute of Criminology, 1980.

Weiss, Robert, Richard Berk, Wenzhi Li, and Margaret Farrell-Ross. "Death Penalty Charging in Los Angeles County: An Illustrative Data Analysis Using Skeptical Priors." 28 *Sociological Methods and Research* 91 (1999).

Wilbanks, William. *The Myth of a Racist Criminal Justice System.* Monterey, Calif.: Brooks-Cole, 1987.

Williams, Marian, and Jefferson Holcomb. "Racial Disparity and Death Sentences in Ohio." 29 *Journal of Criminal Justice* 207 (2001).

Winfree, L. Thomas. "Attica." In *Encyclopedia of American Prisons,* ed. Marilyn D. McShane and Frank P. Williams III. New York: Garland, 1996.

Wolfgang, Marvin E. *Patterns in Criminal Homicide.* Philadelphia: Univ. of Pennsylvania Press, 1958.

Wolfgang, Marvin E., Robert M. Figlio, and Thorsten Sellin. *Delinquency in a Birth Cohort.* Chicago: Univ. of Chicago Press, 1972.

Wolfgang, Marvin E., Arlene Kelly, and Hans C. Nolde. "Comparison of the Executed and the Commuted among Admissions to Death Row." 53 *Journal of Criminal Law, Criminology, and Police Science* 301 (1962).

Wolfgang, Marvin E., and Marc Reidel. "Race, Judicial Discretion, and the Death Penalty." 407 *Annals of the American Academy of Political and Social Science* 119 (1973).

Wolfson, Wendy P. "The Deterrent Effect of the Death Penalty upon Prison Murder." In *The Death Penalty in America,* 3rd ed., ed. Hugo Bedau. New York: Oxford Univ. Press, 1982.

Wooldredge, John D. "Correlates of Deviant Behavior among Inmates of U.S. Correctional Facilities." 14 *Journal of Crime and Justice* 1 (1991).

Yunker, James A. "Is the Death Penalty a Deterrent to Homicide? Some Time Series Evidence." 5 *Journal of Behavioral Economics* 45 (1976).

————. "A New Statistical Analysis of Capital Punishment Incorporating Post-Moratorium Data." 82 *Social Science Quarterly* 297 (2001).

Zimmerman, Paul R. "State Executions, Deterrence, and the Incidence of Murder." 7 *Journal of Applied Economics* 163 (2004). Available at http://www.cema.edu.ar/publicaciones/download/volumen7/zimmerman.pdf

Codes and Statutes

Civil Rights Act of 1965. Public Law 101-576. *U.S. Statutes at Large* 104: 2838. Codified as amended in scattered sections of *U.S. Code* 2, *U.S. Code* 28, and *U.S. Code* 42.

Oregon Revised Statutes (1997 ed.).

Texas Code of Criminal Procedure Annotated. West, 1985, 2001.

Texas Government Code Annotated. Vernon, 2002.

Texas Statutes and Codes Annotated. West, 1977.

Texas Penal Code Annotated. Vernon, 1974; West, 1993, 1994, 1999, 2001.

Virginia Code Annotated. Michie, 1999.

Court Cases

Note: The full text of most Supreme Court cases can be found on FindLaw.com. Recent cases from other federal appellate courts, U.S. district courts, and some state appellate courts are also available there.

Adams v. State, 577 S.W.2d 717 (Tex. Crim. App. 1979).

Adams v. State, 448 U.S. 38 (1980).

Adams v. State, 624 S.W.2d 568 (Tex. Crim. App. 1981).

Atkins v. Virginia, 536 U.S. 304 (2002).

Barefoot v. Estelle, 463 U.S. 880 (1983).

Bell v. Ohio, 438 U.S. 637 (1978).

Beltran v. State, 728 S.W.2d 382 (Tex. Crim. App. 1987).

Beltran v. State, No. 70,888 (Tex. Crim. App., Apr. 28, 1993).

Boulware v. Texas, No. 52,139 (Tex. Crim. App. 1991 [1974]).

Branch v. Texas, 447 S.W.2d 932 (Tex. Crim. App. 1969).

Branch v. Texas, 408 U.S. 238 (1972).

Brandley v. Keeshan, 64 F.3d 196 (5th Cir. 1995).

Brandley v. State, 691 S.W.2d 699 (Tex. Crim. App. 1985).

Brown v. Texas, 118 S.Ct. 366 (1997).

Callin v. Collins, 510 U.S. 1141 (1994).

Coker v. Georgia, 433 U.S. 584 (1977).

Deeb v. State, 815 S.W.2d 692 (Tex. Crim. App. 1991).

Eddings v. Oklahoma, 455 U.S. 104 (1982).

Edmund v. Florida, 458 U.S. 782 (1982).

Estelle v. Smith, 451 U.S. 454 (1981).

Ex parte Adams, 768 S.W.2d 281 (Tex. Crim. App. 1989).

Ex parte Brandley, 781 S.W.2d 886 (Tex. Crim. App. 1990).

Ex parte Davis, 947 S.W.2d 216 (Tex. Crim. App. 1996).

Ex parte Granviel, 561 S.W.2d 503 (Tex. Crim. App. 1978).

Ford v. Wainwright, 477 U.S. 399 (1986).

Fowler v. North Carolina, 428 U.S. 904 (1976).

Furman v. Georgia, 408 U.S. 238 (1972).

Gregg v. Georgia, 428 U.S. 153 (1976).

Guerra v. Collins, 916 F.Supp. 620 (S.D. Tex. 1995).

Guerra v. Johnson, 90 F.3d 1075 (5th Cir. 1996).

Guerra v. State, 771 S.W.2d 453 (Tex. Crim. App. 1988).

Houston Chronicle Publishing Co. v. McMaster, 598 S.W.2d 864 (Tex. Crim. App. 1980).

In re Stanford, 537 U.S. 968 (2002).

Jurek v. Texas, 428 U.S. 262 (1976).

Kleasen v. State, 560 S.W.2d 938 (Tex. Crim. App. 1977).

Lockett v. Ohio, 438 U.S. 586 (1978).

Macias v. State, 733 S.W.2d 192 (Tex. Crim. App. 1987).

Martinez–Macias v. Collins, 810 F.Supp. 782 (W.D. Tex. 1991).

McCleskey v. Kemp, 481 U.S. 279 (1987).

McGautha v. California, 402 U.S. 183 (1971).

McManus v. State, 591 S.W.2d 505 (Tex. Crim. App. 1980).

Penry v. Lynaugh, 492 U.S. 302 (1989).

Penry v. Johnson, 532 U.S. 782 (2001).

Profitt v. Florida, 428 U.S. 242 (1976).

Pugh v. Locke, 406 F.Supp. 318 (D. Ala. 1976).

Pulley v. Harris, 465 U.S. 37 (1984).

Ramos v. Lamm, 485 F.Supp. 122 (D. Colo. 1979).

Ring v. Arizona, 536 U.S. 584 (2002).

Roberts v. Louisiana, 428 U.S. 325 (1976).

Roberts v. Louisiana, 431 U.S. 633 (1977).

Rodriguez v. Texas, No. 62,274 (Tex. Crim. App. 1978).

Roe v. Wade, 410 U.S. 113 (1973).

Roper v. Simmons, 112 S.W.3d 397 (Mo. 2003).

Satterwhite v. Texas, 486 U.S. 249 (1988).

Simmons v. South Carolina, 512 U.S. 154 (1994).

Skelton v. State, 795 S.W.2d 162 (Tex. Crim. App. 1989).

Skipper v. South Carolina, 476 U.S. 1 (1986).

Spence v. State, 795 S.W.2d 743 (Tex. Crim. App. 1990).

Stanford v. Kentucky, 492 U.S. 361 (1989).

Stogsdill v. State, 552 S.W.2d 481 (Tex. Crim. App. 1977).

Thompson v. Oklahoma, 108 S.Ct. 2687 (1988).

Tison v. Arizona, 481 U.S. 137 (1987).

Trop v. Dulles, 356 U.S. 86 (1958).

Witherspoon v. Illinois, 391 U.S. 510 (1968).

Woodson v. North Carolina, 428 U.S. 280 (1976).

Index